Excel

Get the Results You Want!

Years 5–6

Selective Schools and Scholarship Mathematical Reasoning Tests

Allyn Jones
& Alan Horsfield

Completely new edition incorporating 2020 Selective School test changes

Reprinted 2024, 2025 (twice)

ISBN 978 1 74125 632 1

Pascal Press Pty Ltd
PO Box 250
Glebe NSW 2037
www.pascalpress.com.au

Publisher: Vivienne Joannou
Project editor: Rosemary Peers
Edited by Rosemary Peers
Proofread by Barbara Bessant and Mark Dixon
Answers checked by Peter Little
Cover by DiZign Pty Ltd
Typeset by Grizzly Graphics (Leanne Richters) and lj Design (Julianne Billington)
Printed by Vivar Printing/Green Giant Press

Contents

All tests are generally of the same format. Mostly you will be given information and asked one question about it. Sometimes you might get more than one question.

What kinds of questions will be in the test?

All tests use multiple-choice questions where you have to choose the best answer from the given options.

What mathematics topics will be covered in the test?

The test includes questions involving number, patterns, measurement, geometry, statistics, probability and working mathematically. This means you will be familiar with the topics covered in the test but the questions may be more difficult or of a type you may not have seen before.

Do I have to study these areas before the test?

No. The best preparation is to know what to expect on the day of the test and to practise the types of questions in the test.

What kinds of questions will I be asked?

You will be given some information and asked one question about it. The information might be given in words or might involve a diagram, graph or table.

You will be familiar with most question types from classroom work and from other tests you have done, such as the NAPLAN tests.

Do I have to answer all the questions?

Yes, you should try to answer every question. However, it is possible you will not have time to do them all. Some questions will take less than one minute to answer, while others will take longer. You will have to work quite quickly to answer all the questions. Many students don't manage to do this.

How can I make the best use of my time?

Here are a few tips to help you get through the test and to make the best use of your time.

- Don't waste too much time on any one question. If you are not sure, guess the answer but mark it so you can come back to it later if you have time. If it seems impossible to choose, select the answer you first thought was right.
- Answer every question. Don't leave any out. You have a chance of getting the right answer, even if you guess.

If you do have some time to spare, go over your answers. Sometimes you will realise the correct answer to a question after answering other questions.

ADVICE TO PARENTS/ GUARDIANS

Every child has their own talents which need to be discovered and nurtured. Some children are high achievers or have special talents which are not reflected in the results of these tests.

This is because these tests focus on predicting the overall educational achievement of high scorers but may not be accurate in predicting how well a particular student might perform. In fact some students with high scores in these tests may not ultimately do well in high school, while some who were not selected will go on to attain excellent academic results.

Children need to be interested in taking these tests. This will be a significant and memorable event for them and they need support as the tests are very competitive.

INTRODUCTION

It is advisable that children should not undertake the NSW Selective High School Placement Test unless some of the following criteria are satisfied:

- they are among the top of their class at school
- they attend an Opportunity Class
- they are very good at English and Mathematics
- they read widely
- it is their decision to apply for a selective school
- the preparation for the test is not stressful for them.

MAXIMISE YOUR RESULTS IN THE SELECTIVE SCHOOL TEST

You can be confident that ***Excel*** books will help students succeed in the Selective School test. We have over 35 years of experience in helping students prepare for tests and all our writers are experienced educators.

How *Excel* can help you prepare for the online Selective School tests

STEP 1: Use this book

Remember the advantages of revising in book form. There are many benefits to a student using books to prepare for the online tests:

- Writing on paper helps students retain information; it is an effective way to memorise. High-quality educational research has shown that writing by hand is more effective than using a keyboard for retention of information.
- Students will be able to prepare thoroughly for topic and test revision. They will only succeed with sound knowledge of content; this requires study and focus. Students will not succeed in tests simply because they know how to answer questions digitally.
- Some students find it easier to concentrate when reading a page in a book than when reading on a screen.
- It can be more convenient to use a book, especially when a student doesn't have ready access to a computer.

STEP 2: Practise on *Excel Test Zone*

Get online practice to prepare for these online tests. Once you have completed this book, we recommend you go to www.exceltestzone.com.au and register for practice in the Selective School–style tests.

- For optimal performance in Selective School tests we recommend students gain valuable practice in completing tests online, as well as tests in book form, as the actual tests will be taken online, on a computer.
- Students will be able to complete multiple tests and therefore practise answering questions on a computer in order to become confident with this process.
- Students will be able to practise tests under similar timed conditions to the real tests, giving them valuable preparation.

SAMPLE TEST 1

12 Miranda wrote a sequence of numbers. The 3rd term was 138, the 4th term 135 and the 5th term was 132. What is the 13th term?

A 129
B 113
C 108
D 105
E 103

13 Here is a number sentence.

$$20 - \boxed{?} \div 2 \times 3 + 5 = 7$$

What is the value of the missing number?

12	6	18	8	16
A	**B**	**C**	**D**	**E**

14 Eight more than twice a number is 12 more than the number itself. What is the number?

4	6	8	10	20
A	**B**	**C**	**D**	**E**

15 The rectangle contains two identical shaded squares. What fraction of the rectangle is shaded?

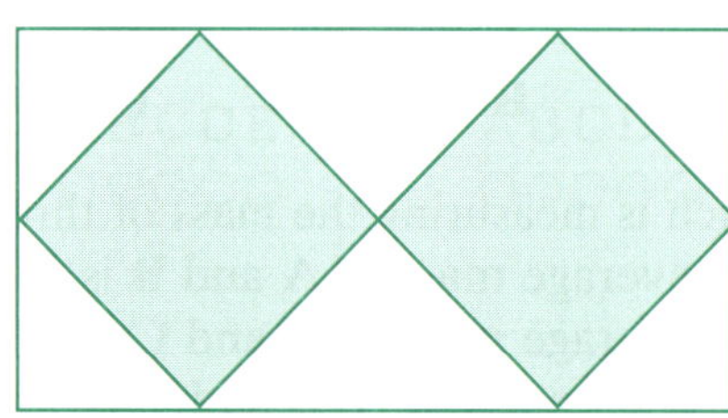

(Not to scale)

$\frac{1}{2}$	$\frac{1}{4}$	$\frac{3}{4}$	$\frac{1}{3}$	$\frac{2}{3}$
A	**B**	**C**	**D**	**E**

16 A container of water is leaking. When it is one-fifth empty it holds 120 L. What amount of water is in the container when it is one-fifth full?

24 L	25 L	30 L	40 L	50 L
A	**B**	**C**	**D**	**E**

17 Rectangles P and Q have perimeters 80 cm and 64 cm respectively.

P

Q

Not to scale

A square is formed when the rectangles are joined.

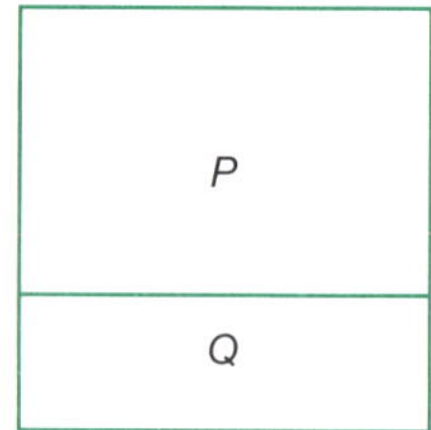

How much wider is rectangle P than rectangle Q?

4 cm	8 cm	10 cm	12 cm	16 cm
A	**B**	**C**	**D**	**E**

18 A long-distance train travels at a constant speed. It takes 20 minutes to travel 25 km. How long will it take to travel 175 km?

A 2 hours 10 minutes
B 2 hours 15 minutes
C 2 hours 20 minutes
D 2 hours 30 minutes
E 2 hours 40 minutes

19 A bag contains 30 balls, numbered 1 to 30. A ball is chosen at random. What is the probability the number is a multiple of 3 and between 10 and 25?

$\frac{1}{6}$	$\frac{1}{5}$	$\frac{1}{4}$	$\frac{13}{30}$	$\frac{33}{30}$
A	**B**	**C**	**D**	**E**

20 After Lauren sprinkles some food into her fishpond her goldfish eat for 5 minutes. If she feeds them twice a day every day, about how long do the fish spend eating every year?

A 15 hours
B 16 hours
C 25 hours
D 30 hours
E 60 hours

Answers and explanations on pages 81–82

SAMPLE TEST 1

21 Aubrey bought three apples and two bananas for $3.65. At the same shop, Sarah bought two apples and four bananas for $4.30. What did Michaela pay for an apple and a banana?

$1.45	$1.50	$1.55	$1.60	$1.65
A	**B**	**C**	**D**	**E**

22 The mass of one can of beans is the same as the mass of seven eggs. The mass of three loaves of bread is the same as the mass of 35 eggs. How many cans of beans has the same mass as 12 loaves of bread?

18	20	22	24	28
A	**B**	**C**	**D**	**E**

23 During a pandemic, the number of people who have been vaccinated doubles every 3 months. The number of people vaccinated at the end of a year is how many times the number vaccinated at the start of the year?

3	4	6	12	16
A	**B**	**C**	**D**	**E**

24 This is a square pyramid.

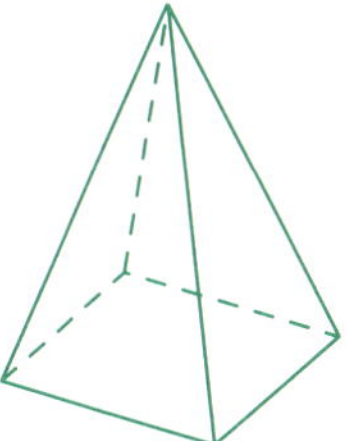

The apex is cut off parallel with the base and discarded. Which is the correct table of information for the new shape?

	Edges	Vertices	Faces
A	12	4	5
B	8	8	8
C	9	9	5
D	12	8	6
E	12	7	6

25 Darcy left his home and travelled to Goulburn before returning home. The travel graph shows the distance Darcy is from home between 10:30 am and 3 pm.

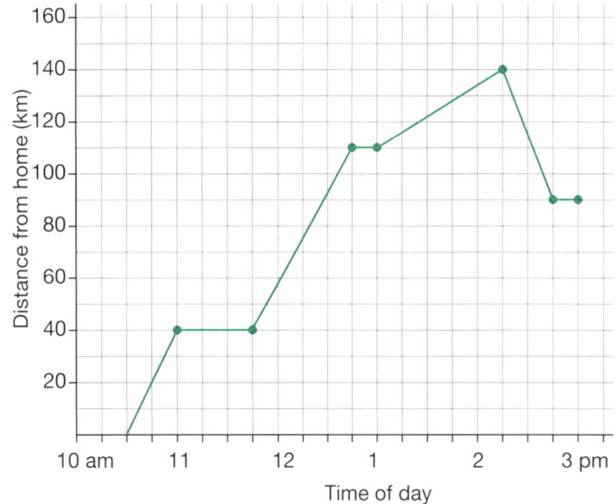

What was the fastest average speed recorded?

A 90 km/h
B 70 km/h
C 100 km/h
D 80 km/h
E 60 km/h

26 The diagram shows three circles with a square inside the largest circle. How many lines of symmetry can be drawn on the shape?

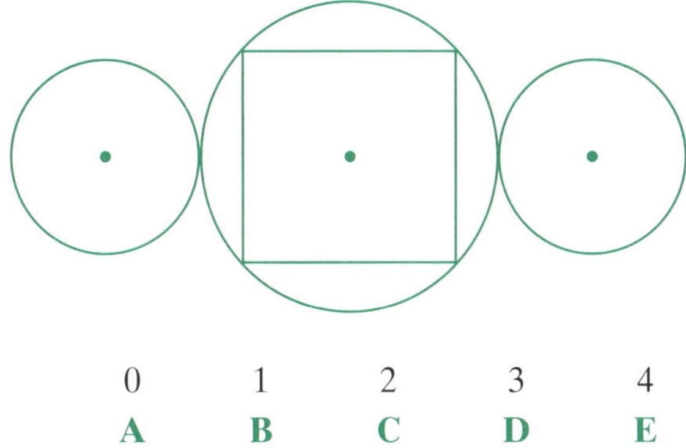

0	1	2	3	4
A	**B**	**C**	**D**	**E**

Answers and explanations on pages 81–82

SAMPLE TEST 1

27 This clock is rotated 90° anticlockwise. What will its new position be?

A

B

C

D

E

28 The area of the circle is 240 cm^2. What is the shaded area?

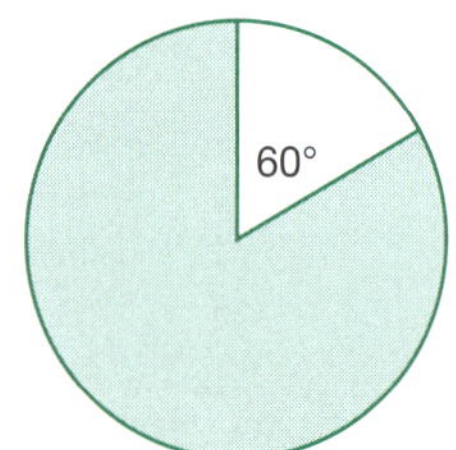

A 175 cm^2
B 180 cm^2
C 192 cm^2
D 200 cm^2
E 210 cm^2

29 The net of a square-based pyramid is made up of a square and triangles. The area of the square is 36 cm^2 and the area of each triangle is 48 cm^2. What is the total area of the net?

A 132 cm^2
B 192 cm^2
C 216 cm^2
D 228 cm^2
E 264 cm^2

30 Max usually rides his bike home from school at an average speed of 15 km/h. The trip takes him 20 minutes. This afternoon he needs to arrive home 5 minutes earlier.
At what average speed does he need to cycle?

A 11 km/h
B 16 km/h
C 20 km/h
D 21 km/h
E 24 km/h

31 Elsie made this spinner with four colours. The arrow is spun.

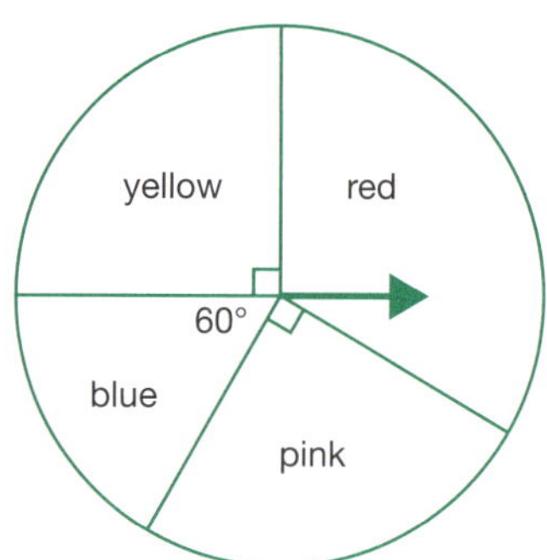

Which of the following statements is/are correct?

X The probability of spinning a red is twice the probability of spinning a blue.
Y The probability of spinning a pink is 0.25.
Z The probability of spinning a yellow or a blue is $\frac{5}{12}$.

A statement X only
B statement Y only
C statement Z only
D statements Y and Z only
E statements X, Y and Z

☞ Answers and explanations on pages 81–82

SAMPLE TEST 1

32 The diagram shows three squares P, Q and R which border a triangle. The area of P is 9 cm^2, the area of Q is 49 cm^2 and the area of R is 25 cm^2.

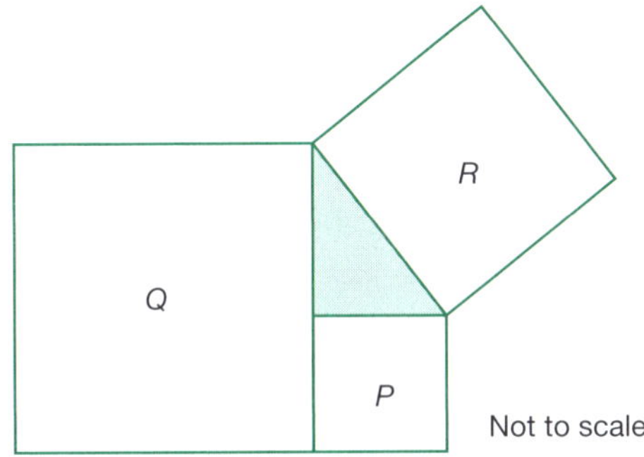

What is the area of the shaded triangle?

A 8 cm^2 **B** 12 cm^2 **C** 10 cm^2
D 6 cm^2 **E** 10 cm^2

33 A group of students were asked for their favourite colour.

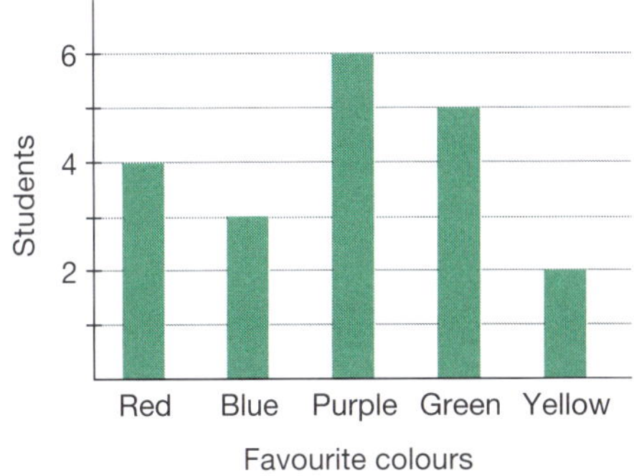

Here are three statements about the graph.

1 Two more students liked purple than yellow.
2 Half of the students like red or purple.
3 15% of the students liked blue.

Which of these statements is/are correct?

A statement 1 only
B statement 2 only
C statement 3 only
D statements 2 and 3 only
E statements 1, 2 and 3

34 The length of a rectangle is halved and its width doubled to form a square. Which of the following statements is/are true?

1 The perimeter of the rectangle and the square are equal.
2 The area of the rectangle and the square are equal.
3 The perimeter of the rectangle is greater than the perimeter of the square.

A statement 1 only
B statement 2 only
C statement 3 only
D statements 2 and 3 only
E statements 1 and 2 only

35 A container is in the shape of a rectangular prism.

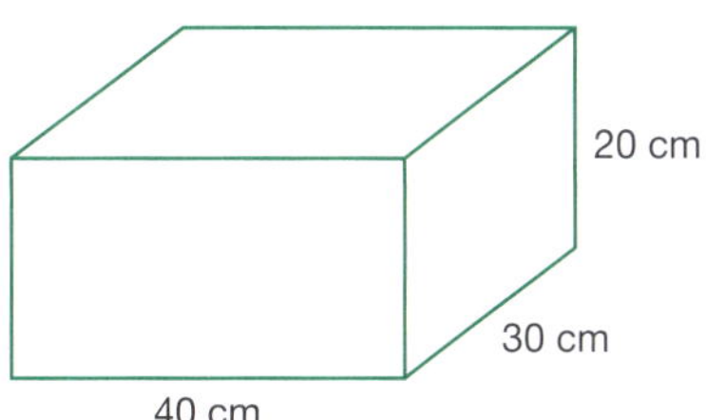

Not to scale

The container is half filled with water. A small stone with a volume of 3600 cm^3 is placed in the container and sinks to the bottom. What is the new height of water in the container?

A 13 cm
B 14 cm
C 15 cm
D 16 cm
E 17 cm

Answers and explanations on pages 81–82

SELECTIVE SCHOOL-STYLE TEST **Mathematical Reasoning**

SAMPLE TEST 2

1 The diagram shows four boxes containing balls. Dane wants each box to have the same number of balls. What is the smallest number of balls Dane needs to move so that the same number of balls are in each box?

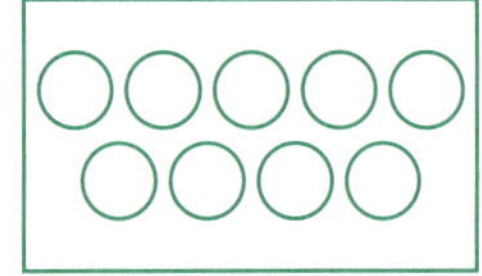

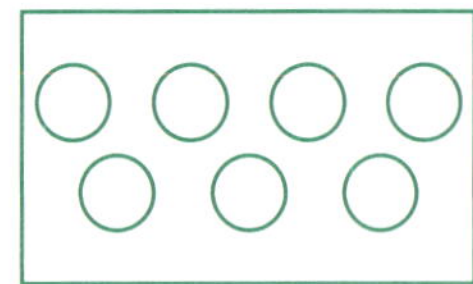

5	6	7	8	10
A	**B**	**C**	**D**	**E**

2 16 more than half the square of a number is 48. What is the number?

6	8	12	16	24
A	**B**	**C**	**D**	**E**

3 How many axes of symmetry are in this design?

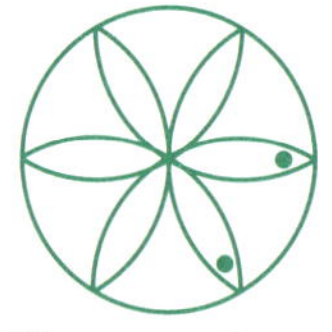

1	3	6	12	2
A	**B**	**C**	**D**	**E**

4 The diagram shows the tile pattern for a section of floor.

Each white triangular tile costs $9 and a grey triangular tile costs $2 more than a white tile. What is the total cost of the tiles?

A $180 **B** $132 **C** $160
D $260 **E** $240

5 For a special assembly, chairs have been arranged in the school hall in equal rows. Oscar looked from the stage at his mother sitting in the audience. There are:

- six chairs on her left and eight chairs to her right.
- seven rows ahead of her and twelve rows behind her.

How many chairs are in the hall?

266	110	210	335	300
A	**B**	**C**	**D**	**E**

6 A number has a remainder of 3 when divided by 6, a remainder of 2 when divided by 5 and a remainder of 1 when divided by 4. What is the smallest number that fits these conditions?

117	93	87	57	69
A	**B**	**C**	**D**	**E**

7 Jason and Scott both had $8. Jason gave 25% of his money to Scott. Later Scott gave 25% of his money to Jason. How much does Jason have?

A $6.00
B $7.50
C $8.00
D $8.50
E $8.75

8 Liam, William and Jacob all work casual jobs. Last week Liam earned $46 more than William and $87 less than Jacob. If William earned $387, what was the total earned by all three boys?

A $941 **B** $944 **C** $1340
D $1379 **E** $1381

9 Eden is following a cake recipe which requires $\frac{3}{4}$ of a cup of flour. How many cakes can she make using 6 cups of flour?

3	6	8	4	9
A	**B**	**C**	**D**	**E**

Answers and explanations on pages 83–85

SAMPLE TEST 2

10 Carolyn multiplied the largest three-digit odd number by the smallest three-digit even number and then subtracted this result from a million. What was her answer?

A 90 100
B 99 100
C 900 100
D 990 100
E 999 100

11 A crate containing 20 identical boxes has a mass of 44 kg. When 6 boxes are removed the mass is 32 kg. What is the mass of the crate containing 8 boxes?

A 20 kg
B 17 kg
C 21 kg
D 19 kg
E 18 kg

12 Sam and Alice and their four children go to the movies. The price of a child's ticket is half the price of an adult. The total price of admission was $72. What will be the price for Tom and his 12-year-old daughter's admission?

$6	$12	$18	$24	$27
A	**B**	**C**	**D**	**E**

13 In the magic square, numbers in each row, column and diagonal add to the same number. What is the number that is represented by the *?

	1.25		12.25
	10.25	9.25	7.25
*		5.25	11.25
3.25		14.25	0.25

8.25	1.25	4.25	2.25	15.25
A	**B**	**C**	**D**	**E**

14 Alice is using matchsticks to make a pattern of triangles. Here are the first three shapes in the pattern:

She summarises the number of triangles and matches in the table below.

triangles	1	2	3	4	5
matches	3	5	7	9	11

If Alice continues the pattern, how many triangles will be in the shape if she uses 191 matches?

95	96	190	380	383
A	**B**	**C**	**D**	**E**

15 Which piece will complete this chequered square?

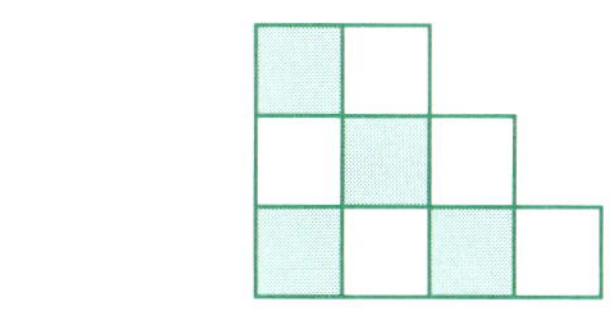

A

B

C

D

E

16 Here is a number sentence:

$(\boxed{?} + 5)^2 - 4 \times 6 = 5 + 5 \times 4$, where $\boxed{?}$ represents a positive integer. What is the value of the missing number?

1	2	3	4	5
A	**B**	**C**	**D**	**E**

Answers and explanations on pages 83–85

SAMPLE TEST 2

17 When the product of a certain number and 4 is subtracted from 20 the answer is the sum of the number and 10. What is the number?

3	8	5	2	10
A	**B**	**C**	**D**	**E**

18 The diagram shows a shape comprised of four squares. The areas of the squares are 1 cm^2, 4 cm^2, 16 cm^2 and 64 cm^2.

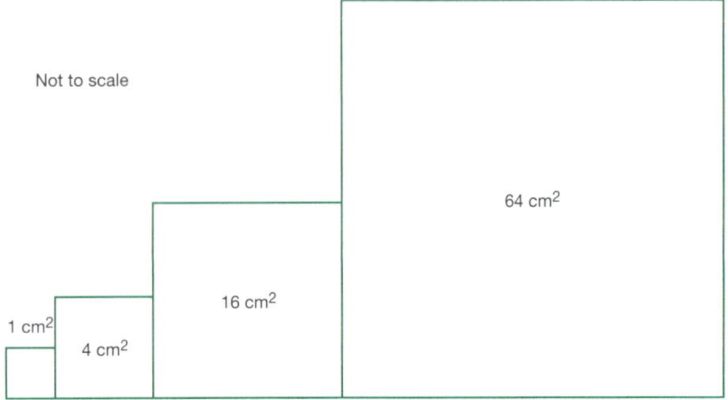

What is the perimeter of the shape?

A 46 cm
B 30 cm
C 340 cm
D 120 cm
E 170 cm

19 Look at the numbers:

$$2^1 = 2, 2^2 = 4, 2^3 = 8, 2^4 = 16,$$
$$2^5 = 32, 2^6 = 64, 2^7 = 128 \ldots$$

What would be the last digit of 2^{24}?

2	4	8	0	6
A	**B**	**C**	**D**	**E**

20 This large block has been made up of cubic centimetre blocks and then painted. How many of the centimetre blocks have only one face painted?

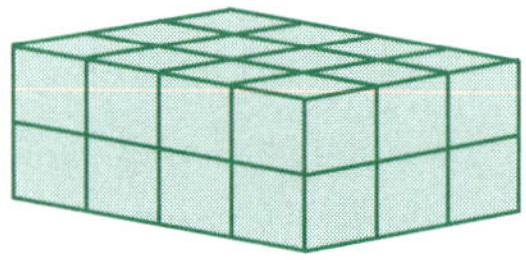

2	4	8	12	15
A	**B**	**C**	**D**	**E**

21 Results in a test for five students are recorded in the graph below.

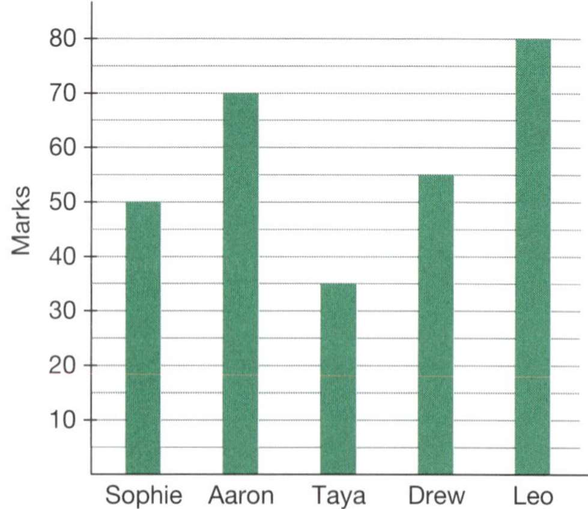

Here are three statements about the graph.

1 Aaron scored 15 marks more than Drew.
2 The average of Sophie's mark and Leo's mark is 65.
3 Taya scored half as many marks as Leo.

Which of these statements is/are correct?

A statements 1 and 2 only
B statement 1 only
C statement 2 only
D statement 3 only
E statements 1, 2 and 3

22 The shape is comprised of five identical rectangles. The length of each rectangle is twice the width.

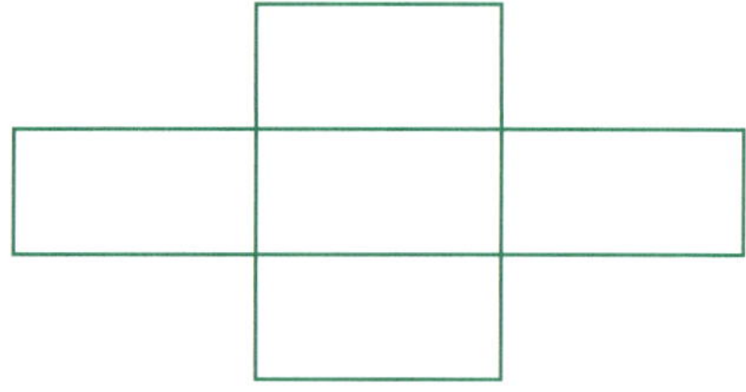

If the total area of the shape is 1000 cm^2, what is the perimeter of the shape?

A 180 cm
B 200 cm
C 250 cm
D 275 cm
E 300 cm

Answers and explanations on pages 83–85

SAMPLE TEST 2

23 Container P is filled with water and all the water is poured into an empty container Q.

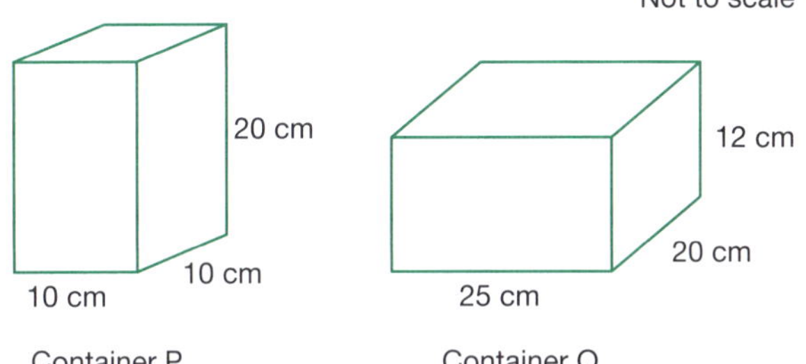

What fraction of container Q is filled?

$\frac{1}{6}$	$\frac{1}{3}$	$\frac{1}{2}$	$\frac{2}{3}$	$\frac{5}{6}$
A	**B**	**C**	**D**	**E**

24 Here is a cube with side length 12 cm:

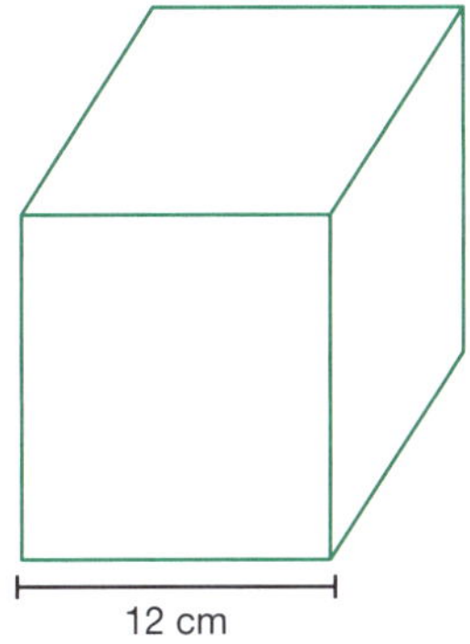

How many small cubes with side length 4 cm can be removed from the cube?

3	6	9	27	64
A	**B**	**C**	**D**	**E**

25 Oscar drove his car from Blacktown to Bathurst. Initially Oscar averaged a speed of 80 km/h for 1 hour 15 minutes. He then increased his speed for the last 70 km. If his average speed for the entire trip was 85 km/h, how long did he drive for?

A 2 hours
B 1 hour 40 minutes
C 2 hours 10 minutes
D 1 hour 45 minutes
E 1 hour 55 minutes

26 If it takes 1 hour 12 minutes to paint $\frac{9}{20}$ of a wall, how much more time will it take to finish the job?

A 1 hour 20 minutes
B 1 hour 28 minutes
C 1 hour 30 minutes
D 1 hour 36 minutes
E 1 hour 40 minutes

27 Edward and Josie entered a triathlon which started at 11:47 am. Josie took 3 hours 14 minutes to complete the race. Edward finished 31 minutes before Josie. At what time did Edward finish the triathlon?

A 2:43 pm
B 2:30 pm
C 3:00 pm
D 3:32 pm
E 3:28 pm

28 The diagram shows a rectangle with length 20 cm and perimeter 72 cm. Two identical triangles are drawn inside the rectangle.

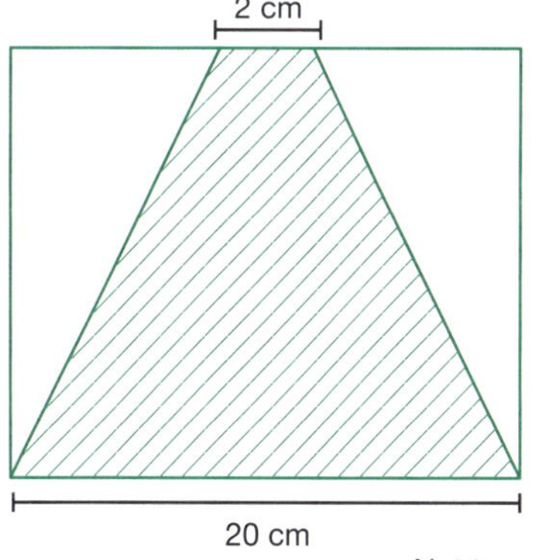

What is the area of the shaded trapezium?

A 32 cm^2
B 148 cm^2
C 176 cm^2
D 248 cm^2
E 320 cm^2

SAMPLE TEST 2

29 Keiran investigated some quadrilaterals and here are some of his conclusions.

1 All squares are rhombuses.
2 All rhombuses are kites.
3 All parallelograms are rectangles.

Which of Keiran's conclusions is/are correct?

A conclusion 1 only
B conclusion 2 only
C conclusions 1 and 2 only
D conclusions 1 and 3 only
E conclusions 1, 2 and 3

30 Elijah made a spinner with three different coloured sectors. When the arrow is spun, the probability of spinning a red is four times the probability of spinning a yellow. The probability of spinning a blue is $\frac{1}{4}$. What is the size of the angle that is yellow?

44°	50°	48°	56°	54°
A	**B**	**C**	**D**	**E**

31 The diagram shows a triangular prism, with two isosceles triangles, each with an area of 108 cm^2.

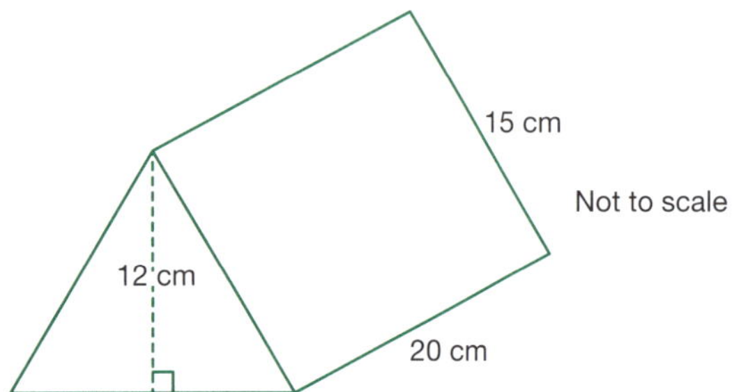

What would be the area of the net of the prism?

A 888 cm^2
B 906 cm^2
C 936 cm^2
D 972 cm^2
E 1176 cm^2

32 The sum of two angles in a triangle is 56°. What is the size of the third angle?

34°	44°	124°	134°	144°
A	**B**	**C**	**D**	**E**

33 The price of a digital currency coin at the end of each week is shown in the line graph below.

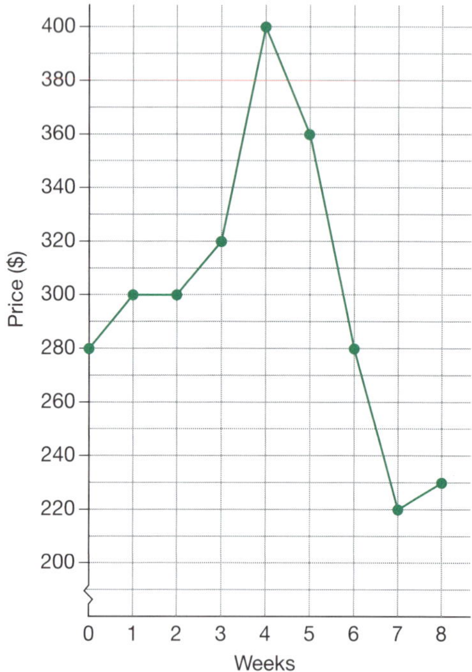

Here are three statements about the graph.

1 During week 7 the price dropped $70.
2 The maximum price was at the end of week 4.
3 The greatest change in price was during week 6.

Which of these statements is/are true?

A statement 1 only
B statement 2 only
C statements 2 and 3 only
D statements 1, 2 and 3
E statement 3 only

Answers and explanations on pages 83–85

SAMPLE TEST 2

34 Darcie walks one-third of a distance at 5 km/h. She then runs the remainder of the distance. If the total distance of 15 km takes 2 hours, at what speed does Darcie run?

A 7 km/h
B 7.5 km/h
C 8 km/h
D 12 km/h
E 10 km/h

35 There are 12 marbles in a bag. The marbles are either red, blue or green. Two of the marbles are red. There are three times as many green marbles as red marbles. A marble is chosen at random.

Which of these statements is/are correct?

1 The probability of choosing a red marble is $\frac{1}{3}$.

2 The probability of choosing a green marble is $\frac{1}{2}$.

3 If a blue marble is removed, the probability of now choosing a blue marble is $\frac{1}{3}$.

A statement 1 only
B statement 2 only
C statement 3 only
D statements 1 and 2 only
E statements 2 and 3 only

Answers and explanations on pages 83–85

SELECTIVE SCHOOL–STYLE TEST **Mathematical Reasoning**

SAMPLE TEST 3

1 Populations are rounded off to the nearest million. The population of a small African nation was rounded off to twenty million. Which one of the following could be the actual population of the nation?

A 19 290 974
B 19 701 794
C 20 598 340
D 20 901 100
E 19 099 999

2 I start counting backwards by sevens from 5. What is the fifth number I will say?

–7	–16	–23	–35	–30
A	**B**	**C**	**D**	**E**

3 Every week Amy does a 10-word spelling test. After 4 weeks her average is 7.5 correct. How many does she have to get correct in the fifth week to bring her average up to 8?

0.5	2.5	8	10	9
A	**B**	**C**	**D**	**E**

4 3 apples and 1 pineapple cost $3.25. The pineapple is twice as expensive as 1 apple. What is the price of an apple?

A 55c
B 65c
C 75c
D $1.05
E $1.25

5 There are between 30 and 40 ducks in a pond. If I count them by twos there is one over. When I count them by threes there are two left over. How many ducks are in the pond?

31	33	35	37	39
A	**B**	**C**	**D**	**E**

6 What is the difference between $\frac{3}{6}$ and $\frac{6}{3}$?

$\frac{1}{2}$	$1\frac{1}{2}$	$2\frac{1}{3}$	3	2
A	**B**	**C**	**D**	**E**

7 36 L of water is poured into an empty drum which is then $\frac{2}{3}$ full of water. How much does the drum hold?

48 L	54 L	60 L	72 L	64 L
A	**B**	**C**	**D**	**E**

8 A sports instructor purchased a volleyball, a softball and a soccer ball from a sports store. The softball was $3 more expensive than the volleyball but $3 cheaper than the soccer ball. The total cost was $45 dollars. What did the soccer ball cost?

A $12
B $21
C $15
D $18
E $19

9 A student's ferry fare is half the teacher's fare. On an excursion the total fare charged for two teachers and ten students is $42. What is the fare for one teacher?

A $4.20
B $3.00
C $9.00
D $12.00
E $6.00

10 In the magic square, numbers in each row, column and diagonal add to the same number. What is the number that is represented by the *?

*	3		14
		11	9
10			
5	15	16	2

4	13	6	12	17
A	**B**	**C**	**D**	**E**

Answers and explanations on pages 85–86

SAMPLE TEST 3

11 Paula made the following stacks of blocks. If she continues to use the same pattern, how many blocks will she need for the next stack?

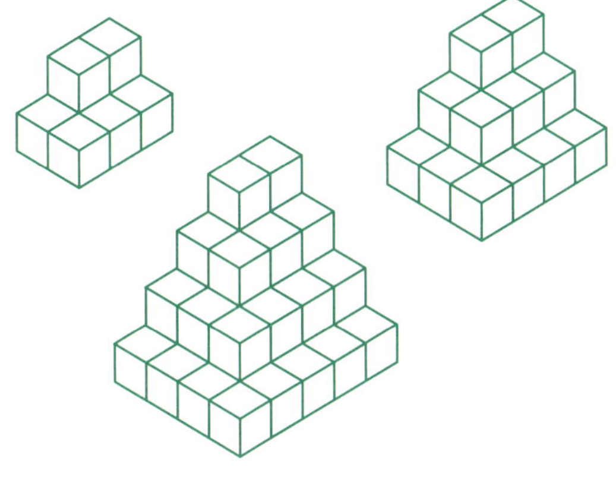

66	70	80	96	100
A	**B**	**C**	**D**	**E**

12 In a sequence the second number is 11, the fourth is 25 and the sixth is 39. The sequence continues. Which of these is also in the sequence?

108	109	110	111	112
A	**B**	**C**	**D**	**E**

13 In the addition, different letters stand for different digits.

$$\begin{array}{r} AB \\ +\quad A \\ \hline BCC \end{array}$$

What does BCC represent?

A 100
B 111
C 122
D 233
E 211

14 If 6480 × 3600 = 23 328 000, what is 23 328 ÷ 648?

0.36	3.6	36	360	1000
A	**B**	**C**	**D**	**E**

15 This figure is made up of 2 cm squares. What is its perimeter?

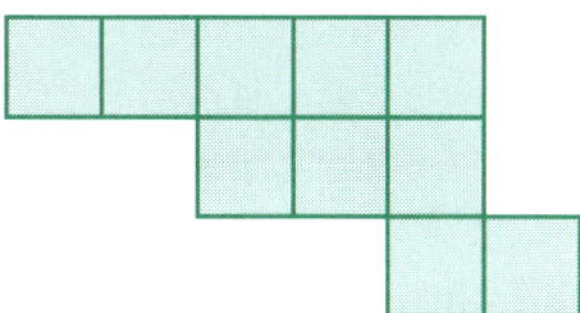

A 20 cm
B 24 cm
C 36 cm
D 40 cm
E 32 cm

16 What is the area of the shaded part of this diagram? Each square represents 1 cm^2.

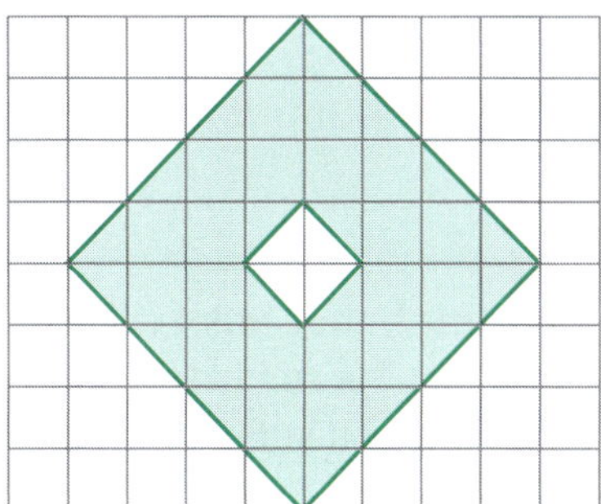

A 30 cm^2 **B** 32 cm^2 **C** 62 cm^2
D 64 cm^2 **E** 48 cm^2

17 Mrs Martin decides to paint one side of her front door. The door has a 50 cm square glass window in the centre of the door. It is 50 cm from the top.

What area of the door has to be painted?

A 0.75 m^2
B 1.25 m^2
C 1.5 m^2
D 2.25 m^2
E 1.7 m^2

Answers and explanations on pages 85–86

SAMPLE TEST 3

18 A rectangular fish tank holds 20 000 L. If it is 2 m high and 2 m deep, how long is the tank?

A 20 m **B** 50 m **C** 0.5 m
D 5 m **E** 0.25 m

19 This solid shape is made using 1 cm^3 cubes. What is its volume?

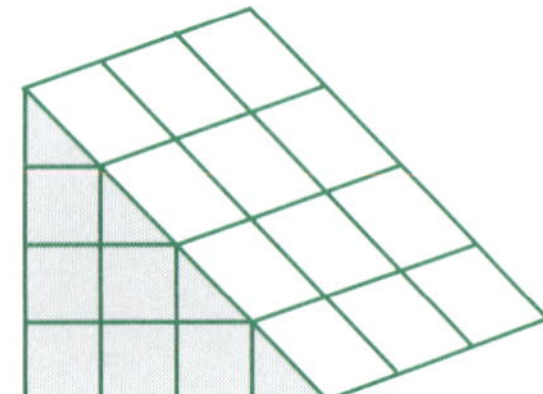

A 7 cm^3
B 8 cm^3
C 24 cm^3
D 36 cm^3
E 18 cm^3

20 On a peanut butter label it lists 5.6 g of protein and 1.5 g sugar for every 20 g serve. How much sugar is in a 360 g jar?

A 3 kg **B** 27 g **C** 30 g
D 54 g **E** 100.8 g

21 A train travels 96 km in 40 minutes. What is its average speed?

A 144 km/h
B 192 km/h
C 80 km/h
D 96 km/h
E 160 km/h

22 On this balance each square marked • has the same mass. The other squares show their mass in kilograms.

What does • stand for?

A 11 kg **B** 7 kg **C** 3.5 kg
D 3 kg **E** 1.5 kg

23 A clock shows the correct time at 8 am. If it gains four minutes in every hour, what time will it show five and a half hours later?

A 12.38 pm
B 1.22 pm
C 1.52 pm
D 2.22 pm
E 2:02 pm

24 What is the area of the shaded section of these overlapping squares?

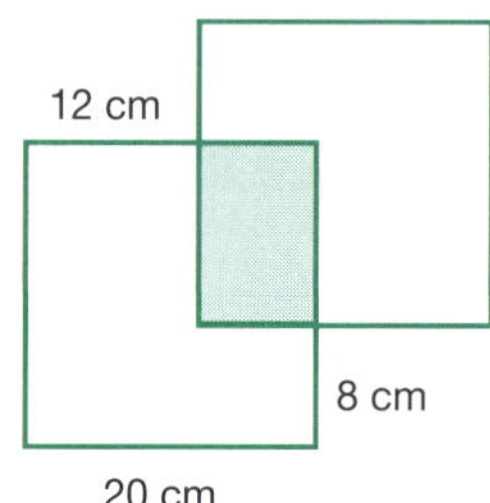

A 64 cm^2
B 96 cm^2
C 144 cm^2
D 276 cm^2
E 304 cm^2

25 If this shape was viewed in a mirror, it would look like which of the following?

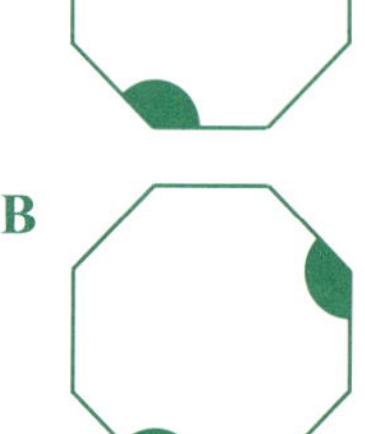

A

B

C

D

E

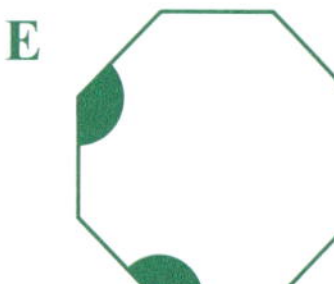

Answers and explanations on pages 85–86

SAMPLE TEST 3

26 This shape is reflected in the mirror. The mirror acts as a line of symmetry.

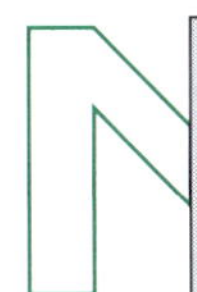

What image will be seen in the mirror?

A

B

C

D

E

27 The table shows the admissions charged at a Holiday Fun Park. For example, the cost of admission of two adults and one child is $25.

		Adults		
Children		0	1	2
	0	–	$10	$19
	1	$6	$16	$25
	2	$11	$21	$30
	3	$15	$25	$34
	More than 3	$18	$28	$37

How much more will Mr and Mrs Brown and their four children pay than Jason and his two children?

$19	$37	$21	$18	$16
A	**B**	**C**	**D**	**E**

28 The Nour family have three children: two girls and one boy. What are the chances of the next child being a girl?

$\frac{1}{2}$	$\frac{1}{3}$	$\frac{1}{4}$	$\frac{3}{4}$	$\frac{2}{5}$
A	**B**	**C**	**D**	**E**

29 Islands stretch across the Pacific Ocean. When the time on Pirate Island is 10:30 am, the time on Tui Island is 3:00 pm. What will the time be on Pirate Island when the time is 3.30 am Tuesday on Tui Island?

A 11 pm Monday
B 11 am Monday
C 8 am Tuesday
D 8.30 pm Tuesday
E 10 pm Monday

30 The numbers around the edge of a dart board range from 1 to 20. What are the chances of getting a number divisible by three with one dart?

$\frac{1}{3}$	$\frac{3}{10}$	$\frac{1}{20}$	$\frac{3}{20}$	$\frac{1}{6}$
A	**B**	**C**	**D**	**E**

31 Which of the following shapes, when rotated through 180°, would still appear the same?

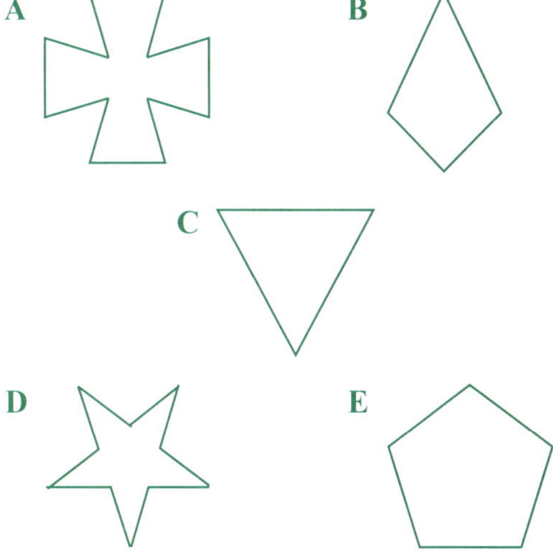

Answers and explanations on pages 85–86

SAMPLE TEST 3

32 A circle is divided into 12 equal parts as shown. What is the size of the angle at X?

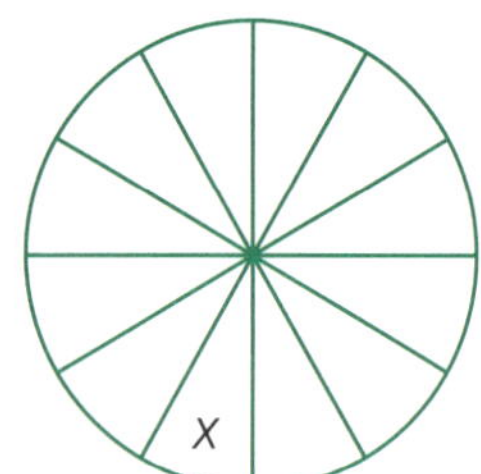

A 15°
B 20°
C 30°
D 36°
E 18°

33 Which of the following would **not** fold to make this pyramid?

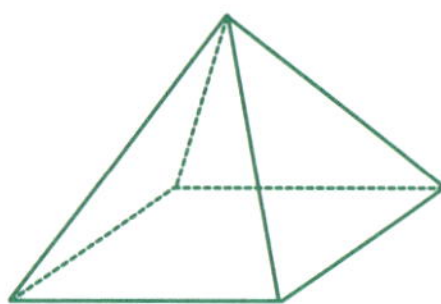

A
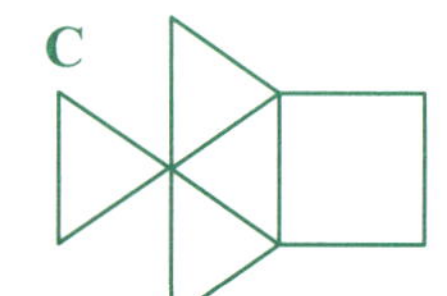

B
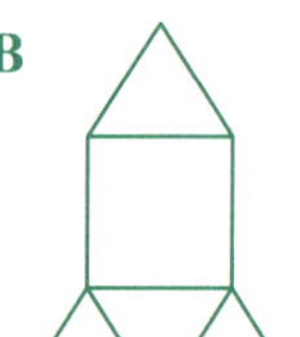

C

D

E
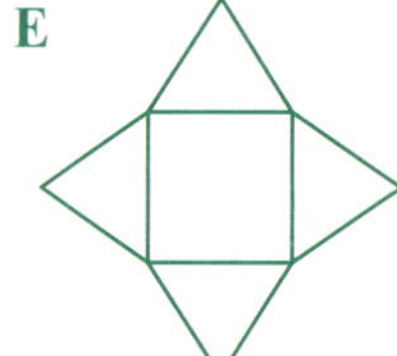

34 Twenty-seven cubes have been glued together to make one large cube (as shown). It was painted all over before being pulled apart. How many cubes will have only two faces painted?

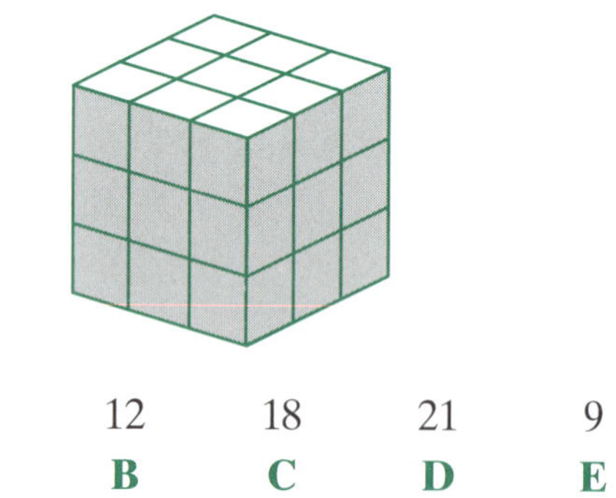

8	12	18	21	9
A	B	C	D	E

35 The graph shows the number of absent days for students in class 6K in the month of August.

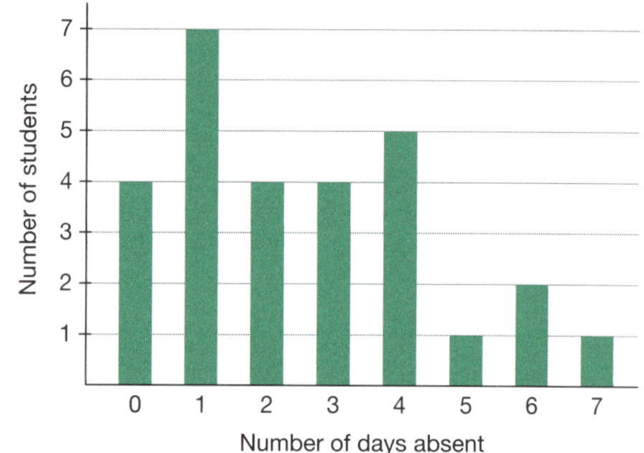

Here are three statements about the graph.

1 Most students were absent for four days.
2 There are 28 students in the class.
3 More than half the students in the class had fewer than three absent days.

Which of these statements is/are correct?

A statement 1 only
B statement 2 only
C statement 3 only
D statements 1, 2 and 3
E statements 2 and 3 only

☞ Answers and explanations on pages 85–86

SELECTIVE SCHOOL-STYLE TEST **Mathematical Reasoning**

SAMPLE TEST 4

1

```
   2878
    679
   [  ]
+  3025
   7085
```

[ ] =

A 503
B 623
C 1503
D 1623
E 603

2 Greg's batting average after three innings in cricket is 35. He scored twice as many runs in both his second and third innings as he did in his first innings. What was his lowest score?

42	35	25	21	23
A	**B**	**C**	**D**	**E**

3 Three freight trains arrive in Perth. Each carries 20 containers. In each container there are 20 cartons. Each carton contains 200 packets of band aids.
How many packets were taken to Perth?

A 24 000
B 48 000
C 80 000
D 240 000
E 83 000

4 How many numbers between 1 and 150 are divisible by both 8 and 5 without remainders?

3	6	15	30	48
A	**B**	**C**	**D**	**E**

5 Tony and Bill both do a maths test with 20 questions. Tony gets 60% right and Bill gets 75% right. How many more questions did Bill get right than Tony?

3	5	7.5	15	4
A	**B**	**C**	**D**	**E**

6 Mrs Moon purchased 25 m of material at $5.96 a metre. Mrs Moon only has $20 notes. How many notes will she need to pay for the material?

3	5	6	8	7
A	**B**	**C**	**D**	**E**

7 I divide a payment of $460 between three contractors and a supervisor. The supervisor gets twice as much as each of the contractors. How much does the supervisor get?

A $115
B $153.33
C $184
D $230
E $92

8 What fraction of this hexagon is shaded?

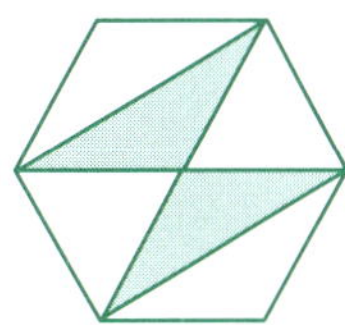

A one-third
B one-sixth
C one-quarter
D one-half
E one-fifth

9 In this puzzle, letters represent numbers. The total of each row is written on the right and the total of each column is written on the bottom. What number is represented by *X*?

a	*b*	*d*	*c*	*X*
a	*d*	*c*	*c*	25
d	*d*	*d*	*d*	20
d	*b*	*a*	*d*	21
18	24	22	26	

21	25	23	22	24
A	**B**	**C**	**D**	**E**

Answers and explanations on pages 86–88

SAMPLE TEST 4

10 Pauline made the following stacks of blocks. If she continues to use the same pattern, how many blocks will she need for the next stack?

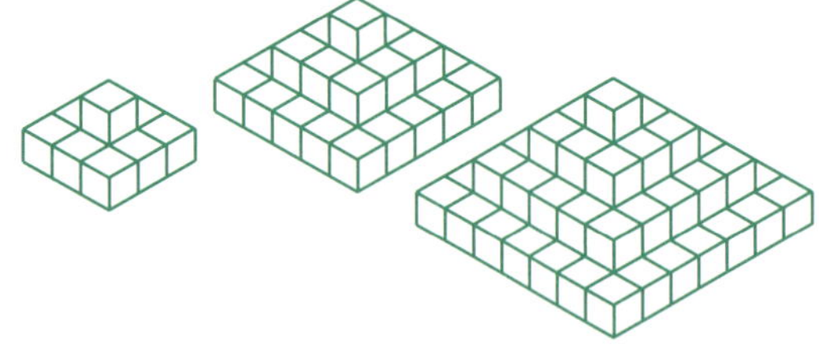

81	84	133	165	148
A	**B**	**C**	**D**	**E**

11 Erica wrote this number sentence.

$\boxed{?} + 23 - 4 + 2 \times 5 = 31$

What is the missing number?

8	18	22	76	2
A	**B**	**C**	**D**	**E**

12 Which number sentence describes the statement 'Twice the sum of five and the product of three and two is greater than the difference between twenty and the quotient of twelve and four'.

A $2 \times 5 + 3 \times 2 > 20 - 12 \div 4$
B $2 \times (5 + 3 + 2) > 20 - 12 \div 4$
C $2 \times (5 + 3 \times 2) > 20 - 12 \div 4$
D $2 \times (5 + 3 \times 2) > (20 - 12) \div 4$
E $2 \times 5 + 3 \times 2 > (20 - 12) \div 4$

13 This shape has an axis of symmetry as shown. What is its total area?

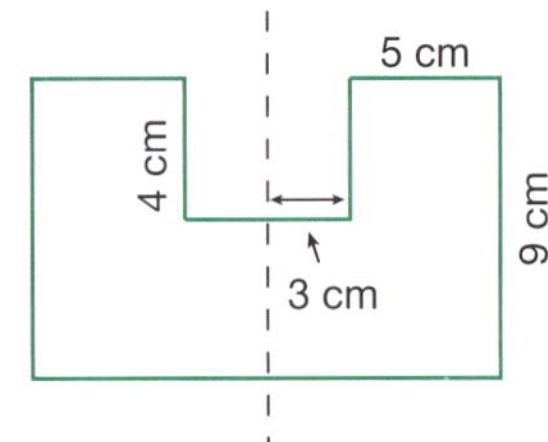

A 50 cm^2
B 127 cm^2
C 99 cm^2
D 120 cm^2
E 94 cm^2

14 How many lines of symmetry does this shape have?

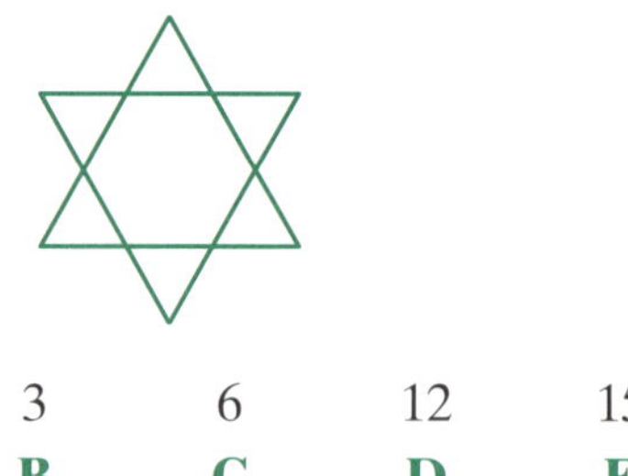

2	3	6	12	15
A	**B**	**C**	**D**	**E**

15 The total area of the small squares in this figure is 52 cm^2. What is its perimeter?

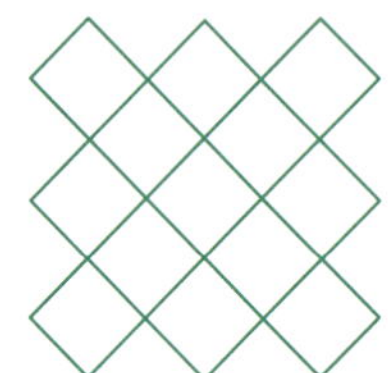

A 13 cm
B 20 cm
C 26 cm
D 40 cm
E 39 cm

16 Four square tables are pushed together to form one long table.

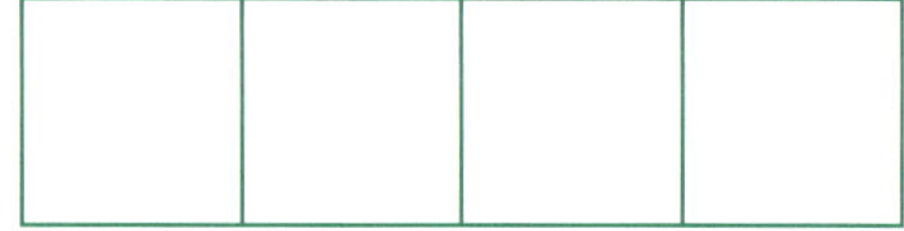

The perimeter of the new table is 20 m. What is the total perimeter of the four small tables?

A 8 m
B 20 m
C 26 m
D 32 m
E 28 m

17 24 L of milk are poured into an empty vat. The vat is then $\frac{3}{4}$ full. How many litres does that vat hold?

A 18 L **B** 30 L **C** 32 L
D 36 L **E** 40 L

Answers and explanations on pages 86–88

SAMPLE TEST 4

18 Suppose a Prime Minister wins an election on a Saturday. What day of the week will it be 100 days later?

A Friday
B Saturday
C Sunday
D Monday
E Tuesday

19 There are 52 cards in a pack: two black suits (clubs and spades) and two red suits (hearts and diamonds). Elaine has a pack of shuffled cards. She deals from the top of the pack and turns up a black card. What are the chances of turning up a second black card?

$\frac{1}{2}$	$\frac{2}{13}$	$\frac{2}{51}$	$\frac{25}{51}$	$\frac{26}{51}$
A	**B**	**C**	**D**	**E**

20 1 L of carrot juice cost $5.60. What would 1.75 L cost?

A $7.00
B $8.40
C $9.80
D $10.20
E $10.80

21 Look at this shape. Which row on the table represents its properties?

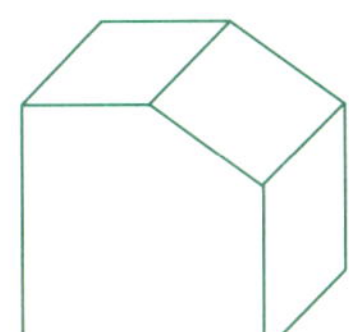

	Edges	Faces	Vertices
A	10	8	9
B	15	6	8
C	12	9	8
D	15	7	10
E	15	7	12

22 Andy wants to cycle 5 km in 35 minutes. He cycles the first 4 km at 8 km/h. How fast must he go in the fifth kilometre?

A 4 km/h
B 8 km/h
C 12 km /h
D 15 km/h
E 10 km/h

23 On this balance each box marked with a • has the same mass. The other boxes show their weight in kilograms. What is the weight of a box marked with •?

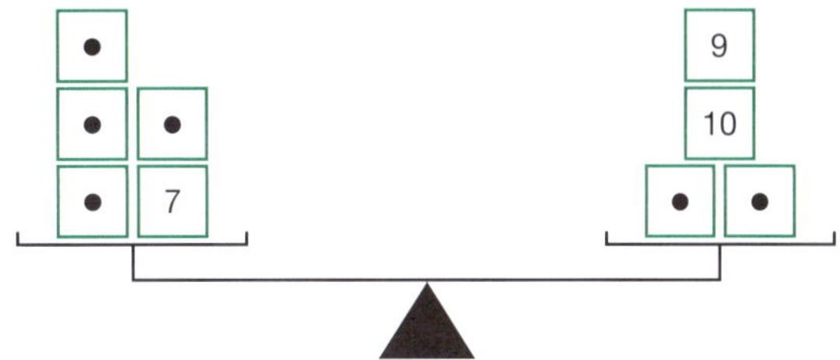

A 3 kg
B 6 kg
C 7 kg
D 12 kg
E 4 kg

24 When the time in England is 4 am on Tuesday the time in Melbourne is 2 pm on the same day. What will the time be in Melbourne when the time is 9 pm on Friday in England?

A 7 am Thursday
B 7 am Saturday
C 11 pm Saturday
D 9 am Friday
E 9 am Saturday

25 A cyclist can ride 4 km in 5 minutes. What is his speed?

A 12 km/h
B 15 km/h
C 48 km/h
D 60 km/h
E 72 km/h

Answers and explanations on pages 86–88

SAMPLE TEST 4

26 Which shapes would I have to use to make this figure?

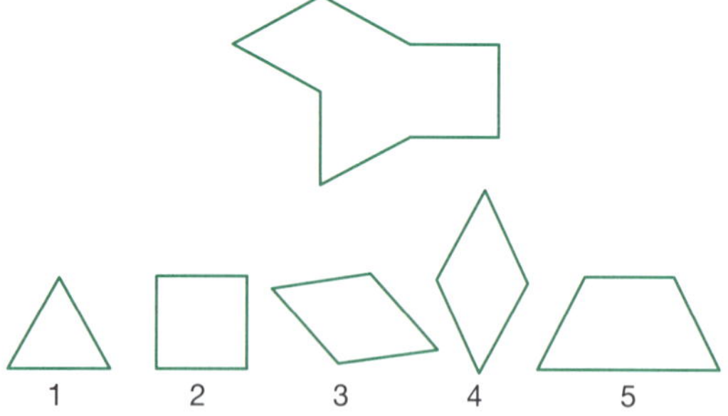

A 1, 3 and 5
B 2, 3 and 4
C 3, 4 and 5
D 1, 3 and 4
E 1, 2 and 3

27 Look at the first shape. Next to it is the same shape that has been rotated clockwise. Through how many degrees has it been rotated?

 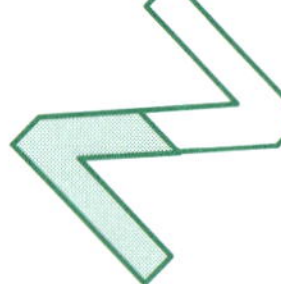

A 90°
B 135°
C 180°
D 225°
E 270°

28 Using the rays in this diagram, how many different acute angles can be found?

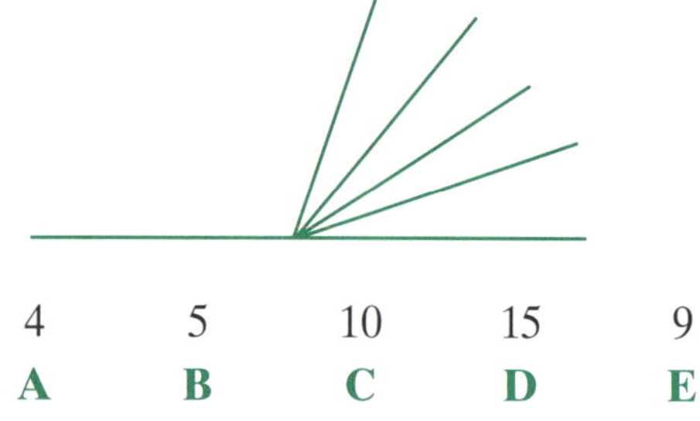

4	5	10	15	9
A	**B**	**C**	**D**	**E**

29 The Stolen Stones rock group get $1200 to share between the four members. The leader gets $100 more than the keyboard player who gets $100 more than the drummer. The bass player gets $100 less than the drummer. How much does the bass player receive?

A $200
B $150
C $125
D $90
E $300

30 A farmer has two square paddocks side by side. Each side of each paddock is 100 metres long. If he fences both paddocks and uses posts 5 m apart, how many posts will he need?

138	140	139	160	124
A	**B**	**C**	**D**	**E**

31 Jack's travel graph is shown below.

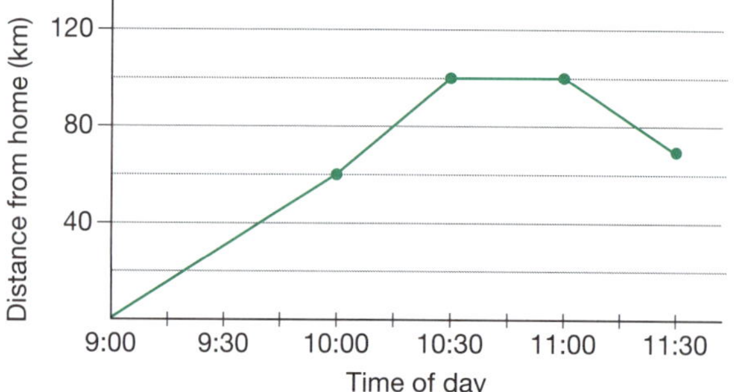

What was Jack's fastest speed?

A 100 km/h
B 60 km/h
C 40 km/h
D 90 km/h
E 80 km/h

32 In a large bag there are hundreds of red, green, white and black marbles. How many must be withdrawn from the bag to be sure of getting two the same colour?

2	3	4	5	1
A	**B**	**C**	**D**	**E**

Answers and explanations on pages 86–88

SAMPLE TEST 4

33 Lilly used a net to construct this rectangular prism.

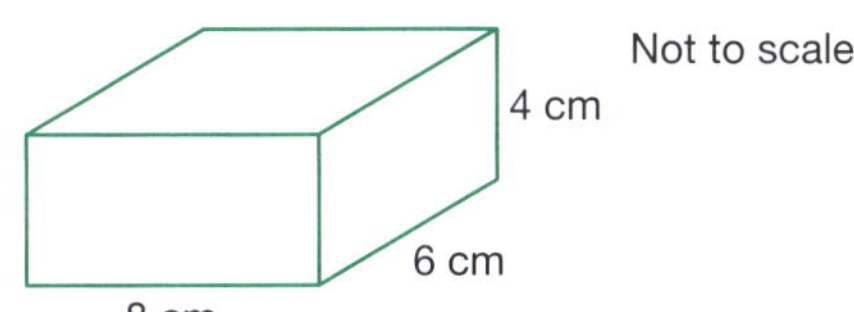

What would be the total area of the net of the prism?

A 208 cm^2
B 104 cm^2
C 192 cm^2
D 144 cm^2
E 160 cm^2

34 Two navigation lights are in a harbour. One light flashes 40 times a minute and the other light flashes 15 times a minute. If they flash simultaneously at 9 pm, how many more times will they flash simultaneously by 10 pm?

120	60	320	360	300
A	**B**	**C**	**D**	**E**

35 Students in a class collected data about the number of children in their own families and recorded the information on the graph below.

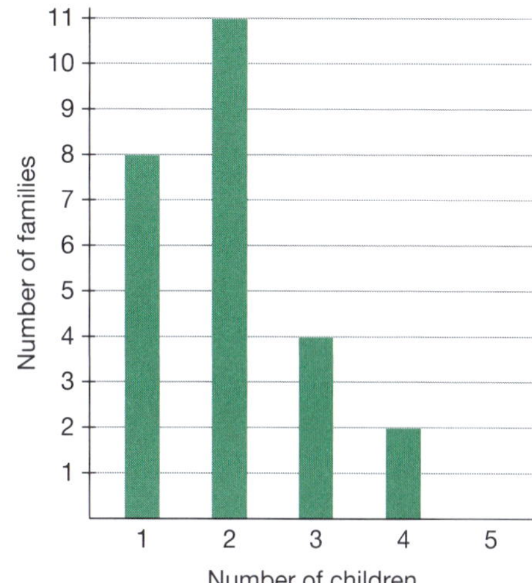

Here are three statements about the graph.

1 25 students were surveyed.
2 17 students were in a family of at least two children.
3 The average number of children in a family is exactly two.

Which of these statements is/are correct?

A statement 1 only
B statement 2 only
C statement 3 only
D statements 2 and 3 only
E statements 1, 2 and 3

Answers and explanations on pages 86–88

SELECTIVE SCHOOL-STYLE TEST **Mathematical Reasoning**

SAMPLE TEST 5

1 Adding consecutive even numbers commencing with 2, Hoa gets a total of 90. What is the last number added?

16	18	20	22	24
A	**B**	**C**	**D**	**E**

2 9 × (7 + ☐) – 10 = 98

☐ =

5	45	52	108	12
A	**B**	**C**	**D**	**E**

3 Jody and Emily went to a netball match. Jody bought seat number 33 and Emily bought seat number 186. If there are 25 seats in each row, how many rows is Emily behind Jody?

5	6	25	153	4
A	**B**	**C**	**D**	**E**

4 Gavin leaves Townsville and flies to Hobart. The temperature in Townsville was 23 °C. The temperature in Hobart, on arrival, was –4 °C. What was the difference in temperature?

A 19 °C
B 23 °C
C 27 °C
D –19 °C
E –23 °C

5 What is the lowest number that leaves a remainder of 1 when divided separately by 4, 5 or 6?

13	21	61	121	181
A	**B**	**C**	**D**	**E**

6 A motorcycle can travel approximately 100 km on 5.5 L of fuel. About how far will it travel on 10 L?

A 110 km
B 165 km
C 180 km
D 220 km
E 550 km

7 What percentage of this square is shaded?

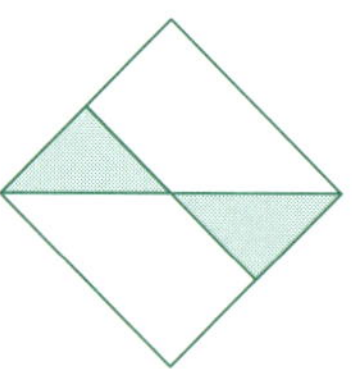

A 20%
B 25%
C 33.3%
D 50%
E 12.5%

8 I am thinking of a certain number. When I increase it by one-quarter then decrease that number by two-thirds I finish up with 5. What number did I start with?

8	12	16	24	20
A	**B**	**C**	**D**	**E**

9 How many lines of symmetry are there in this design?

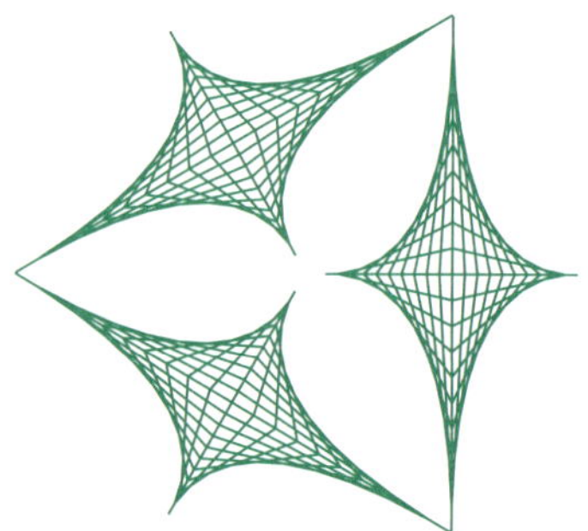

0	1	3	6	2
A	**B**	**C**	**D**	**E**

10 A country train travels at 72 km/h between two towns. The trip takes three-quarters of an hour. What is the distance between the towns?

A 54 km
B 81 km
C 96 km
D 108 km
E 90 km/h

Answers and explanations on pages 88–90

SAMPLE TEST 5

11 A Vedic Square is a nine-by-nine square where the numbers formed are the result of multiplication, with the answer to each multiplication being replaced by its digital sum. For example, $4 \times 8 = 32$, and $3 + 2 = 5$. Sometimes the digital sum requires the digits to be added a second time. For example, $8 \times 7 = 56$, and $5 + 6 = 11$, which then requires $1 + 1 = 2$.

This Vedic Square is partly completed.

	1	2	3	4	5	6	7	8	9
1	1	2	3	4	5	6	7	8	9
2	2	4	6	8	1	3	5	7	9
3	3	6	9	3					
4	4	8					X	5	
5	5	1							
6	6	3			Y				
7	7								
8	8								Z
9	9								

What is the value of $X + Y \times Z$?

40	24	27	36	28
A	**B**	**C**	**D**	**E**

12 Kate made a pattern of balls. The order was two reds, then a green, two blues, a yellow and then purple, and then the pattern repeats many times. What colour is the 45th ball?

A red
B blue
C yellow
D purple
E green

13 Toby has been saving 5c, 10c and 50c coins. He has thirteen 5c coins and twice as many 10c coins. Half his coins are 50c coins. How much has Toby got?

A \$9.45
B \$14.95
C \$22.75
D \$29.25
E \$13.00

14 Here is a number sentence.

$10 - (▲ - 15 \div 5) = 4$.

What is the missing number represented by ▲?

3	25	19	9	15
A	**B**	**C**	**D**	**E**

15 Look at this stack of cubes (each row is complete).

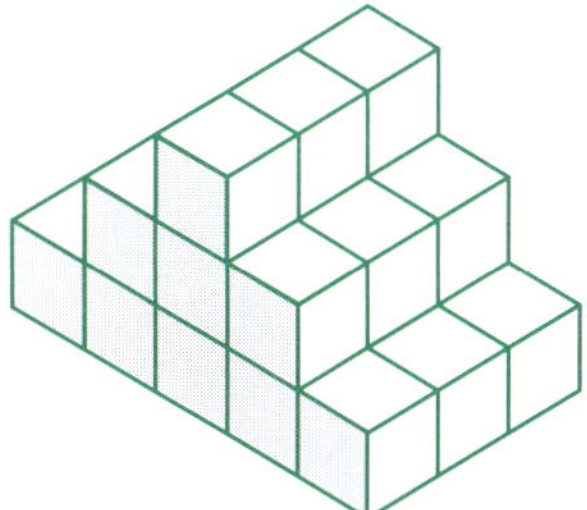

If you could look at it from all sides, how many cubes are completely hidden from view?

1	3	5	7	4
A	**B**	**C**	**D**	**E**

16 The perimeter of a square city block is 1200 m. What is its area?

A 6 ha
B 9 ha
C 12 ha
D 90 ha
E 120 ha

Answers and explanations on pages 88–90

SAMPLE TEST 5

17 What percentage of this square is shaded?

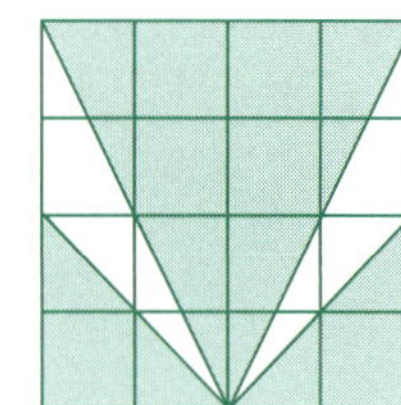

50%	60%	66.6%	75%	80%
A	**B**	**C**	**D**	**E**

18 In this addition each letter represents a digit. Different letters represent different digits.

```
     UP
+   TUB
   BOOT
```

What number does BOOT stand for?

A 1009
B 2115
C 2551
D 1224
E 2113

19 An equilateral triangle has a side length of 6 cm. An isosceles triangle has a perimeter twice as long as the equilateral triangle. If one side is 3 cm longer than another side, which of these could not be a side length of the isosceles triangle?

A 10 cm
B 12 cm
C 14 cm
D 13 cm
E 11 cm

20 750 mL of chilli sauce costs $4.47. What would 1.25 L cost?

A $7.45
B $8.94
C $13.41
D $17.88
E $8.35

21 This was originally a complete 10 cm cube. A 5 cm cube was removed from one corner as shown. What fraction of it has been removed?

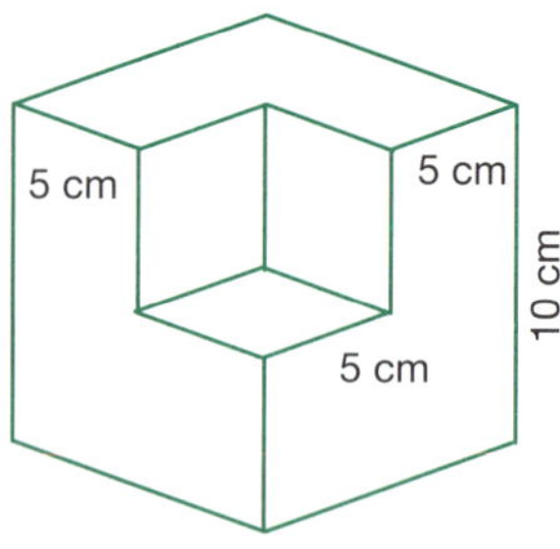

A one-half
B one-quarter
C one-eighth
D one-sixteenth
E three-quarters

22 A Boeing 737 flies 250 km in 25 minutes. How far will it fly in one and a half hours?

A 1800 km
B 1200 km
C 750 km
D 900 km
E 1000 km

23 Rod had a stopwatch. Timing the chimes from the town hall clock at 5 o'clock, Rod found it chimed five times in 4 seconds. How long would it take to chime at 10 o'clock?

A 8 seconds
B 9 seconds
C 9.5 seconds
D 10 seconds
E 8.5 seconds

24 The perimeter of a square is 2 m. What is its area?

A 0.25 m^2
B 0.5 m^2
C 1 m^2
D 4 m^2
E 2 m^2

Answers and explanations on pages 88–90

SAMPLE TEST 5

25 The last day of July is a Thursday. What was the last day of June?

A Tuesday
B Thursday
C Saturday
D Monday
E Friday

26 A group of students were surveyed to find the number of cars owned by people who live at their household. A dot plot shows the results of the survey.

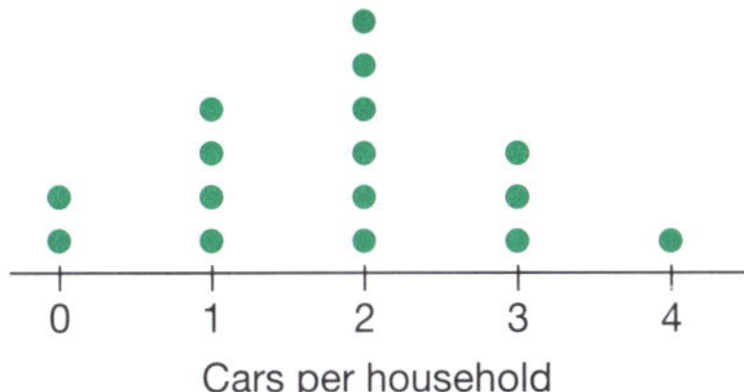

Here are three statements about the graph.

1. Two students had six cars at their household.
2. Twice as many students had one car than those students who did not have a car.
3. The students had a total of 31 cars at their households.

Which of these statements is/are correct?

A statement 1 only
B statement 2 only
C statement 3 only
D statements 1 and 2 only
E statements 1, 2 and 3

27 At a party Nina is blindfolded and faced to the North. She is then rotated 135° clockwise, 180° anticlockwise, 90° clockwise and 180° anticlockwise. What direction is she now facing?

A south
B south-west
C west
D south-east
E north-west

28 A marathon runner can cover 7 km in 20 minutes. What is his average speed?

A 2.8 km/h
B 14 km/h
C 20 km/h
D 21 km/h
E 35 km/h

29 What is the small angle between the hands of a clock at 6.30?

0°	5°	15°	30°	6.5°
A	**B**	**C**	**D**	**E**

30 In a bag there are 24 green balls, 20 red balls and 16 yellow balls. A ball is chosen at random. What is the probability that the ball is yellow?

$\frac{1}{3}$	$\frac{1}{16}$	$\frac{3}{16}$	$\frac{8}{15}$	$\frac{4}{15}$
A	**B**	**C**	**D**	**E**

31 The net of an open-top cube has a total area of 80 cm^2.

What is the volume of the cube?

A 125 cm^3
B 27 cm^3
C 216 cm^3
D 343 cm^3
E 64 cm^3

Answers and explanations on pages 88–90

SAMPLE TEST 5

32 Consider this pattern.

$2^2 - 0^2 = 4$

$3^2 - 1^2 = 8$

$4^2 - 2^2 = 12$

$5^2 - 3^2 = 16$

What is the value of $121^2 - 119^2$?

460	480	490	492	520
A	**B**	**C**	**D**	**E**

33 The graph shows the number of screen-time hours for a group of Year 6 students throughout a week. The time has been rounded to whole hours.

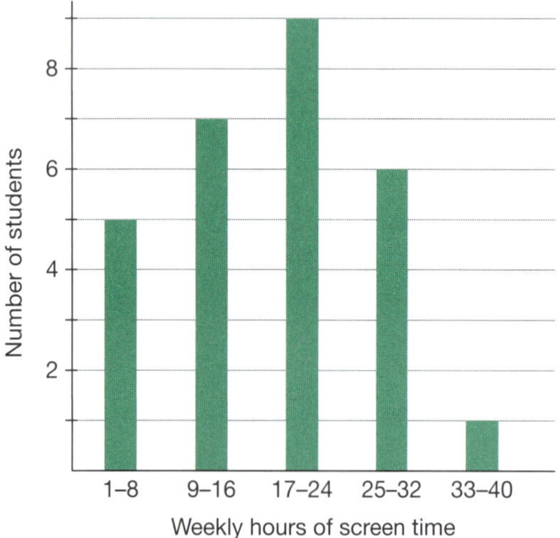

Which of these statements is/are correct?

1 Twenty-eight students were surveyed.

2 The majority of students spent between 9 and 24 hours on screen time.

3 Three more students spent less than 17 hours of screen time than the number of students who spent between 17 and 24 hours.

A statement 1 only
B statement 2 only
C statement 3 only
D statements 1 and 2 only
E statements 1, 2 and 3

34 A board game uses two four-sided dice, numbered 1, 2, 3 and 4. The dice are rolled and the results are added to give a score. What is the probability of getting a score of at least 7?

$\frac{1}{16}$	$\frac{1}{8}$	$\frac{3}{16}$	$\frac{1}{4}$	$\frac{1}{3}$
A	**B**	**C**	**D**	**E**

35 Here is a sequence of numbers:

1, 4, 9, 16, 25, 36, 49 …

Katie picks two consecutive numbers in the sequence. The difference is 41. What is the sum of the numbers?

761	841	1200	1241	1681
A	**B**	**C**	**D**	**E**

Answers and explanations on pages 88–90

SELECTIVE SCHOOL–STYLE TEST **Mathematical Reasoning**

SAMPLE TEST 6

1 A hundred cards are numbered 1 to 100. The cards are arranged in order. The three even cards that add to 78 are discarded. What is the sum of the **next** three consecutive even numbers?

81	84	96	98	101
A	**B**	**C**	**D**	**E**

2 What is the difference between $(3^3 + 2^3)$ and $(3 + 2)^3$?

0	9	80	90	100
A	**B**	**C**	**D**	**E**

3 $4 \times (\square + 9) = 3 \times (\square + 11) + 3$.

$\square =$

3	2	1	0	4
A	**B**	**C**	**D**	**E**

4 If the first and last digits of the number 345 are interchanged, the difference between the two numbers will be

202	102	200	198	298
A	**B**	**C**	**D**	**E**

5 If Elena gives Layla \$10 and Layla gives Avery \$8, the three girls will have the same amount of money. If Layla originally had \$20, how much more money did Elena have than Avery at the start?

A \$8
B \$10
C \$12
D \$16
E \$18

6 What is the total length of the edges of a rectangular prism measuring 4 cm × 3 cm × 5 cm?

A 24 cm
B 40 cm
C 48 cm
D 60 cm
E 36 cm

7 The shape has been formed using identical rectangles arranged to form a square.

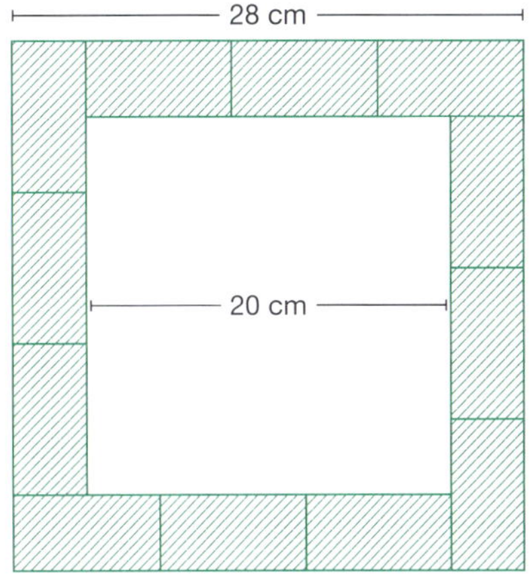

What is the area of each rectangle?

A 20 cm^2
B 25 cm^2
C 30 cm^2
D 32 cm^2
E 28 cm^2

8 A bag of marbles can be shared equally among 2, 3, 4, 5, or 6 players with no marbles left over. What is the smallest number of marbles that can be in the bag?

720	120	60	30	240
A	**B**	**C**	**D**	**E**

9 If 30% of a number is 12, what is that number?

48	40	36	4	360
A	**B**	**C**	**D**	**E**

10 The width of a rectangle is two-thirds of the length. If the length is 12 cm, which of these is the number sentence used to find the perimeter, in centimetres, of the rectangle?

A $12 \times 12 \div 3 \times 2$
B $2 \times 12 + 12 \div 2 \times 3$
C $2 \times 12 + 12 \div 3 \times 2$
D $2 \times (12 + 12 \div 3 \times 2)$
E $2 \times (12 + 12 \div 2 \times 3)$

Answers and explanations on pages 90–92

SAMPLE TEST 6

11 One-quarter of a book is read on Saturday. One-third of the book is read on Sunday. There are 50 pages left to read. How long was the book?

A 90 pages
B 120 pages
C 180 pages
D 240 pages
E 250 pages

12 In this diagram what fraction of the first square is the third square?

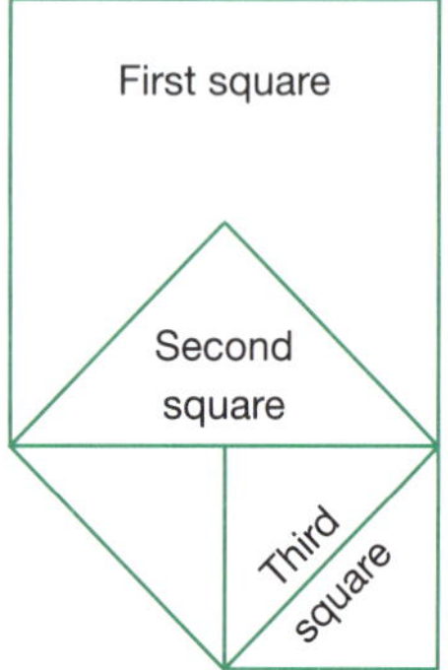

A one-half
B one-quarter
C one-third
D one-eighth
E two-thirds

13 How many lines of symmetry are in this design?

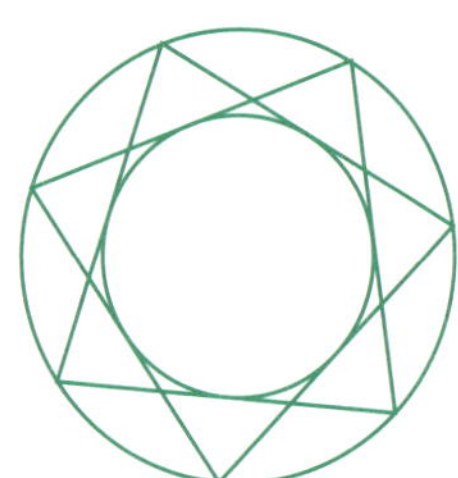

0	6	7	14	12
A	**B**	**C**	**D**	**E**

14 In the magic square, numbers in each row, column and diagonal add to the same number. What is the number that is represented by the *?

	6	3	16
		10	*
14		8	
7		13	2

5	4	1	9	11
A	**B**	**C**	**D**	**E**

15 $\frac{5}{7}$ can be written as the repeating decimal 0.714 285 714 28… Which of these will be the 101st digit to the right of the decimal point?

5	7	8	4	2
A	**B**	**C**	**D**	**E**

16 Two adults and three children go to the movies. An adult ticket costs \$18 and a child ticket is half price. Each person has an ice cream which costs \$4. Which of these gives the number sentence used to find the total cost, in dollars, for the family?

A $4[18 \times 2 + (18 \times 3) \div 2]$
B $18 + 4 \times 2 + (18 \times 3) \div 2 + 4$
C $(18 + 4) \times 2 + (18 \times 3) \div 2 + 4$
D $18 \times 2 + (18 \times 3) \div 2 + 5 \times 4$
E $(18 + 4) \times 2 + (18 \times 3) \div (2 + 4)$

17 Four identical small squares of side length 4 cm are removed from the corners of a square with side 10 cm. What percentage of the original square remains?

32%	36%	40%	64%	72%
A	**B**	**C**	**D**	**E**

Answers and explanations on pages 90–92

SAMPLE TEST 6

18 Two identical cubes are stacked on top of each other. The total volume of the stack is 250 cm^3. What is the sum of the areas of the faces on each cube?

A 75 cm^2
B 25 cm^2
C 125 cm^2
D 300 cm^2
E 150 cm^2

19 Matt makes two identical cardboard squares with slits as shown below.

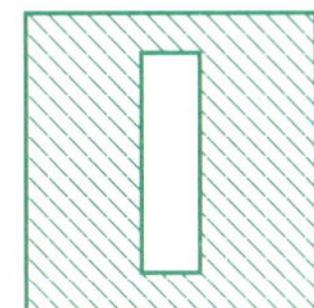

He rotates the second through 90°.

He then places one on top of the other without changing the direction of the slits. What is the shape of the opening?

A 
B 
C 
D 
E 

20 Taylor and Lincoln are reading the same book title. Taylor has read $\frac{1}{4}$ of the book and has 180 pages remaining. If Lincoln has read $\frac{2}{3}$ of the book, how many pages remain?

90	60	80	120	100
A	**B**	**C**	**D**	**E**

21 A metal container is filled with 40 L of olive oil and has a mass of 63 kg. When 10 L of olive oil is poured from the container, the mass is now 49 kg. What is the mass of the empty container?

A 6 kg
B 7 kg
C 8 kg
D 9 kg
E 10 kg

22 The odometer in Marin's car shows 198761. He drives for 3 hours 30 minutes at an average speed of 90 km/h. What does the odometer read now?

A 198764
B 198765
C 199031
D 199058
E 199076

23 A timer beeps every 2 minutes. A second timer beeps every $2\frac{1}{2}$ minutes. Both timers beeped at 11 am. What is the first time after noon they will beep together?

A 12.05
B 12.10
C 12.25
D 12.21
E 12:20

24 In our bathroom the hot tap can fill a container in 3 minutes. The cold tap can fill the same container in 2 minutes. If both taps are running, how long will it take to fill the container?

A 5 minutes
B 2 minutes 30 seconds
C 1 minute 12 seconds
D 40 seconds
E 2 minutes 20 seconds

Answers and explanations on pages 90–92

SAMPLE TEST 6

25 The arrows on the two spinners are spun. The numbers the arrows land on are multiplied. What is the probability that the product is odd?

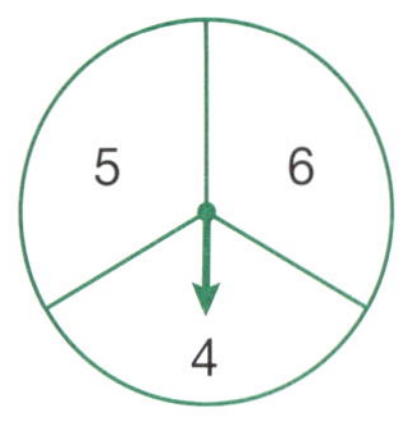

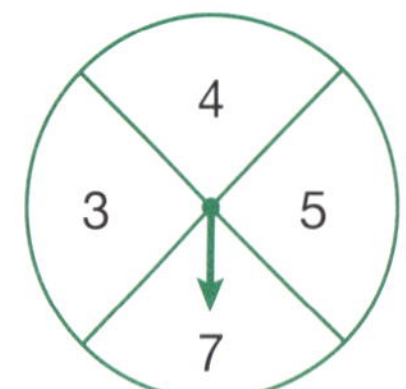

$\frac{1}{12}$	$\frac{1}{6}$	$\frac{1}{4}$	$\frac{1}{3}$	$\frac{5}{12}$
A	**B**	**C**	**D**	**E**

26

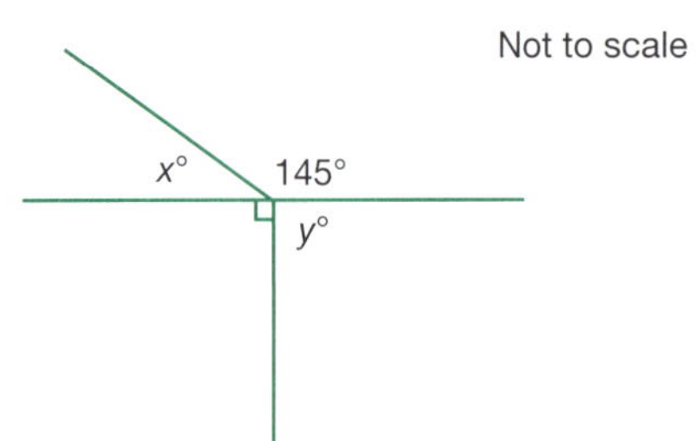

What is the sum of x and y?

130	115	135	145	125
A	**B**	**C**	**D**	**E**

27 Zoe took 3 hours to drive from Mitchell to Glendon. Her average speed for the trip was 80 km/h. How much longer would the trip have been if she decreased the average speed by 20 km/h?

A 10 minutes
B 20 minutes
C 30 minutes
D 45 minutes
E 60 minutes

28 The width of a rectangle is $\frac{1}{5}$ of the perimeter. If the perimeter is 20 cm, what is the area?

A 8 cm^2 **B** 12 cm^2 **C** 16 cm^2
D 24 cm^2 **E** 32 cm^2

29 Here are two views of a cube which has faces labelled *S*, *T*, *V*, *W*, *X* and *Y*.

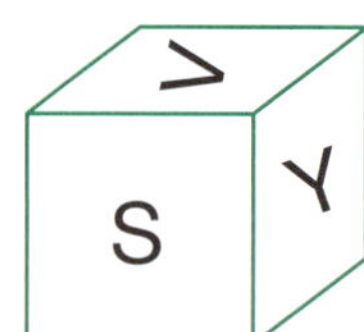

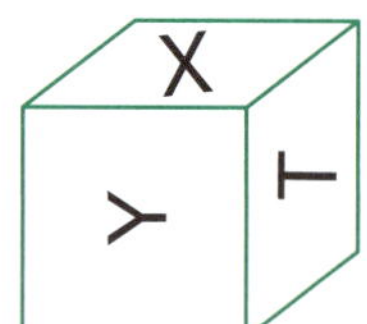

Which letter will be on the front face when *Y* is on the rear face?

W	*S*	*T*	*V*	*X*
A	**B**	**C**	**D**	**E**

30 An auditorium has a wall measuring 25 m by 3 m. Theo is using paint that covers 6 m^2 per 500 mL. The paint is available in 4 L cans. How many cans will Theo require if he uses two coats of paint?

1	2	3	4	5
A	**B**	**C**	**D**	**E**

31 A survey of one hundred 18-year-old students throughout NSW was conducted to find the proportion who owned a driver's licence.

	Licensed	**Not licensed**
Live in Sydney	18	32
Live outside of Sydney	28	22

Here are three statements about the table.

1 28% of the students surveyed live outside Sydney and have a driver's licence.
2 54% of the students surveyed do not have a driver's licence.
3 36% of the students surveyed who live in Sydney have a driver's licence.

Which of these statements is/are correct?

A statements 1, 2 and 3
B statements 1 and 2 only
C statement 1 only
D statement 2 only
E statement 3 only

☞ Answers and explanations on pages 90–92

SAMPLE TEST 6

32 The diagram shows three squares. Each side of square Q is 1 cm longer than the sides of square P.

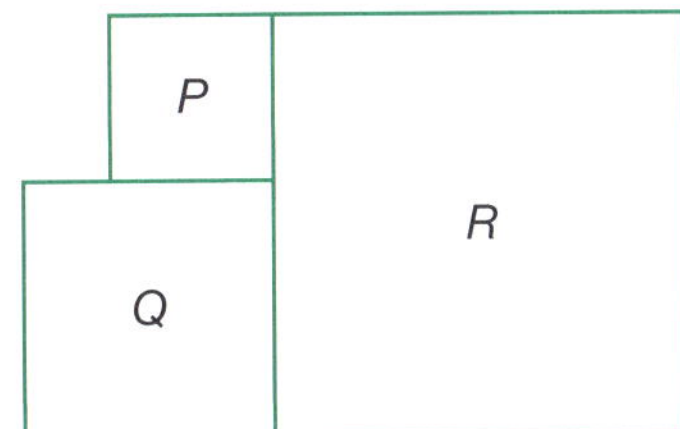

If square P has an area of 16 cm^2, what is the total area of the three squares?

A 77 cm^2
B 93 cm^2
C 100 cm^2
D 105 cm^2
E 122 cm^2

33 Each team in a sports competition plays 36 games. Halfway through the competition, the Tigers have won seven games and the Kangaroos have won twice as many. If the Kangaroos win one-third of the remaining games, how many more games will the Tigers need to win to finish equal with the Kangaroos on the points table, assuming there are no draws in the competition?

20	14	13	15	12
A	**B**	**C**	**D**	**E**

34 There are eight balls in a bag. The chance of selecting a red ball from the bag is $\frac{3}{4}$. Two red balls are removed from the bag. If a ball is now selected at random, what is the probability that it is red?

$\frac{1}{6}$	$\frac{1}{3}$	$\frac{2}{3}$	$\frac{1}{2}$	$\frac{1}{4}$
A	**B**	**C**	**D**	**E**

35 The sector graph shows the hair colour of 36 students.

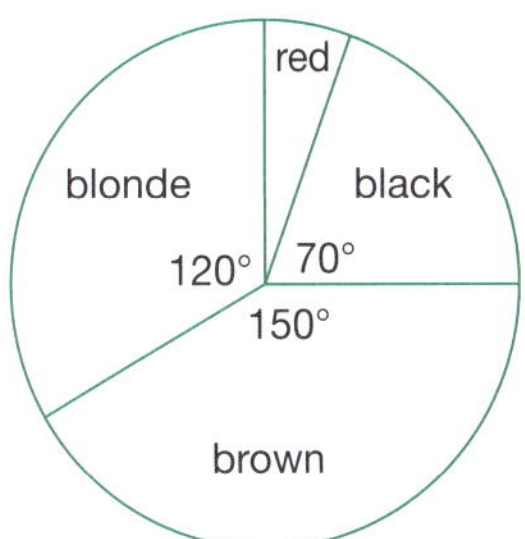

Which of these statements is/are correct?

1 12 students had blonde hair.
2 25% of the students had either red or black hair.
3 Fewer students had blonde or black hair than brown hair.

A statement 1 only
B statement 2 only
C statement 3 only
D statements 1 and 2 only
E statements 1, 2 and 3

Answers and explanations on pages 90–92

SELECTIVE SCHOOL-STYLE TEST **Mathematical Reasoning**

SAMPLE TEST 7

1 Marco's average on his first three tests was 84. His average increased by three marks after the next two tests. If Marco scored 88 in his fourth test, what was his result in the fifth test?

91	92	93	94	95
A	**B**	**C**	**D**	**E**

2 What is the value of 80 less than the sum of 75 and the product of 25 and 5?

120	130	420	150	275
A	**B**	**C**	**D**	**E**

3 If 11 May was a Tuesday, what day of the week was 1 August in the same year?

A Saturday **B** Sunday **C** Monday
D Tuesday **E** Wednesday

4 The average of four numbers is 8. If 4 is subtracted from two of the numbers, what is the change to the average?

A decreases by 4
B decreases by 2
C decreases by 1
D no change
E increases by 2

5 In a TV quiz show there are 10 questions; 5 points are given for a correct answer and 2 points deducted for an incorrect answer. (Unanswered questions are treated as incorrect.)

Mrs Warren attempted all 10 questions and scored 29 points. How many questions did she get wrong?

7	6	4	3	5
A	**B**	**C**	**D**	**E**

6 Which is the greatest amount?

A 50% of $6.50
B 40% of $8.40
C 25% of $14.00
D 100% of $3.10
E 200% of $1.70

7 What fraction of this square is shaded?

A 0.5
B 0.75
C 0.8
D 1.5
E 0.6

8 Robbie finishes the second half of a book in two-thirds the number of days he spent reading the first half. If the whole book took 30 days to read, how long did it take Robbie to read the second half of the book?

12	10	16	15	18
A	**B**	**C**	**D**	**E**

9 What is the missing number?

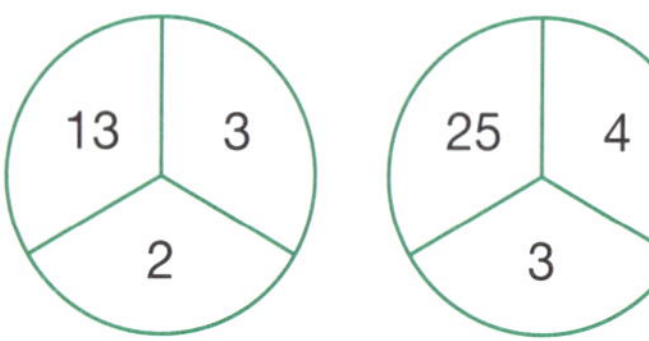

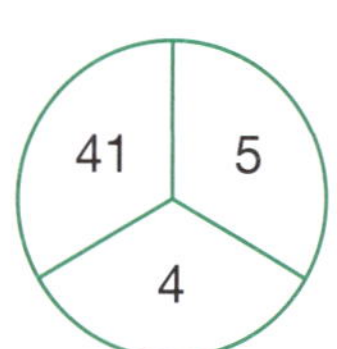

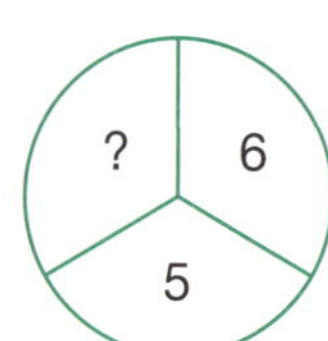

61	57	59	63	65
A	**B**	**C**	**D**	**E**

10 $\boxed{?} - (8 + 2 \times 2) = \boxed{?} \div 4.$

What is the value of $\boxed{?}$?

12	16	20	24	28
A	**B**	**C**	**D**	**E**

Answers and explanations on pages 92–94

SAMPLE TEST 7

11 The grid has some shaded squares. What is the smallest number of additional squares that need to be shaded for the grid to have one line of symmetry?

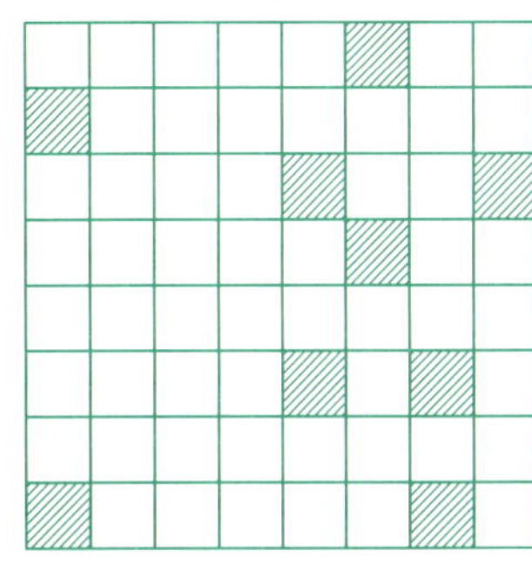

9	3	7	6	2
A	**B**	**C**	**D**	**E**

12 In a Mathematics competition, a correct answer earns 3 marks, an unanswered question is awarded 0 marks and 2 marks are deducted for each incorrect answer. Ashleigh sat the test and answered 20 of the 30 questions. If Ashleigh scored 45 in the test, how many questions did she answer correctly?

14	15	16	17	18
A	**B**	**C**	**D**	**E**

13 Last night in Thredbo the temperature dropped 2 °C every 3 hours. If it was 4 °C at 9 pm, what was the temperature at 6 am this morning?

–2 °C	–5 °C	–3 °C	–4 °C	–6 °C
A	**B**	**C**	**D**	**E**

14 A farmer built a straight fence using 40 equally spaced posts. The distance from the fifth post to the tenth post was 20 m. What is the length of the fence?

A 80 m
B 160 m
C 156 m
D 800 m
E 164 m

15 The diagram shows a square of side 12 cm. Four identical triangles are drawn in the square. A trapezium is shaded inside the square.

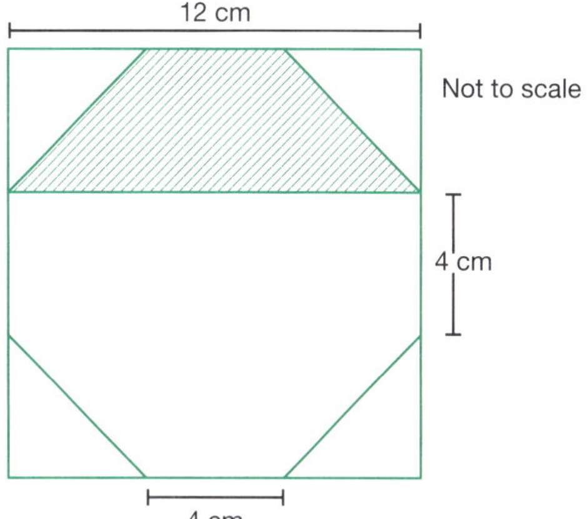

What is the area of the trapezium?

A 32 cm²
B 24 cm²
C 36 cm²
D 48 cm²
E 40 cm²

16 One-third of X equals Y. 50% of Y equals Z.

If $X = 24$, what is $\frac{X}{Y + Z}$?

$\frac{1}{2}$	4	2	$\frac{1}{4}$	7
A	**B**	**C**	**D**	**E**

17 An antique vase is valued at $600. It increases in value by 5% per year. What is its value after two years?

A $661.50
B $660.00
C $630.00
D $610.00
E $666.00

18 Justin's water tank is presently quarter full and contains 1500 L. After a rainy day, the tank has filled to two-thirds full. How much water has been added to the tank during the day?

A 2500 L **B** 1500 L **C** 2000 L
D 1600 L **E** 2400 L

Answers and explanations on pages 92–94

SAMPLE TEST 7

19 A cube has a volume of 64 m^3. The cube is cut into eight smaller identical cubes. These cubes are now placed on top of each other to make a stack. How high is the stack of cubes?

A 8 m
B 12 m
C 16 m
D 24 m
E 32 m

20 Jonah has one hour to cycle 18 km. After 20 minutes he has already cycled $\frac{2}{3}$ of the distance. What speed should he now average to arrive on time?

A 9 km/h
B 10 km/h
C 12 km/h
D 14 km/h
E 15 km/h

21 The diagram shows a large square split into rectangles and squares. The four small squares are identical in size.

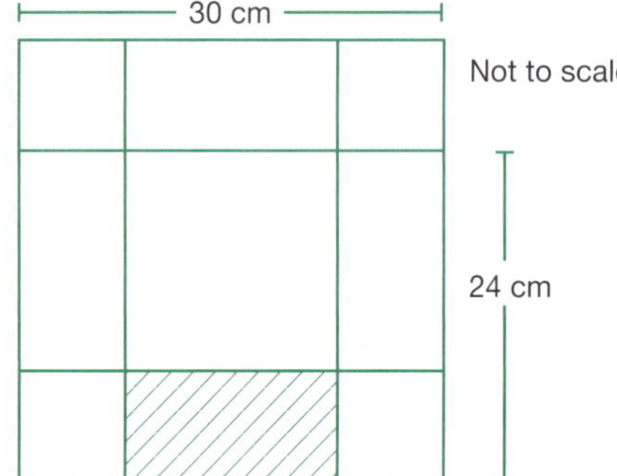

What is the area of the shaded rectangle?

A 72 cm^2
B 112 cm^2
C 108 cm^2
D 144 cm^2
E 120 cm^2

22 The graph shows the mass of a jar containing different amounts of water. The total capacity of the jar is 800 mL.

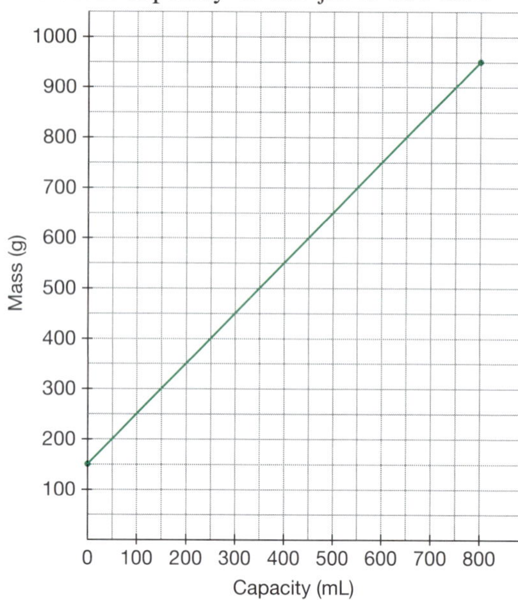

Here are three statements about the graph.

1 The mass of the container when empty is 150 g.
2 When the container is half full its mass is 450 g.
3 When there is 600 mL of water in the container, two-thirds of the water is poured out and the mass of the container decreases by less than 50%.

Which of these statements is/are correct?

A statement 1 only
B statement 2 only
C statement 3 only
D statements 1 and 2 only
E statements 1, 2 and 3

23 A bag contains green, blue and red balls. The probability of choosing a red ball at random is $\frac{3}{8}$ and the chance of choosing a blue ball is $\frac{3}{5}$. What is the smallest possible number of green balls in the bag?

1	2	3	4	6
A	**B**	**C**	**D**	**E**

☞ Answers and explanations on pages 92–94

SAMPLE TEST 7

24 The timetable for buses between the towns of Dalwood and Luskintyre is shown below.

Dalwood to Luskintyre		Luskintyre to Dalwood	
Depart	Arrive	Depart	Arrive
7:15	8:35	6:20	7:45
8:55	10:15	8:15	9:40
11:05	12:25	10:55	12:20
14:45	16:10	14:40	16:05
18:20	19:45	16:55	18:15

Oliver catches the third bus of the day from Luskintyre to Dalwood. He returns to Luskintyre on the next bus. How long was he away from Luskintyre?

A 3 hours 30 minutes
B 3 hours 55 minutes
C 4 hours 5 minutes
D 5 hours 10 minutes
E 5 hours 15 minutes

25 A crate contains 40 boxes. The boxes are identical except they are different colours. One box is chosen at random from the crate. The table shows the probability of choosing each colour. The probability of choosing a blue box is not shown.

Colour	Probability
red	0.3
blue	
green	0.2
yellow	0.3

How many blue boxes are in the crate?

4	5	8	10	12
A	**B**	**C**	**D**	**E**

26 What is the area of the shaded trapezium?

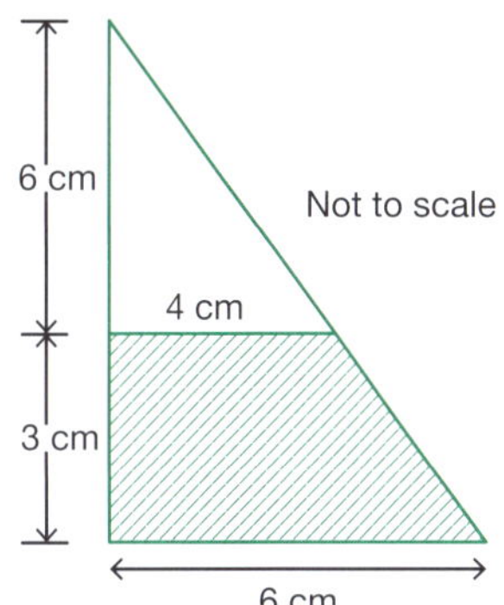

A 10 cm^2
B 11 cm^2
C 12 cm^2
D 14 cm^2
E 15 cm^2

27 A cube has side length of 4 cm and a mass of 128 kg. A square prism is made from the same metal as the cube and has a mass of 1200 kg. If two edges of the prism have a length of 10 cm, what is the length of the other edge?

A 6 cm
B 8 cm
C 10 cm
D 12 cm
E 16 cm

28 Here are the prices displayed at a parking station.

Parking costs			
Weekday		Weekend	
First 2h	\$24	First 4h	\$18
Each additional hour	\$9	Each additional hour	\$7

How much is the total cost of parking Friday, Saturday and Sunday from 9 am to 3 pm?

A \$132 **B** \$92 **C** \$148
D \$124 **E** \$180

Answers and explanations on pages 92–94

SAMPLE TEST 7

29 I make this shape up from small cubes. If the shape was painted, how many cubes would have only one face painted?

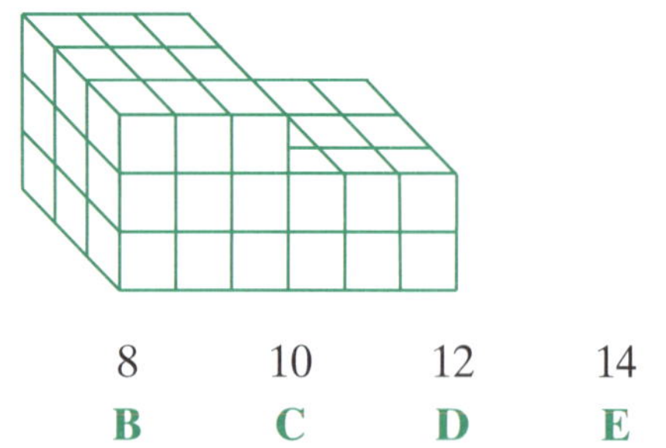

6	8	10	12	14
A	**B**	**C**	**D**	**E**

30 How many lines of symmetry can be drawn on this shape?

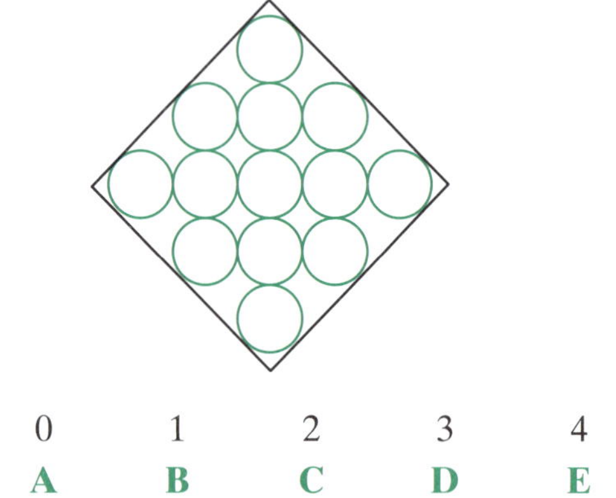

0	1	2	3	4
A	**B**	**C**	**D**	**E**

31 The diagram shows an equilateral triangle inside a square. The two angles represented by the dots are the same size. What is the size of each of these angles?

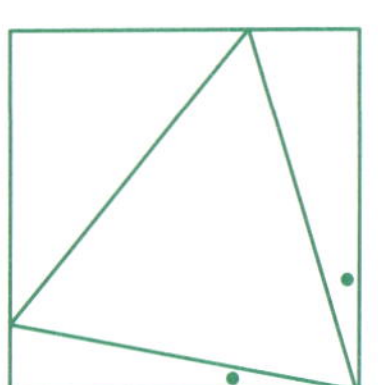

A 12°
B 15°
C 20°
D 10°
E 30°

32 When Karen arrived in the city she checked the time on an analog clock on the Town Hall. The time showed 11 o'clock. By the time she left the hour hand had rotated 120°. What time did Karen leave?

A quarter past 11
B 12 o'clock
C 3 o'clock
D quarter past 2
E 4 o'clock

33 The quiz results of a group of students are recorded in the graph below.

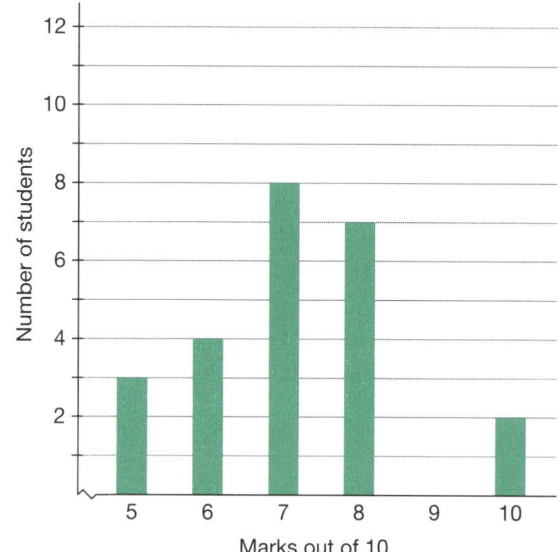

Which of these statements is/are correct?

1 Twenty-four students took the quiz.
2 50% of the students scored 6 or 7.
3 Nine students scored at least 80% on the quiz.

A statement 1 only
B statement 2 only
C statement 3 only
D statements 1 and 2 only
E statements 1, 2 and 3

☞ Answers and explanations on pages 92–94

SAMPLE TEST 7

34 The length of rectangle *P* is half the length of rectangle *Q*, which is half the length of rectangle *R*. All three rectangles have the same width. How many rectangle *P*s would need to cover rectangle *R*?

2	4	8	12	16
A	**B**	**C**	**D**	**E**

35 Benji and Eli have a combined mass of 100 kg. Eli and Ned have a combined mass of 125 kg, and Benji and Ned have a combined mass of 141 kg. What is Eli's mass?

56	39	58	83	42
A	**B**	**C**	**D**	**E**

Answers and explanations on pages 92–94

SELECTIVE SCHOOL-STYLE TEST **Mathematical Reasoning**

SAMPLE TEST 8

1 Three boys have an average mass of 51 kg. If two of the boys have a total mass of 110 kg, what is the mass of the third boy?

A 38 kg
B 39 kg
C 43 kg
D 51 kg
E 55 kg

2 How many whole numbers are between $\sqrt{15}$ and $\sqrt{150}$?

9	10	100	134	135
A	**B**	**C**	**D**	**E**

3 In which of these is the dotted line a line of symmetry?

E MM

4 Halle has 71 bracelets. She arranges them into groups of four and five bracelets. What is the smallest possible number of groups of five she can have?

1	2	3	4	5
A	**B**	**C**	**D**	**E**

5 There are 168 students attending a Year 7 orientation day. There are two activities. Activity *A* involves forming teams of four students and Activity *B* involves teams of six students. How many more teams will be formed for Activity *A* than Activity *B*?

14	8	12	18	16
A	**B**	**C**	**D**	**E**

6 Here is a 3D shape.

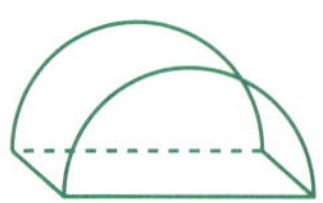

Which of these is the net of the shape?

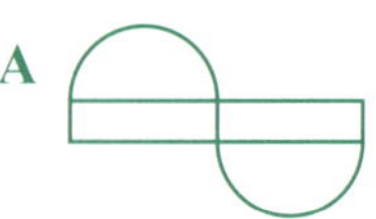

7 The price of an ice cream is $4.80. This is 50% of my money and 40% of Kevin's money. How much do we have altogether?

A $14.40
B $18.00
C $21.60
D $24.00
E $33.60

8 What is three-quarters of an amount if two-thirds of the amount is $1280?

A $1380 **B** $1300 **C** $1320
D $1480 **E** $1440

9 Look at this stack of cubes. There are no gaps or holes. If you could look at it from all sides, how many cubes are completely hidden from view?

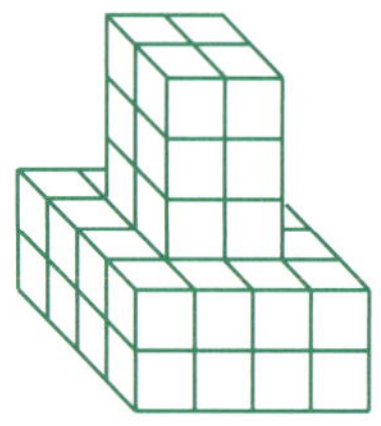

2	3	4	6	5
A	**B**	**C**	**D**	**E**

Answers and explanations on pages 94–96

SAMPLE TEST 8

10 Last week the price of a cryptocurrency coin was \$2000. This week the price increased to \$6000. What is the percentage increase?

A 50%
B 100%
C 200%
D 300%
E 400%

11 Theo, Cleo and Leo enter a competition. A win or a draw earns some points while a loss earns 0 points. Theo wins 4 games, draws 1 game and has 22 points. Cleo wins 3 games, draws 2 games and has 19 points. How many points has Leo after he wins 2 games and draws 3 games?

14	16	17	18	19
A	**B**	**C**	**D**	**E**

12 Lucinda added the highest common factor of 12 and 18 to the lowest common multiple of 18 and 12. What was Lucinda's answer?

30	32	40	42	48
A	**B**	**C**	**D**	**E**

13 Two-fifths of the 40 chocolates in a box are dark chocolate and the remainder are milk chocolate. After the box was passed around a group of friends, a dark chocolate and four milk chocolates had been taken and eaten. What fraction of the remaining chocolates were milk?

$\frac{5}{8}$	$\frac{7}{10}$	$\frac{4}{7}$	$\frac{3}{5}$	$\frac{5}{6}$
A	**B**	**C**	**D**	**E**

14 For her flight to Singapore, Sarah had a 22-kg baggage allowance. The airline has an excess baggage charge of \$12.50 per kg. How much did Sarah's baggage weigh if she had to pay \$100?

A 4 kg
B 8 kg
C 26 kg
D 28 kg
E 30 kg

15 What is the missing number?

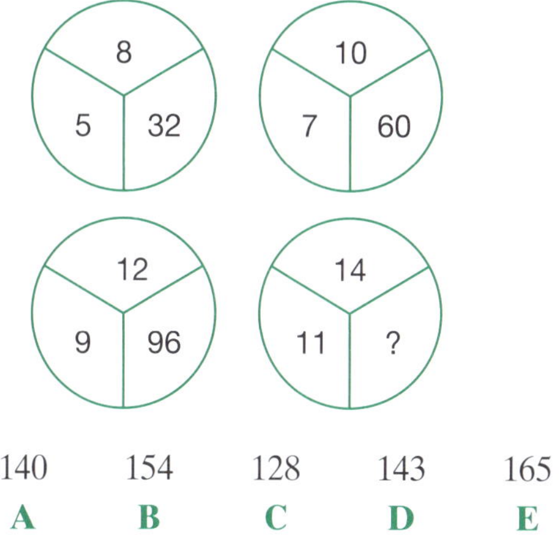

140	154	128	143	165
A	**B**	**C**	**D**	**E**

16 Adrian used grey squares to make this sequence of figures.

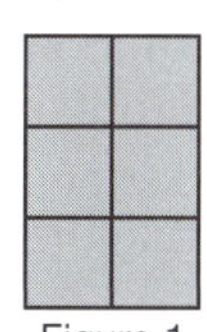
Figure 1

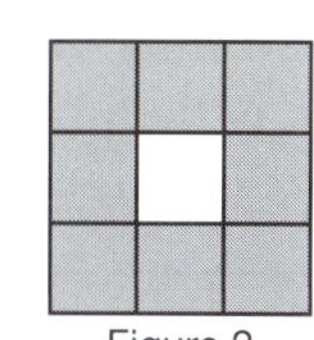
Figure 2

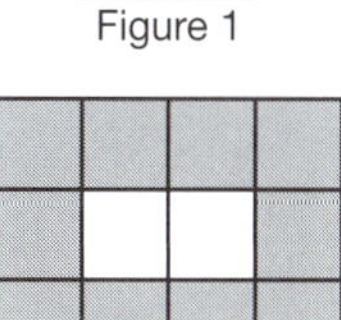
Figure 3

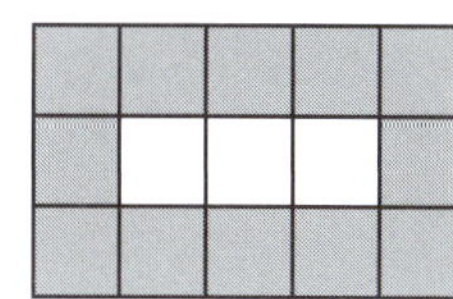
Figure 4

How many grey squares would be needed to make Figure 25?

48	50	52	54	56
A	**B**	**C**	**D**	**E**

Answers and explanations on pages 94–96

SAMPLE TEST 8

17 When she babysits, Ella charges \$20 for the first hour and \$12 for every hour after that. What is the number sentence she can use to find the amount, in dollars, she charges to babysit for 4 hours?

A $20 + 12 \times 4$
B $20 + 12 \times (4 - 1)$
C $(20 + 12) \times (4 - 1)$
D $(20 + 4) \times (12 - 1)$
E $20 + 4 \times (12 - 1)$

18 In a rectangle the length is $1\frac{1}{2}$ times the width. If the perimeter is 100 cm, what is the area?

A 600 cm^2
B 750 cm^2
C 900 cm^2
D 1200 cm^2
E 150 cm^2

19 Here is a sequence of numbers. 13, 21, 29, 37 … What is the twenty-first number in the sequence?

168	165	181	218	173
A	**B**	**C**	**D**	**E**

20 The diagram shows a pool measuring 8 m by 4 m. Two-metre wide paving is laid around the outside of the pool. A glass fence is then built around the outside of the paved area.

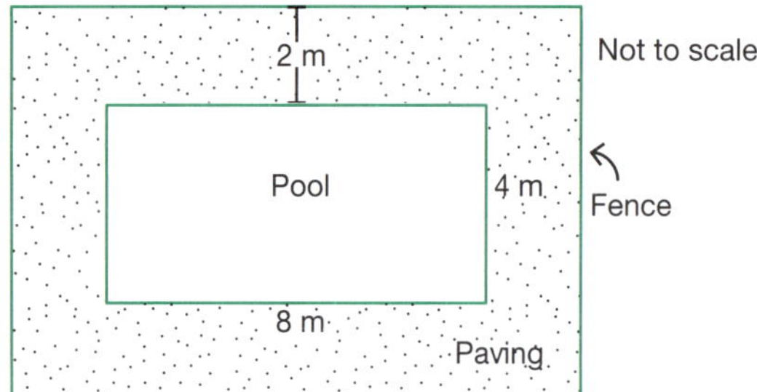

If the cost of the glass fence is \$300 per metre, what is the total cost of the fence?

A \$7200
B \$9600
C \$12 000
D \$14 400
E \$16 000

21 If ⬬ + ⬬ + ⬬ + ⬬ + ■ + ■ = 40 and ⬬ = 6, what is the value of ⬬ + ■ × ⬬?

42	64	54	84	102
A	**B**	**C**	**D**	**E**

22 Logan has three sticks. The sticks are 9 cm, 13 cm and 15 cm in length. He wants to use these sticks to measure the length of other objects. Which of these measurements **cannot** be measured?

A 4 cm **B** 23 cm **C** 24 cm
D 28 cm **E** 37 cm

23 The average length of the sides of a right-angled triangle is 10 cm. If the longest side is 13 cm and the difference between the shortest and longest side is 8 cm, what is the area of the triangle?

A 30 cm^2 **B** 24 cm^2 **C** 32 cm^2
D 48 cm^2 **E** 40 cm^2

24 Morgan has a dozen glasses, each with a capacity of 250 mL. He pours juice from a 2-litre container into the glasses. He decides to fill the glasses to only $\frac{4}{5}$ of their total capacity to prevent spillage. How many of the glasses will remain empty?

4	1	2	3	5
A	**B**	**C**	**D**	**E**

Answers and explanations on pages 94–96

SAMPLE TEST 8

25 The letter Z has been drawn. Which of these transformations will result in an image identical to the original Z?

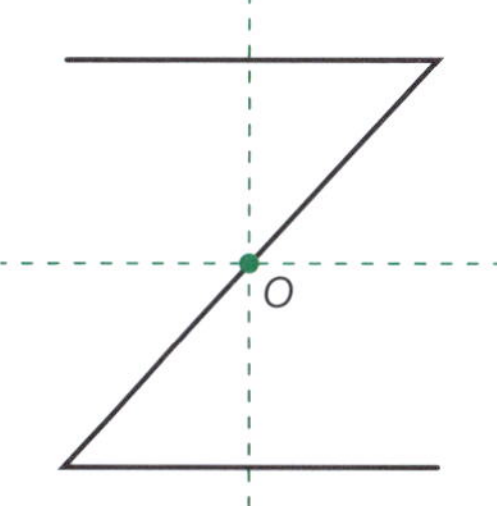

A a rotation of 90° in a clockwise direction around O

B a reflection about the vertical line

C a reflection about the horizontal line

D a rotation of 180° around O

E a rotation of 90° in an anticlockwise direction about O

26 The graph shows the distance travelled by a motorist over a period of time.

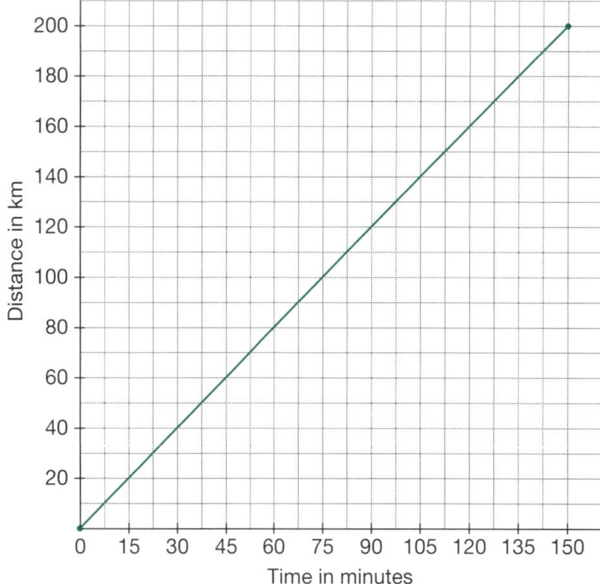

Here are three statements about the graph.

1 It took the motorist 45 minutes to travel 60 km.

2 The motorist is travelling at a speed of 80 km/h.

3 At this speed the motorist would travel 250 km in 3 hours 10 minutes.

Which of these statements is/are correct?

A statement 2 only

B statements 1, 2 and 3

C statement 1 only

D statement 3 only

E statements 1 and 2 only

27 An empty rectangular fish tank has a length of 50 cm, a width of 30 cm and a height of 40 cm. William pours 15 L of water into the tank. What is the depth of water in the tank? (Use 1000 cm^3 = 1 L)

15 cm	8 cm	16 cm	20 cm	10 cm
A	**B**	**C**	**D**	**E**

28 A plane took off from city P at 9:20 pm Wednesday. The plane flew for 8 hours 15 minutes to city Q. If city Q is 4 hours ahead of city P, what was the local time in city Q when the plane landed?

A 9:05 am Wednesday

B 1:35 am Thursday

C 9:05 am Thursday

D 9:35 am Thursday

E 11:35 am Thursday

29 A group of students were surveyed to find their favourite colours. The results are shown in the table.

Colour	Students
red	5
blue	4
yellow	7
purple	4

A student is chosen at random. What is the probability that their favourite colour was purple?

0.4	0.1	0.2	0.25	0.5
A	**B**	**C**	**D**	**E**

Answers and explanations on pages 94–96

SAMPLE TEST 8

30 Last Saturday Georgia travelled 480 km from Jacob Junction to Trundle. She drove the first quarter of her journey at an average speed of 60 km/h. For the next quarter of her journey, she increased her average speed by 20 km/h. The rest of her journey was covered in 2 hours 30 minutes. How long was the trip?

A 5 hours 20 minutes
B 5 hours 30 minutes
C 5 hours 40 minutes
D 6 hours
E 8 hours

31 Which of these is the fastest speed?

A 0.3 km/h
B 6 m/min
C 160 cm/min
D 12 mm/sec
E 480 m/h

32 What is the size of the obtuse angle between the hands on an analog clock when the time is 12:30?

180°	175°	172.5°	170°	165°
A	**B**	**C**	**D**	**E**

33 Michael can dig a trench in 20 minutes. Laura can dig the same-sized trench in one hour. If they work together, how long will it take to dig the trench?

A 10 minutes
B 15 minutes
C 12 minutes
D 30 minutes
E 18 minutes

34 Five identical cards numbered 1 to 5 are turned face down on a desk. Zoe chooses two cards at random, one after the other. She multiplies the number on her first card by the number on her second card and calls the result a score. What is the probability that the score is odd?

$\frac{1}{20}$	$\frac{1}{2}$	$\frac{3}{5}$	$\frac{3}{10}$	$\frac{1}{4}$
A	**B**	**C**	**D**	**E**

35 The quiz results of a group of students are recorded in the graph below. One column has been deleted.

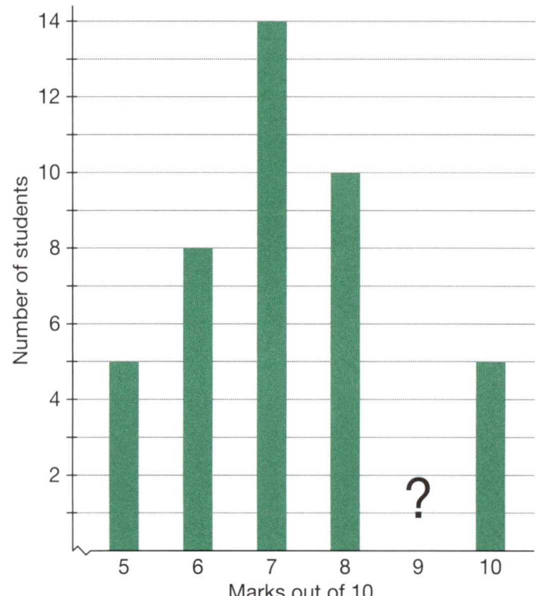

If 74% of the students scored at least 7 out of 10, how many students scored 9?

5	8	9	6	7
A	**B**	**C**	**D**	**E**

☞ Answers and explanations on pages 94–96

SELECTIVE SCHOOL–STYLE TEST **Mathematical Reasoning**

SAMPLE TEST 9

1 How many lines of symmetry can be drawn on this shape?

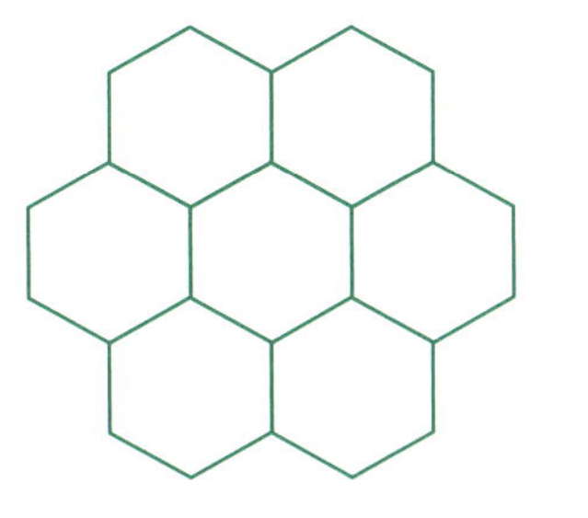

1	2	3	6	12
A	**B**	**C**	**D**	**E**

2 Two years ago, Jesse was five times the age of Freya. Today, Jesse is four times Freya's age. How long will it be until Jesse is three times the age of Freya?

A 2 years
B 4 years
C 6 years
D 8 years
E 10 years

3 Lauren writes down eight different positive integers. The average of the numbers is 10. What is the largest possible number on Lauren's list?

73	48	52	80	54
A	**B**	**C**	**D**	**E**

4 Frankie arranged these five numbers in order from least number of factors to greatest.

16, 24, 36, 50, 64

Which of these is the middle number on the list?

16	24	36	50	64
A	**B**	**C**	**D**	**E**

5 What is the value of $36 - 12 \div 3 \times 2 + 1$?

17	24	29	33	35
A	**B**	**C**	**D**	**E**

6 How many of these are nets of cubes?

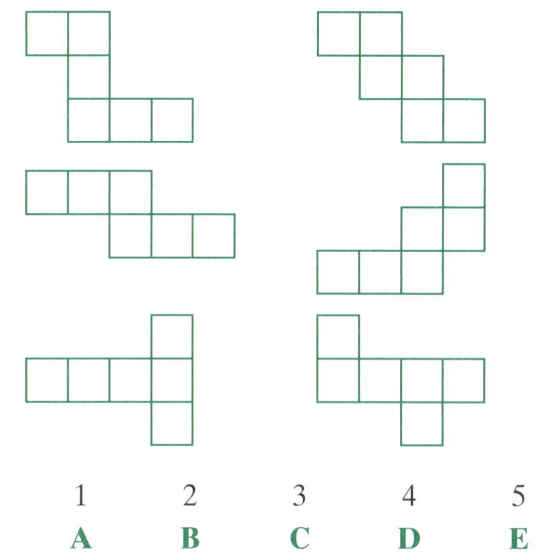

1	2	3	4	5
A	**B**	**C**	**D**	**E**

7 Kate is making a pattern out of white and green tiles. Here is the line of tiles she has already arranged. She wants the pattern to have a vertical line of symmetry. What is the smallest number of tiles she needs to place on the right side of her pattern?

5	4	8	7	6
A	**B**	**C**	**D**	**E**

8 A group of university students who were born overseas was surveyed. The continent they were each born in was recorded.

Continent	Number
Europe	3
North America	5
South America	8
Asia	24
Africa	10

A student is chosen at random. What is the probability that they were born in Asia?

0.48	0.5	0.2	0.24	0.12
A	**B**	**C**	**D**	**E**

Answers and explanations on pages 96–98

SAMPLE TEST 9

9 Lara has \$50 more than Kate. Jannah has twice as much money as Kate. If the girls have a total of \$290, how much money has Lara?

A \$80
B \$140
C \$110
D \$120
E \$130

10 In another world the symbol # is used to find a special result.
If $a\#b = b + a \times b \div (b - a)$, what is the value of 4#8?

32	16	144	48	8
A	**B**	**C**	**D**	**E**

11 A balloon is released at a height of 2 m. Every 2 seconds the balloon rises 5 m in height. At what height is the balloon after one and a half minutes?

A 152 m
B 225 m
C 227 m
D 302 m
E 302.5 m

12 When 2 people shake hands there is 1 handshake. When 3 people shake each other's hands there are 3 handshakes. When 4 people shake each other's hands there are 6 handshakes. How many handshakes are there when 10 people shake each other's hands?

45	40	50	60	55
A	**B**	**C**	**D**	**E**

13 The symbols ■ and ▲ represent numbers.

$\frac{1}{2}$ of ■ = ▲ and $\frac{1}{3}$ of (■ + ▲) = 4

What is the number represented by ▲?

2	3	4	6	8
A	**B**	**C**	**D**	**E**

14 The shape is made of a rectangle and a triangle. The area of the rectangle is three times the area of the triangle.

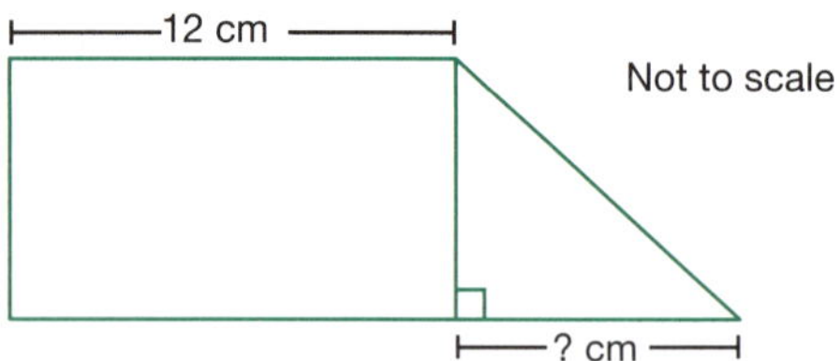

If the area of the rectangle is 72 cm^2, what is the missing length on the triangle?

A 8 cm
B 9 cm
C 10 cm
D 12 cm
E 18 cm

15 Emily's car uses petrol at the rate of 8 L per 100 km. How far will she travel using 54 L?

A 600 km
B 615 km
C 625 km
D 650 km
E 675 km

16 Jenna makes a box with dimensions 80 cm by 40 cm by 20 cm. Leilani makes another box which has one-quarter the volume of Jenna's box. Which of these could be the dimensions of Leilani's box?

A 40 cm by 20 cm by 10 cm
B 20 cm by 10 cm by 5 cm
C 80 cm by 10 cm by 5 cm
D 40 cm by 40 cm by 10 cm
E 20 cm by 20 cm by 10 cm

17 Symon buys exactly 30 L of petrol every time he visits a petrol station. Last year he used an average of 45 L of petrol every week. About how many times did Symon buy petrol last year?

74	78	81	84	87
A	**B**	**C**	**D**	**E**

Answers and explanations on pages 96–98

SAMPLE TEST 9

18 A container half full of liquid has a mass of 8.2 kg. When it is a quarter full it has a mass of 4.9 kg. What is the mass of the container when it is full?

A 16.4 kg
B 19.6 kg
C 14.8 kg
D 18.0 kg
E 13.2 kg

19 Charlie drove at an average speed of 80 km/h from 11:00 to 11:15. She increased her average speed by 10 km/h for another 20 minutes. How far had she travelled from 11:00 to 11:35?

A 55 km
B 60 km
C 50 km
D 45 km
E 40 km

20 A pan balance is used to find the mass of different combinations of solids.

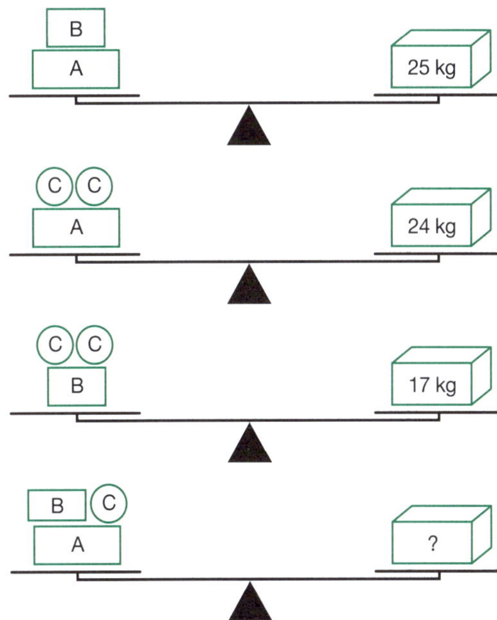

What is the missing mass?

A 29 kg **B** 22 kg **C** 26 kg
D 31 kg **E** 33 kg

21 If $P + Q + R = 50$, $P + Q = 23$ and $R - P = 11$, what is $Q + (R - P)$?

14	16	19	18	21
A	**B**	**C**	**D**	**E**

22 The diagram shows a rectangle measuring 12 cm by 10 cm. A square is removed from the rectangle leaving a shaded part with an area of 56 cm².

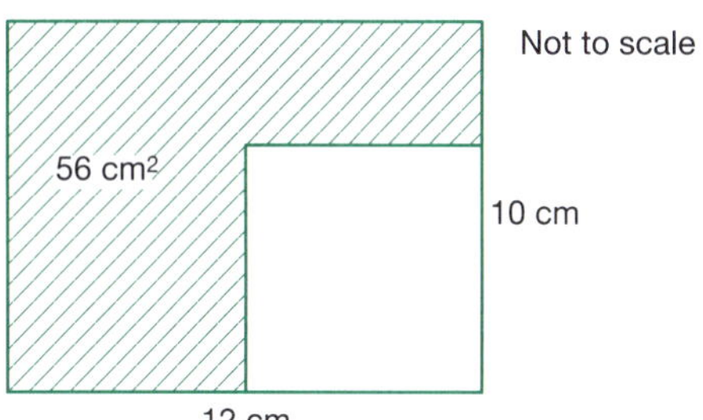

What is the perimeter of the square?

A 64 cm
B 40 cm
C 32 cm
D 48 cm
E 36 cm

23 Raheem left P and walked 5 km east to Q. He then turned and walked 5 km north to R. Raheem then turned and walked 10 km west to S. He finally turned and walked 10 km south to T. What direction is P from T?

A south-east
B south-west
C north-west
D east
E north-east

24 Today Melbourne is 14 hours ahead of New York. New York is 6 hours behind Paris. If it 11:30 pm Wednesday in Paris, what time is it in Melbourne?

A 7:30 am Thursday
B 9:30 am Thursday
C 7:30 pm Thursday
D 9:30 pm Thursday
E 5:30 am Thursday

Answers and explanations on pages 96–98

SAMPLE TEST 9

25 What is the time 16 hours before 16 minutes after midday?

A 1944
B 1916
C 2016
D 1816
E 1744

26 Every week Elle does a 25-question mental arithmetic test. After 4 weeks she has averaged 52% correct. How many does she have to get right in the fifth week to bring her average up to 60%?

8	15	18	23	25
A	**B**	**C**	**D**	**E**

27 In a national competition the first three placegetters receive prize money. The winner is given two-thirds of the total prize money. Second placegetter receives three times as much as the third placegetter. If third place was given $2000, what was the total prize money?

A $12 000
B $24 000
C $15 000
D $18 000
E $30 000

28 In the diagram all whole numbers from 1 to 60 are inside the rectangle. In circle *A* are the multiples of 5, in circle *B* are the multiples of 4 and in circle *C* are the multiples of 3. How many numbers should be in the shaded section?

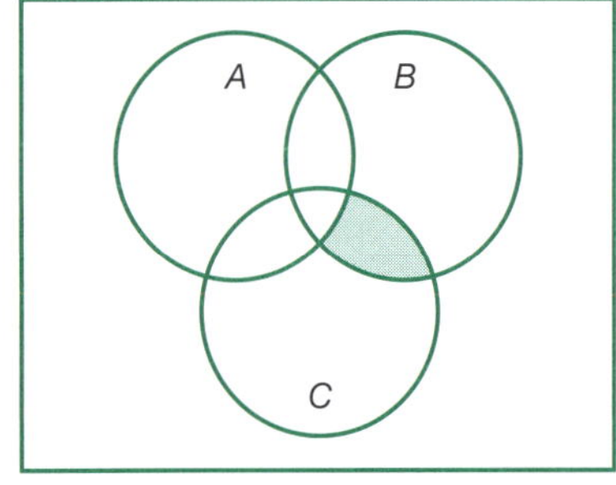

3	4	5	6	8
A	**B**	**C**	**D**	**E**

29 Three families buy tickets to the circus. The Henderson family is two adults and three children and they pay $118. The Harvey family is one adult and two children and they pay $68. The Dann family buy tickets for two adults and one child. How much will the Dann family pay?

$70	$72	$76	$80	$82
A	**B**	**C**	**D**	**E**

30 The arrow is pointing to the letter *T*. The arrow is moved in a clockwise direction to *V*. Through how many degrees is the arrow moved?

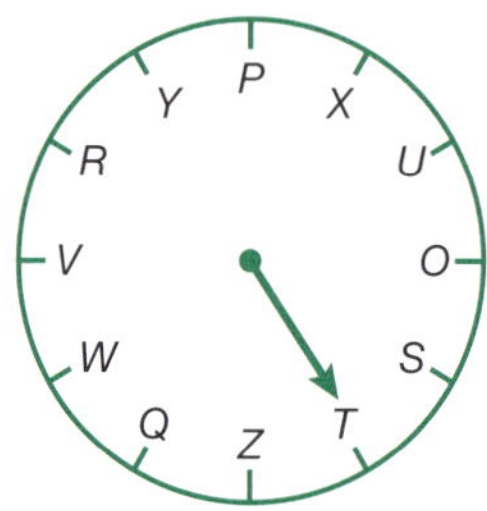

A 90°
B 150°
C 120°
D 270°
E 240°

31 This is an octahedron. Which is the correct table row of information for the shape?

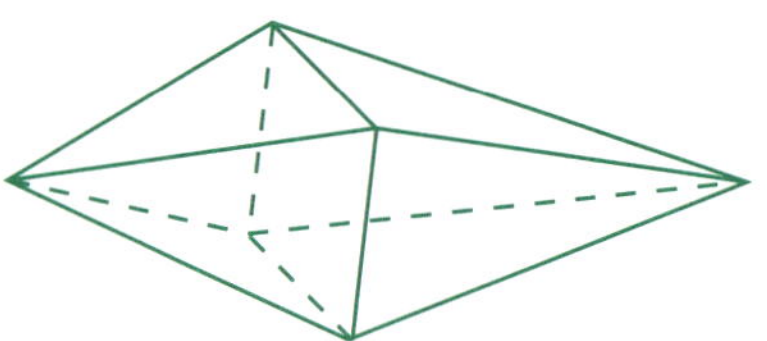

	Edges	Vertices	Faces
A	12	4	8
B	8	6	8
C	8	2	9
D	12	6	8
E	6	6	6

Answers and explanations on pages 96–98

SAMPLE TEST 9

32 Students recorded the colour of 48 cars in the teacher's car park. The results are shown in the sector graph below.

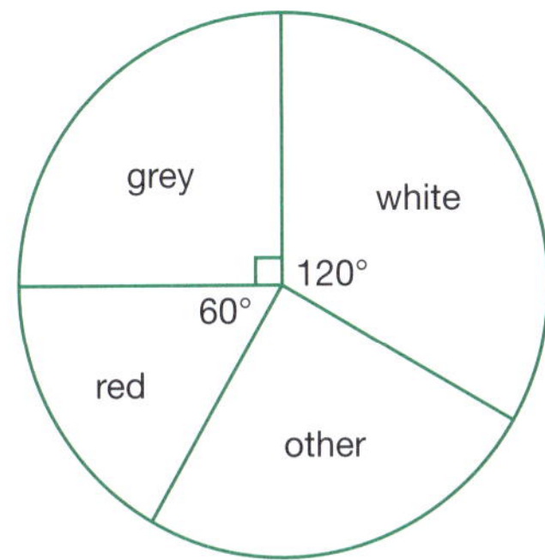

Here are three statements about the graph.

1. There were 12 white cars.
2. 25% of the cars were grey.
3. There were 40 cars that were not red in colour.

Which of these statements is/are correct?

A statements 2 and 3 only
B statement 1 only
C statement 2 only
D statement 3 only
E statements 1, 2 and 3

33 Olivia is in hospital and the chart shows her temperature recorded by nursing staff.

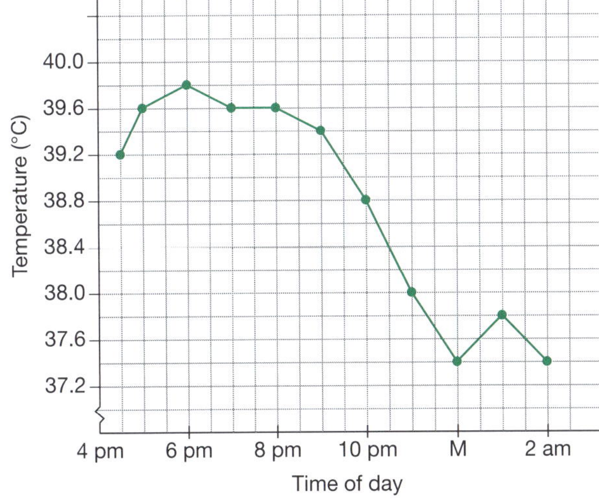

Which of these statements is/are correct?

1. Olivia's temperature was at least 39.6 °C for 3 hours.
2. Olivia's temperature was taken and recorded 10 times.
3. Olivia's temperature was recorded for a total of 10 hours.

A statements 1 and 2 only
B statements 1, 2 and 3
C statement 1 only
D statement 2 only
E statement 3 only

34 A dice is rolled. Which of these is the most likely outcome?

A rolling a 3
B rolling a 6
C rolling a prime number
D rolling a factor of 18
E rolling at least 5

35 A large rectangle has been split into three smaller rectangles. The areas of the smaller rectangles are 20 cm², 18 cm² and 10 cm².

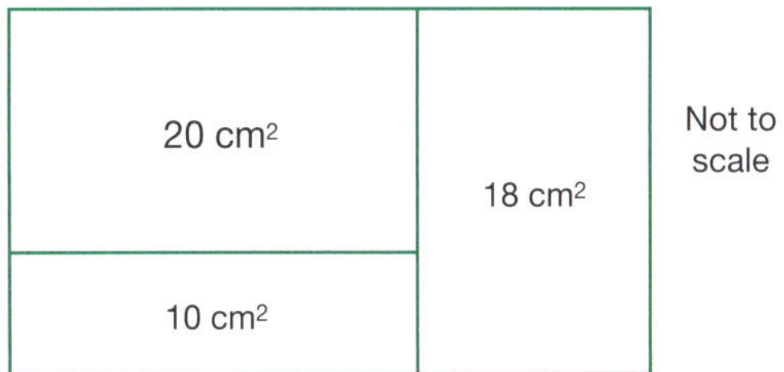

Which of these is a possible perimeter of the original rectangle?

A 20 cm
B 22 cm
C 24 cm
D 26 cm
E 28 cm

Answers and explanations on pages 96–98

SELECTIVE SCHOOL-STYLE TEST **Mathematical Reasoning**

SAMPLE TEST 10

1 At a football game, the number of adult spectators is four times the number of child spectators. Which of these could be the total number of spectators?

A 16 458
B 22 785
C 38 552
D 41 501
E 55 389

2 The sum of two numbers X and Y is 60 and their difference is 36. If $X > Y$, what is $\frac{X}{Y}$?

4	3	2	8	6
A	**B**	**C**	**D**	**E**

3 What is the smallest number that when divided by 3, 4 or 5 has a remainder of 2.

38	44	62	92	122
A	**B**	**C**	**D**	**E**

4 If 45% of a number is 27, what is that number?

30	54	58	60	64
A	**B**	**C**	**D**	**E**

5 Holly decides to have a savings plan. She will deposit \$100 in the first month and increase the amount deposited by 10% each subsequent month. How much will she have saved after three months?

A \$310
B \$321
C \$330
D \$331
E \$311

6 A ride-sharing company has the following charges: Hire charge \$4.00, Distance rate \$2.00/km, Waiting time \$1.50/minute. What is the cost of a journey of 16 km with a 2-minute waiting time?

A \$39
B \$37
C \$41.50
D \$70
E \$43

7 Numbers X and Y are plotted on the number line.

What is $Y - X$?

3	2.6	2.8	2.2	2.4
A	**B**	**C**	**D**	**E**

8 Eve is writing a sequence of numbers on this grid. What is the value of $c - (b - a)$?

1	2	3	4
2	4	6	8
4	8		
a		b	
16			c

42	48	56	60	64
A	**B**	**C**	**D**	**E**

9 Here is a pattern of shapes. How many grey squares are in the pattern when there is a total of 37 squares?

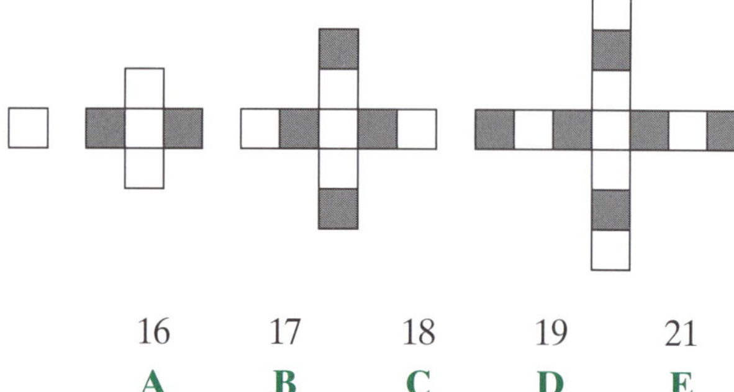

16	17	18	19	21
A	**B**	**C**	**D**	**E**

10 The average height of three women is 172 cm. The average height of five men is 175 cm. Which of these number sentences can be used to find the average height of all the people?

A $(172 + 175) \times (3 + 5) \div 8$
B $(172 \div 3 + 175 \div 5) \times 8$
C $172 \times 3 + 175 \times 5 \div 8$
D $(172 + 175) \div 8$
E $(172 \times 3 + 175 \times 5) \div 8$

Answers and explanations on pages 98–100

SAMPLE TEST 10

11 The pan balance shows that six balls and four cubes has the same mass as three balls and eight cubes.

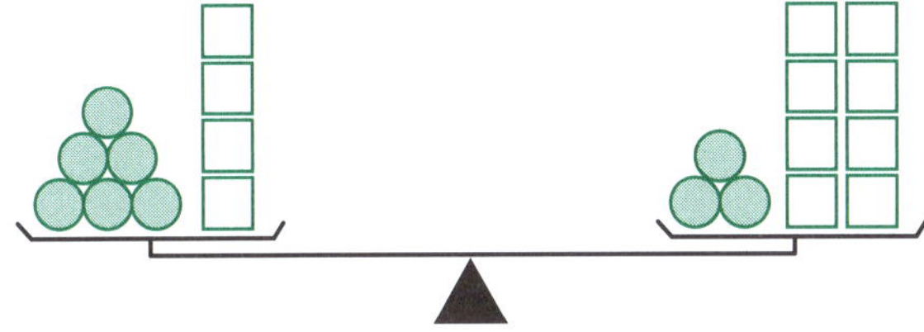

How many balls balance eight cubes?

2	4	6	12	16
A	**B**	**C**	**D**	**E**

12 Eve thinks of a number. She multiplies her number by 4 and then divides this result by 2. She adds 8 and then subtracts 5. She subtracts the first number she thought of. She then adds 3. Again, she subtracts the original number she thought of. What is her answer?

6	11	8	5	2
A	**B**	**C**	**D**	**E**

13 Four identical squares are drawn side by side to form a rectangle with a perimeter of 40 cm.

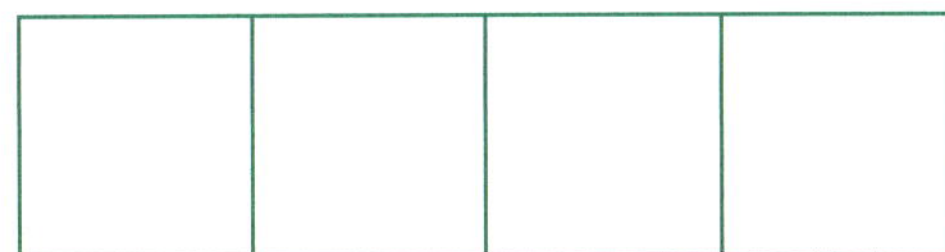

What is the area of the rectangle?

64 cm^2	80 cm^2	96 cm^2	100 cm^2	120 cm^2
A	**B**	**C**	**D**	**E**

14 Which of the following pairs of shapes **both** have **exactly** two lines of symmetry?

A square and rectangle
B rectangle and parallelogram
C parallelogram and rhombus
D rhombus and kite
E rectangle and rhombus

15 The diagram shows a kite split into two identical triangles.

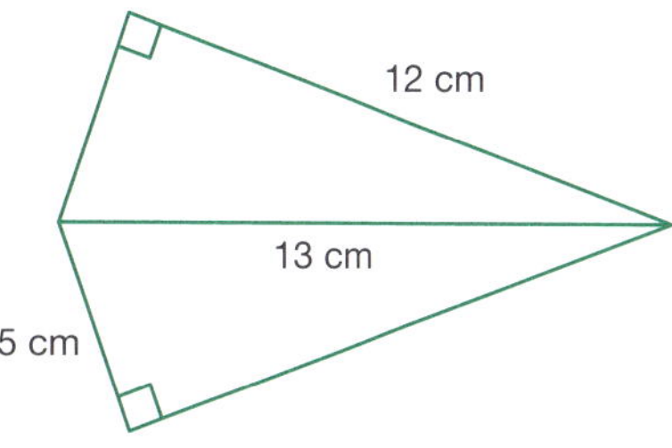

What is the area of the kite?

A 30 cm^2
B 52 cm^2
C 60 cm^2
D 66 cm^2
E 120 cm^2

16 The number of men, women and children who visited a museum last Saturday was recorded. The total number of men and women was 184, the total number of women and children was 250 and the total number of men and children was 286. How many visited the museum on Saturday?

280	360	380	480	720
A	**B**	**C**	**D**	**E**

17 A large square has an area of 36 cm^2. A small square is removed from one corner of the large square. A side of the small square is one-third a side of the large square. What fraction of the large square's perimeter is the small square's perimeter?

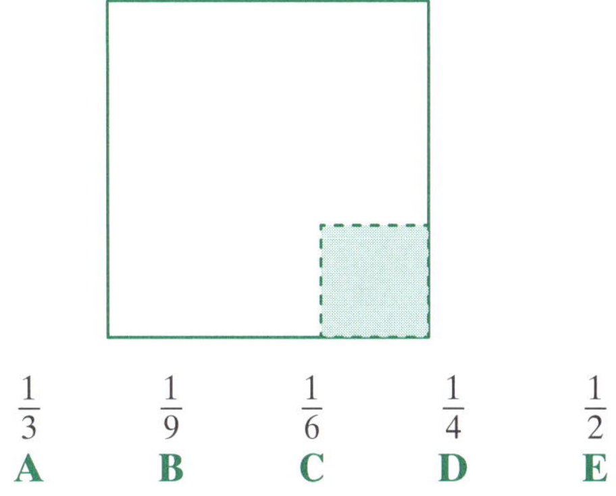

$\frac{1}{3}$	$\frac{1}{9}$	$\frac{1}{6}$	$\frac{1}{4}$	$\frac{1}{2}$
A	**B**	**C**	**D**	**E**

Answers and explanations on pages 98–100

SAMPLE TEST 10

18 Payne has a carton measuring 1.2 m by 1 m by 0.9 m. How many boxes with dimensions 15 cm by 25 cm by 10 cm will fit into the carton?

288	120	144	225	180
A	**B**	**C**	**D**	**E**

19 Water is flowing from a hose at the rate of 5 L/15 seconds. If Kyle starts to fill an empty tank with a capacity of 6000 L at 11:30 am, what time will the tank begin to overflow?

A 5:30 pm
B 5:00 pm
C 4:30 pm
D 4:00 pm
E 3:30 pm

20 A cyclist rides a bike at a constant speed of 40 km/h. In the time he has ridden 100 km, a motorist has driven 160 km. What is the average speed of the motorist?

A 68 km/h
B 65 km/h
C 64 km/h
D 66 km/h
E 60 km/h

21 Adrienne is making a pattern out of white and green tiles. Here is the line of tiles she has already arranged. She wants the pattern to have two lines of symmetry. What is the smallest number of tiles she needs to place on the left side of her pattern?

3	4	5	6	7
A	**B**	**C**	**D**	**E**

22 A clock has a very low battery level and is losing an average 2 minutes every hour. If it is set at the correct time at 3 o'clock in the afternoon, what time will it show at half past 7 the next morning?

A 27 minutes to 7
B 3 minutes past 7
C 27 minutes to 8
D 3 minutes to 7
E 27 minutes past 7

23 The shape is made of small squares. Theo cuts the shape into two pieces so that the pieces form a larger square.

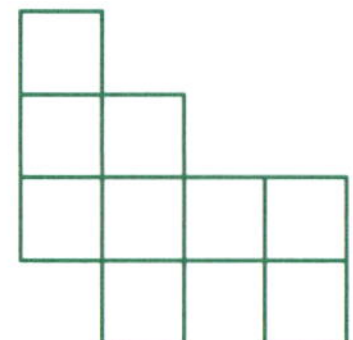

Which of these shows the cutting line?

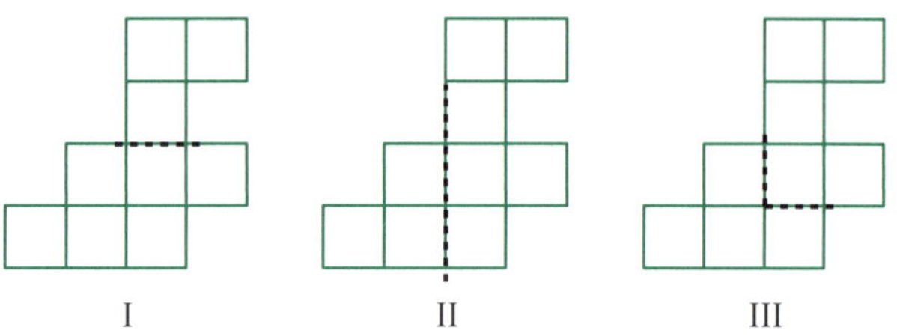

A I only
B II only
C III only
D I and III only
E None

24 Five friends are sitting on the same side of a straight section of river in this order: Alex, Ben, Claire, Daphne and Eddie. Alex is sitting 120 metres from Claire and 220 metres from Eddie. Ben is twice the distance from Alex as he is from Claire. Ben and Daphne are sitting the same distance from Claire. How far apart are Daphne and Eddie sitting?

A 20 metres
B 30 metres
C 40 metres
D 60 metres
E 80 metres

Answers and explanations on pages 98–100

SAMPLE TEST 10

25 Which is the correct table row of information for this hexagonal prism?

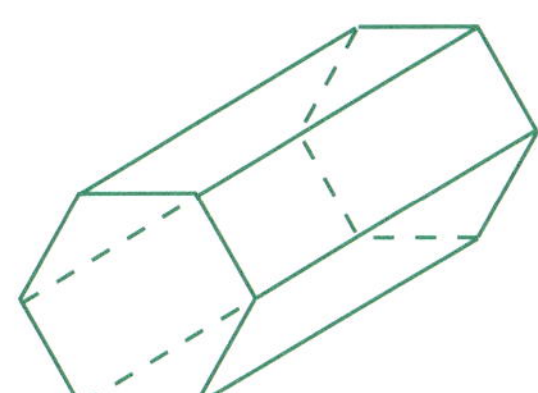

	Edges	Vertices	Faces
A	12	8	8
B	8	12	8
C	12	8	12
D	18	12	8
E	18	12	12

26 The spectators at a soccer match are represented on the sector graph below.

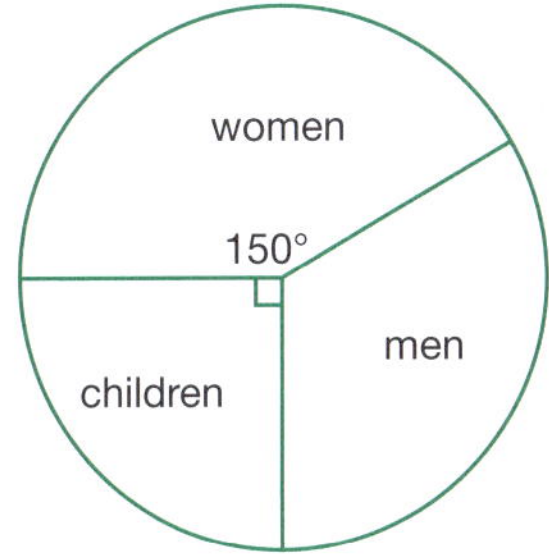

There are 15 children watching the game. Which of these statements is/are correct?

1 There is a total of 60 spectators at the game.

2 There are 25 women at the game.

3 A third of the spectators are men.

A statements 1 and 3 only
B statements 1, 2 and 3
C statement 1 only
D statement 2 only
E statement 3 only

27 Caleb has a spinner made of 12 numbered sectors. He spins the arrow and it lands on 3.

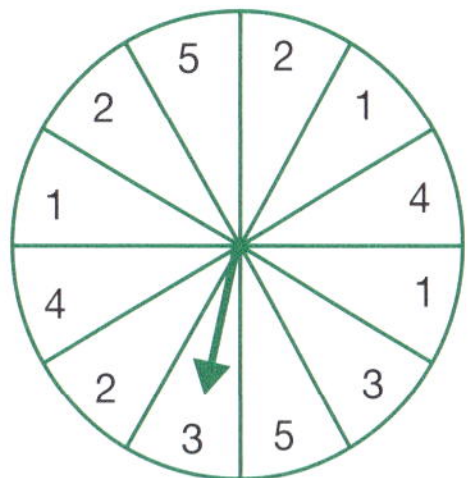

Joel spins the arrow and adds his result to Caleb's number. What is the probability that the total is more than 4?

$\frac{3}{4}$	$\frac{1}{6}$	$\frac{1}{4}$	$\frac{5}{6}$	$\frac{11}{12}$
A	**B**	**C**	**D**	**E**

28 The diagram shows a circle and two radii. A section of the circle is dotted. Aly draws along the (undotted) circle from A to B then through O and then back to A. She estimates this is a distance of 55 cm.

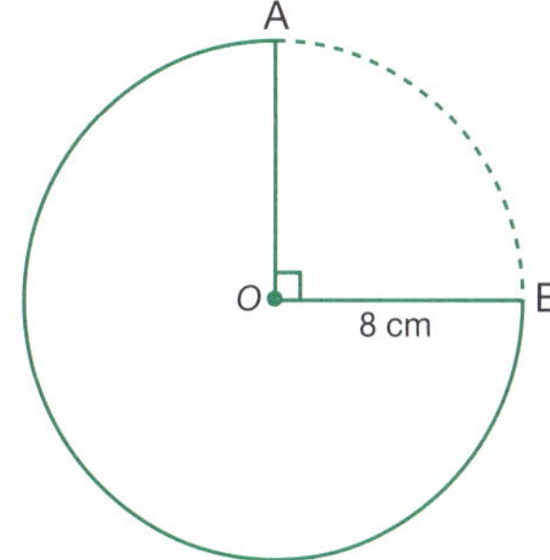

Which of these is the best estimate for the distance along the dotted curve between A and B?

A 16 cm **B** 11 cm **C** 13 cm
D 18 cm **E** 10 cm

29 The smallest angle in a triangle is one-third the size of the largest angle. If the sum of these two angles is 116°, which of these is the size of one of the angles in the triangle?

28°	31°	66°	84°	87°
A	**B**	**C**	**D**	**E**

Answers and explanations on pages 98–100

SAMPLE TEST 10

30 When the time is 2 pm in Chicago it is 9 am in Honolulu on the same day. It takes 8 hours 30 minutes to fly from Chicago to Honolulu. What time will a plane land in Honolulu if it takes off in Chicago at 2:45 pm Sunday?

A 9:15 am Sunday
B 5:45 pm Sunday
C 4:15 am Monday
D 6:15 pm Sunday
E 4:15 am Sunday

31 Emma starts at 8 am on a journey of 200 km. She drives two-fifths of the journey in the first hour and half the distance in the second hour. If she arrives at her destination at 10:15 am, what was Emma's average speed in the final quarter of an hour of her journey?

A 100 km/h
B 90 km/h
C 80 km/h
D 85 km/h
E 60 km/h

32 Christine wrote down 25 consecutive numbers. The sum of the first five consecutive numbers is 60. What is the sum of all 25 numbers?

A 500
B 520
C 525
D 540
E 550

33 A box contains 50 coloured balls of the same size. The chance of randomly selecting a red ball is 0.4 which is twice as great as the chance of selecting a blue ball. There are eight purple balls in the box and the remainder are yellow. How many yellow balls are in the box?

12	8	6	16	10
A	**B**	**C**	**D**	**E**

34 The number of primary-school students from Years 3 to 6 who can swim at least 50 m is recorded below. There are 28 students in each year.

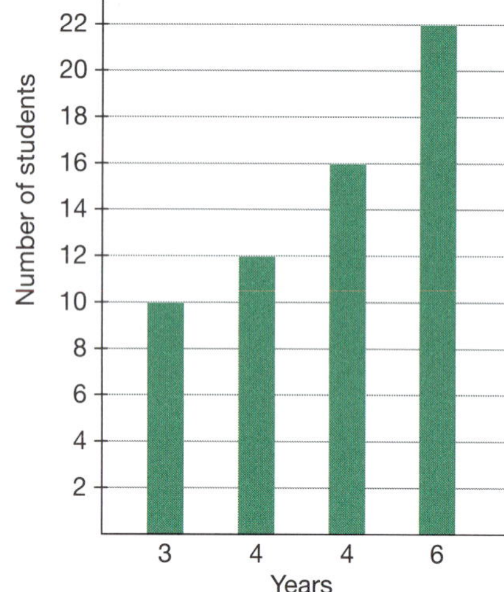

Here are three statements about the graph.

1 Fewer than half of the students in Year 4 can swim 50 m.
2 Exactly twice as many students in Year 6 than in Year 3 can swim 50 m.
3 More than 50% of the students in Years 3 to 6 can swim 50 m.

Which of these statements is/are correct?

A statement 1 only
B statement 2 only
C statements 1 and 3 only
D statement 3 only
E statements 2 and 3 only

35 Here is a pattern of towers made from small cubes, each with volume of 8 cm^3.

 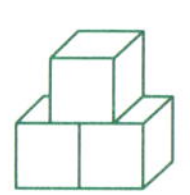 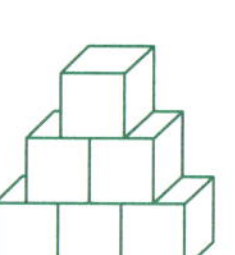 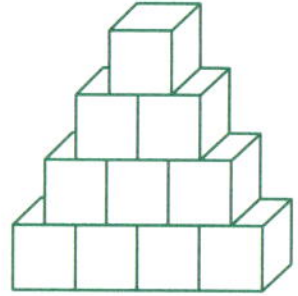

The pattern continues. What is the height of the tower with a volume of 224 cm^3?

A 12 cm **B** 16 cm **C** 10 cm
D 20 cm **E** 14 cm

Answers and explanations on pages 98–100

SELECTIVE SCHOOL–STYLE TEST **Mathematical Reasoning**

SAMPLE TEST 11

1 Here are five numbers: 10, 4, 6, 7, 8. Scott worked out the average of the numbers. When he removed one of the numbers the average did not change. Which number was removed?

10	4	6	7	8
A	**B**	**C**	**D**	**E**

2 What is the smallest number that can be subtracted from 387 to leave a number that is a multiple of 5 and 8?

23	27	32	67	37
A	**B**	**C**	**D**	**E**

3 Grandpa's age is 1 more than a multiple of 2, 3 and 5. Which of these could be his age?

56	66	61	96	81
A	**B**	**C**	**D**	**E**

4 At a lookout Cooper is facing south-west. He turns 90° in a clockwise direction to look at a mountain peak. He then turns in a clockwise direction to face east. From looking at the mountain, through how many degrees has Cooper just turned?

A 135° **B** 90° **C** 180°
D 315° **E** 225°

5 How many of these shapes have more than four lines of symmetry?

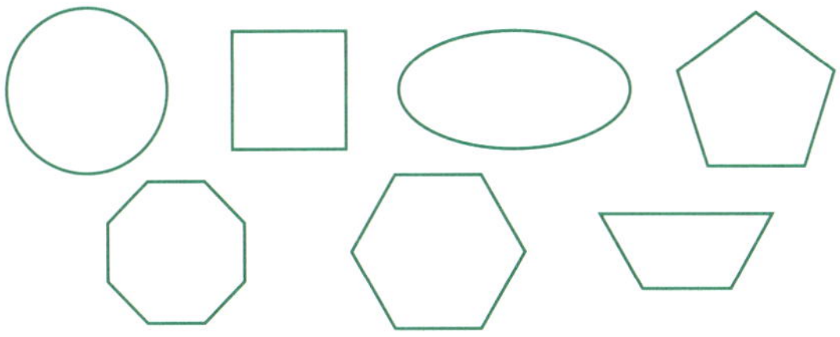

5	3	6	7	4
A	**B**	**C**	**D**	**E**

6 Katherine has read 20% of her book. If she still has 136 pages remaining, how many pages has she read?

34	27	48	28	30
A	**B**	**C**	**D**	**E**

7 There are 10 teams in a hockey competition. During a season, each team plays the other teams twice. Phoebe's team won a third of their games and drew four. How many games did her team lose?

6	7	8	5	9
A	**B**	**C**	**D**	**E**

8 April is listing all five-digit **odd** numbers using the digits 1, 2, 3, 4 and 5. What is the difference between the third biggest and the third smallest numbers on April's list?

A 31 870
B 40 986
C 41 688
D 41 760
E 32 778

9 An electrician charges a call-out fee plus $60 per hour. On Monday he worked for Mr Jenkins for 4 hours and charged $290. On Tuesday he worked for Mrs Roberts for 6 hours. How much will he charge Mrs Roberts?

A $435 **B** $340 **C** $360
D $390 **E** $410

10 Asha is thinking of three-digit numbers which, when divided by 3, 4 or 5, leave a remainder of 1. What is the largest number she can think of?

971	961	999	991	981
A	**B**	**C**	**D**	**E**

11 A large rectangle is cut into two identical squares. One of these squares is cut into two identical triangles. One of these triangles is cut into two smaller identical triangles. What fraction of the original rectangle is one of these smaller triangles?

A one-half
B one-third
C one-eighth
D one-quarter
E one-sixth

Answers and explanations on pages 100–102

SAMPLE TEST 11

12 What is the missing number?

3	2
5	4

8	5
7	3

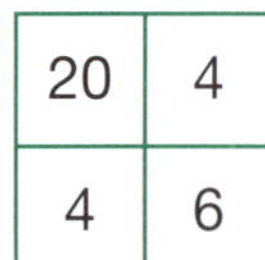

15	?
21	4

6	8	7	9	5
A	**B**	**C**	**D**	**E**

13 A box contains black and white balls. A white ball is removed from the box.

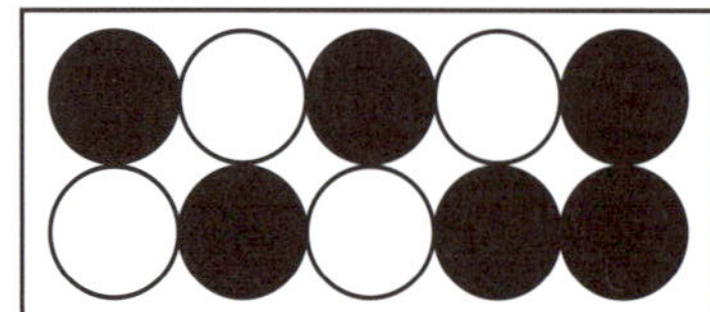

A ball is now chosen at random from the box.
What is the probability that it is black?

$\frac{2}{3}$	$\frac{2}{5}$	$\frac{3}{5}$	$\frac{1}{2}$	$\frac{4}{9}$
A	**B**	**C**	**D**	**E**

14 The sketch shows the net of a 3D shape.

What is the 3D shape?

A cylinder
B cone
C sphere
D ellipse
E none of these

15 Here is a pattern made from squares. Some of the squares are shaded.

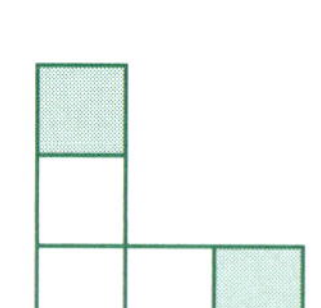
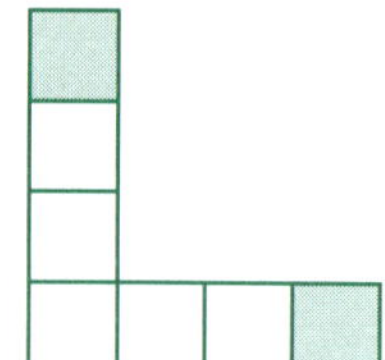

What fraction of the 12th shape will be shaded?

$\frac{2}{25}$	$\frac{1}{12}$	$\frac{1}{13}$	$\frac{2}{27}$	$\frac{1}{14}$
A	**B**	**C**	**D**	**E**

16 Meg is making a necklace of beads. She uses this pattern: 2 red, 1 white, 2 blue, 1 white, 2 green, 1 white, 2 yellow, 1 white and then repeats. If she makes a necklace with 100 beads, what is the colour of the last bead Meg has used?

A white
B red
C blue
D green
E yellow

17 Which of these number sentences describes 9 more than the difference between 24 and the product of 4 and 3 is increased by 2?

A $9 - (24 + 4) \times 3 + 2$
B $9 - (24 - 4 \times 3) + 2$
C $9 - (24 + 4 \times 3) + 2$
D $9 + 24 - 4 \times 3 + 2$
E $9 + 24 - 4 \times (3 + 2)$

18 Darcee starts with a square. She adds 3 cm to one side and subtracts 2 cm from another to form a rectangle with an area of 126 cm^2. What is the perimeter of the rectangle?

A 50 cm
B 52 cm
C 48 cm
D 56 cm
E 46 cm

Answers and explanations on pages 100–102

SAMPLE TEST 11

19 James and Amelia are thinking of the same number. James multiplied the number by 6 and his answer was greater than 20. Amelia multiplied the number by 8 and her answer was less than 50. There is more than one possible number they are thinking of. What is the sum of all the possible numbers they are thinking of?

9	30	22	15	39
A	**B**	**C**	**D**	**E**

20 The diagram shows a large rectangle split into five identical smaller rectangles. The perimeter of the large rectangle is 44 cm.

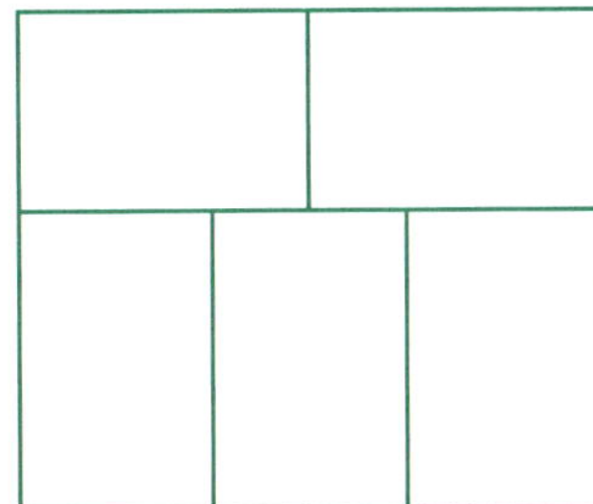

What is the perimeter of each of the small rectangles?

A 20 cm
B 11 cm
C 14 cm
D 24 cm
E 22 cm

21 A cube is made from small cubes of side length 1 cm. The volume of the large cube is 1000 cm^3. Gareth pulls the large cube apart and uses all the small cubes to make cubes of side length 2 cm. How many of these cubes can Gareth make?

5	25	50	125	250
A	**B**	**C**	**D**	**E**

22 One side of a square is increased by 50% and another side decreased by 20%. What change has occurred to the area?

A increased by 50%
B increased by 20%
C decreased by 20%
D decreased by 35%
E increased by 35%

23 A tap is dripping at the rate of two drops every 5 seconds. Every drop contains 0.25 mL of water. Which of these is closest to the amount of water wasted every day?

6 L	7 L	9 L	11 L	15 L
A	**B**	**C**	**D**	**E**

24 What number is missing from this number sentence?

$$\boxed{?} - 4 \times (3 + 2) - 12 \div 2 = \frac{18 - 4 \div 2}{2} + 2$$

24	30	33	36	40
A	**B**	**C**	**D**	**E**

25 Graham walked on an 8-km track up a hill at an average speed of 4 km/h. As soon as he reached the peak he turned around and jogged the same track back down at an average speed of 8 km/h. What was Graham's average speed for the whole trip?

A 5 km/h
B $5\frac{1}{3}$ km/h
C $5\frac{2}{3}$ km/h
D 6 km/h
E $6\frac{1}{3}$ km/h

26 The length of a rectangle is 3 cm longer than three times the width. If the area is 60 cm^2, what is the perimeter?

A 38 cm
B 34 cm
C 36 cm
D 40 cm
E 35 cm

Answers and explanations on pages 100–102

27 The mass of an empty bottle is 80 g. When the bottle is half full it contains 270 mL and has a mass of 410 g. What will be the mass when it is two-thirds full?

A 510 g
B 490 g
C 500 g
D 530 g
E 520 g

28 A plane leaves Dubai at 2340 on Tuesday to fly to Perth. The plane arrives in Perth at 1425 on Wednesday. If Perth is 4 hours ahead of Dubai, how long was the flight?

A 11 hours 45 minutes
B 11 hours 15 minutes
C 10 hours 45 minutes
D 18 hours 15 minutes
E 18 hours 45 minutes

29 The graph shows the amount of rain that fell in Cairns in a week in February.

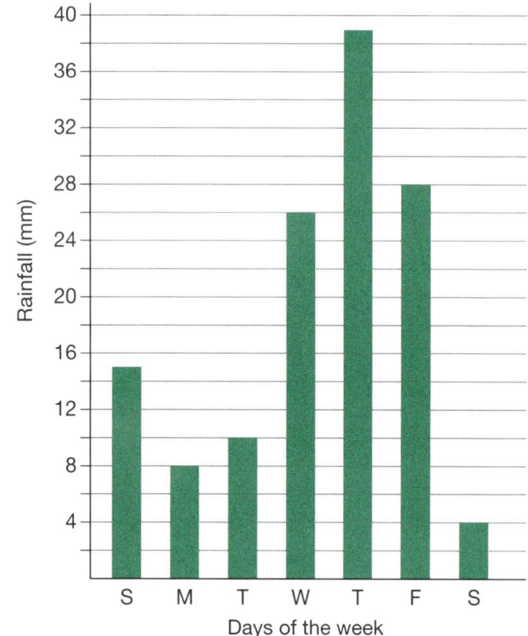

Which of these statements is/are correct?

1 11 mm more rain fell on Sunday than on Wednesday.
2 More rain fell on Thursday and Friday than on Sunday, Monday, Tuesday and Wednesday.
3 The total amount of rain that fell during the week was less than 140 mm.

A statements 2 and 3 only
B statement 2 only
C statement 3 only
D statements 1 and 3 only
E statements 1, 2 and 3

30 Kiah and Matthew are digging 30-cm deep holes for a fence. Kiah can dig three holes in 40 minutes and Matthew can dig two holes in half an hour. The fence is 64 m long and there is a post every 4 m. How long will it take Kiah and Matthew to finish the job?

A 1 hour 50 minutes
B 2 hours
C 2 hours 10 minutes
D 2 hours 15 minutes
E 2 hours 20 minutes

31 The areas of three faces of a rectangular prism are 30 cm^2, 24 cm^2 and 20 cm^2. What is the height h of the prism?

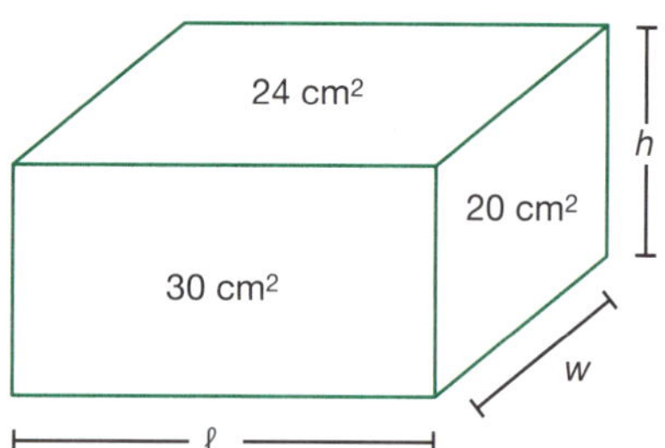

A 2 cm
B 4 cm
C 5 cm
D 6 cm
E 10 cm

☞ Answers and explanations on pages 100–102

SAMPLE TEST 11

32 A journey was completed by travelling at an average speed of 80 km/h for 2 hours 30 minutes. What amount of time would have been saved by averaging 100 km/h for the journey?

A 30 minutes
B 10 minutes
C 20 minutes
D 40 minutes
E 25 minutes

33 Through how many degrees does the minute hand move between 10:40 am and 2:05 pm on the same day?

A 615°
B 1105°
C 1230°
D 1305°
E 1590°

34 The sector graph shows the range of fish Edison owns. He has a total of 72 fish.

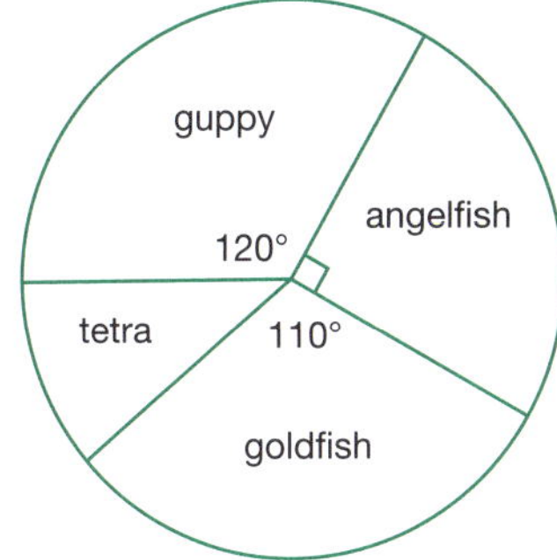

Here are three statements about the graph.

1 There are 18 angelfish.
2 There are four more guppy fish than goldfish.
3 There are nine tetra.

Which of these statements is/are correct?

A statement 1 only
B statements 1 and 2 only
C statements 1 and 3 only
D statements 2 and 3 only
E statements 1, 2 and 3

35 The arrow is spun on a spinner and the result is 2.

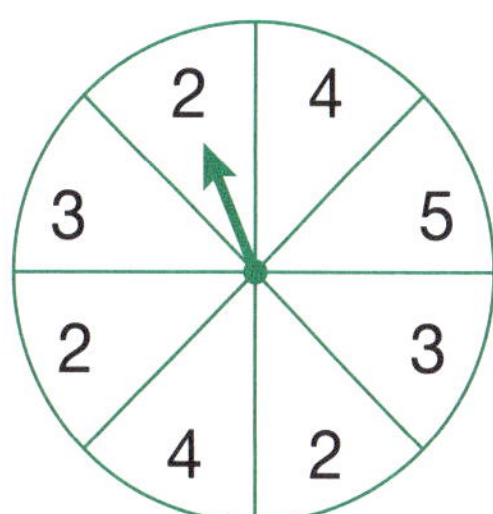

The arrow is spun again.
Which of these statements is/are correct?

1 The probability of spinning 2 again is $\frac{3}{8}$.
2 The probability of spinning an odd number is $\frac{1}{2}$.
3 The probability of spinning a 2, 3 or 5 is $\frac{3}{4}$.

A statement 1 only
B statement 2 only
C statement 3 only
D statements 1 and 2 only
E statements 1 and 3 only

Answers and explanations on pages 100–102

SAMPLE TEST 12

40 MIN

1 In this magic square, numbers in each row, column and diagonal add to 21.

10		
	7	*
6		

What is the number represented by *?

4	5	8	9	11
A	**B**	**C**	**D**	**E**

2 Tristan designed this logo.

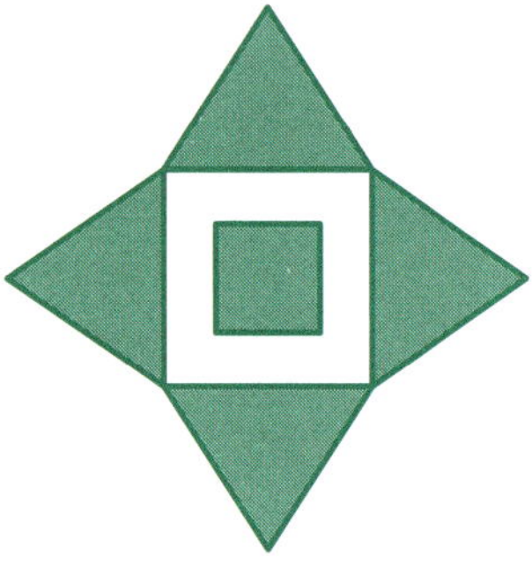

Which of these logos has half as many lines of symmetry as Tristan's logo?

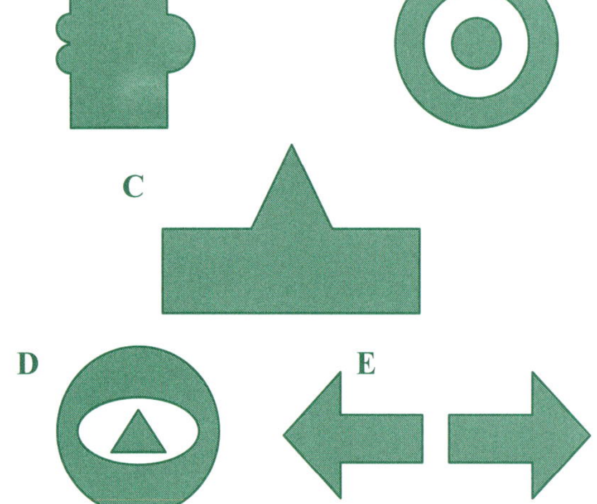

3 Five school friends buy each other Christmas presents. The total cost of the presents is $160. What is the average cost of each present?

A $12
B $8
C $6
D $3.20
E $10

4 Dante is playing with his model cars. When he divides them into groups of five there are three left over. When he divides them into groups of six there are two left over. If he has between 40 and 80 cars, how many are in his collection?

58	73	78	68	53
A	**B**	**C**	**D**	**E**

5 How many integers are less than 6 from 47?

9	10	11	12	13
A	**B**	**C**	**D**	**E**

6 There are eight two-digit numbers that are formed using consecutive digits. How many numbers between 10 and 10 000 can be formed using consecutive digits?

13	21	22	23	24
A	**B**	**C**	**D**	**E**

7 Three friends are counting to 200. Lucinda starts at 3 and counts by 3s. Enya starts at 4 and counts by 4s. Talicia starts at 5 and counts by 5s. Which of these is a number that all girls count?

180	137	125	132	160
A	**B**	**C**	**D**	**E**

8 Here is a number sentence:

$$18 \times 45 = 3 \times \boxed{?} \times 5$$

What is the value of the missing number?

6	15	48	54	75
A	**B**	**C**	**D**	**E**

Answers and explanations on pages 102–104

SAMPLE TEST 12

9 A school's charity day raised $15 200. The expenses for the day amounted to $2700. The remainder was distributed to two charities. Canteen charity was given 80% and the remainder given to Ronald McDonald House. How much money did Ronald McDonald House receive?

A $2500
B $2250
C $2750
D $2600
E $3000

10 A school purchased 250 calculators to sell to students. The calculators cost $17 each and were sold for $22 each. If the school made a profit of $1000, how many calculators were left unsold?

25	20	50	40	75
A	**B**	**C**	**D**	**E**

11 Three-fifths of the chocolates in a box have already been eaten. If 30 chocolates remain, how many chocolates have been eaten?

20	15	45	30	25
A	**B**	**C**	**D**	**E**

12 Last Friday Tyson left his house and cycled three times around his neighbourhood block. Every day since then he has increased the number of laps by 2. Today is the following Wednesday. After he cycles today what is the total distance he has cycled if each lap is 1.5 km?

A 45 km
B 48 km
C 50 km
D 72 km
E 75 km

13 What is the value of
$2 \times [(30 - 3 \times 6) + 16 \div 2] - (3 + 3)$?

26	8	28	36	34
A	**B**	**C**	**D**	**E**

14 A shape is drawn on a grid where each small square has an area of 4 cm^2.

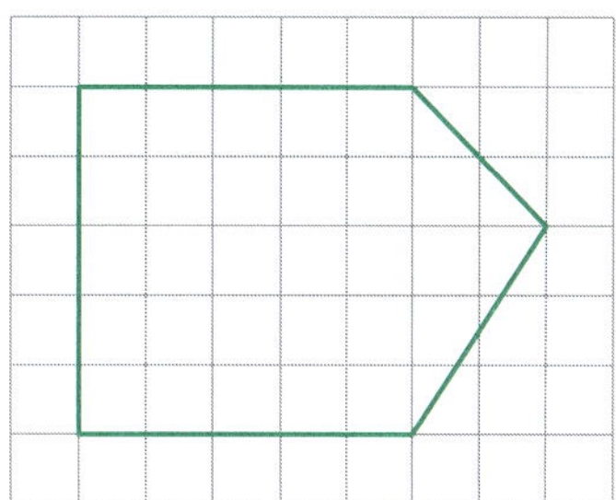

What is the area of the shape?

A 140 cm^2
B 29 cm^2
C 100 cm^2
D 30 cm^2
E 120 cm^2

15 There were 60 oranges in a box. Shyla gave 18 oranges to her sister and two-thirds of the remaining oranges to Maddison. How many oranges remain?

28	14	12	16	18
A	**B**	**C**	**D**	**E**

16 Through how many degrees does the hour hand on an analog clock move from 2:30 pm to 5:00 pm?

25°	35°	75°	65°	80°
A	**B**	**C**	**D**	**E**

17 All the squares of concrete in the school playground have a side length of 2 m. Ella has lots of pieces of square cardboard which have side length of 20 cm. She places one piece of cardboard on the first concrete square, two pieces on the second concrete square, four on the next, eight on the next, and so on. She stops when the number of pieces cannot fit on the concrete square. How many pieces of cardboard did Ella use?

120	400	98	127	200
A	**B**	**C**	**D**	**E**

Answers and explanations on pages 102–104

18 The shape shows two identical triangles inside a rectangle.

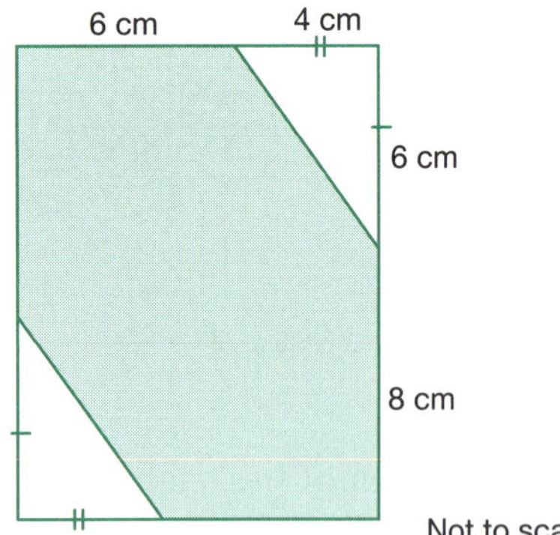

What is the area of the shaded hexagon?

A 88 cm^2
B 84 cm^2
C 116 cm^2
D 92 cm^2
E 128 cm^2

19 For his lawnmower Carl uses fuel which is a mix of oil and petrol. The manufacturer's directions say to pour 200 mL of oil into a 5-L container and then fill the remainder with petrol. If Carl only has 120 mL of oil, how much petrol should he use in the mix?

A 3.24 L
B 3 L
C 2.96 L
D 3.2 L
E 2.88 L

20 When Aastha filled her car with petrol her odometer showed 79 568. After a week she filled up again. She bought 36 L of petrol and her odometer showed 80 018. What rate of petrol did she use, expressed as L/100 km?

A 6 L/100 km
B 8 L/100 km
C 8.5 L/100 km
D 9 L/100 km
E 12 L/100 km

21 A dice is biased. The probability of rolling a 6 is $\frac{3}{8}$. All other numbers are equally likely.
Which of these statements is/are correct?

1 The probability of rolling a 1, 2, 3, 4 or 5 is $\frac{5}{8}$.
2 The probability of rolling an odd number is the same as rolling a 6.
3 The probability of rolling a factor of 6 is 75%.

A statement 1 only
B statement 2 only
C statements 1 and 3 only
D statements 1 and 2 only
E statements 1, 2 and 3

22 What is the area of the pentagon?

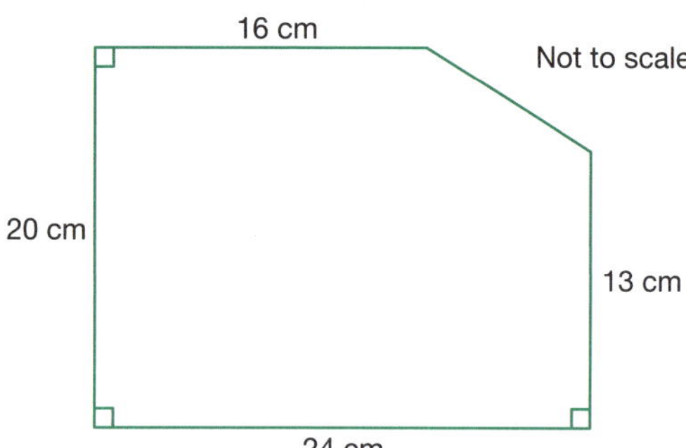

A 380 cm^2
B 452 cm^2
C 408 cm^2
D 432 cm^2
E 424 cm^2

23 There are 30 students standing in a group. One-third of the group are boys and the remainder girls. Half of the girls play netball. If a student is chosen at random, what is the probability that the student is a netball-playing girl?

$\frac{1}{3}$	$\frac{1}{4}$	$\frac{1}{6}$	$\frac{1}{2}$	$\frac{2}{3}$
A	**B**	**C**	**D**	**E**

Answers and explanations on pages 102–104

SAMPLE TEST 12

24 ○ + ○ + ○ + ○ = □

○ × △ = □

□ − △ = 4

What is the value of □ + ○ × △?

12	10	8	16	14
A	**B**	**C**	**D**	**E**

25 Michael and Jenny are 180 km apart. They start to ride towards each other at 10:15 am. Michael rides at an average speed of 40 km/h and Jenny rides at 20 km/h. At what time will they meet?

A 1:15 pm **B** 1:00 pm **C** 1:30 pm
D 2:00 pm **E** 1:45 pm

26 The average mass of four watermelons in a supermarket's display box is 8.6 kg. Another watermelon is placed in the box and the new average is 9.05 kg. What is the mass of the new watermelon?

A 9.05 kg
B 10 kg
C 10.85 kg
D 10.4 kg
E 10.55 kg

27 Ellie drives 16 km in 12 minutes. How far will she travel in 45 minutes at the same speed?

A 56 km
B 60 km
C 64 km
D 65 km
E 72 km

28 A piece of wire is cut into two equal lengths. One piece is bent into a square and the other into an equilateral triangle. If the length of each side of the square is 6 cm shorter than the length of each side of the triangle, what was the length of the original piece of wire?

A 60 cm **B** 72 cm **C** 120 cm
D 144 cm **E** 160 cm

29 Bella, Jasmine and Chelsea are clapping. Bella claps every 10 seconds, Jasmine every 15 seconds and Chelsea every 25 seconds. If they start by clapping together, how long will it be until they clap together again?

A $1\frac{1}{2}$ minutes **B** $2\frac{1}{2}$ minutes
C 2 minutes **D** $2\frac{1}{4}$ minutes
E $1\frac{3}{4}$ minutes

30 The line graph shows the temperatures in Gunnedah over 36 hours in March.

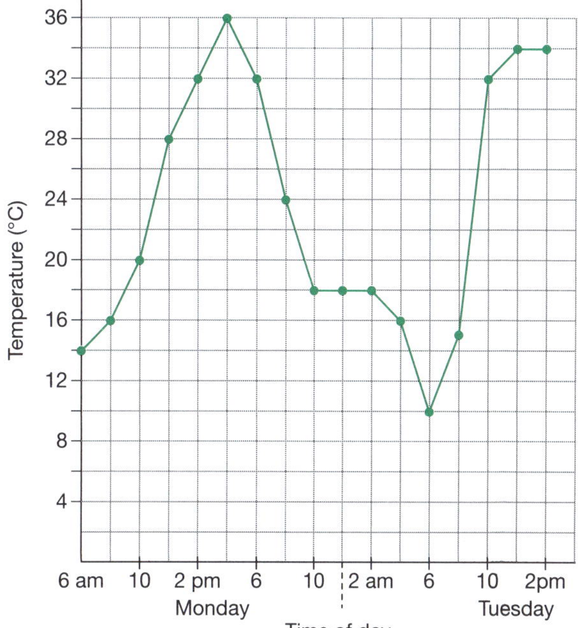

Here are three statements about the graph.

1 The difference between the highest and lowest temperatures was 26°.

2 It was 2° cooler at 8 am on Tuesday than at 8 am on Monday.

3 The temperature halved from 4 pm Monday to 2 am Tuesday.

Which of these statements is/are correct?

A statement 3 only
B statements 1 and 3 only
C statements 1 and 2 only
D statements 2 and 3 only
E statements 1, 2 and 3

Answers and explanations on pages 102–104

SAMPLE TEST 12

31

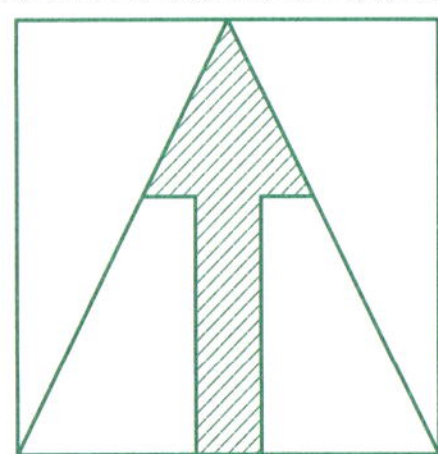

The object is rotated anticlockwise into the position shown below.

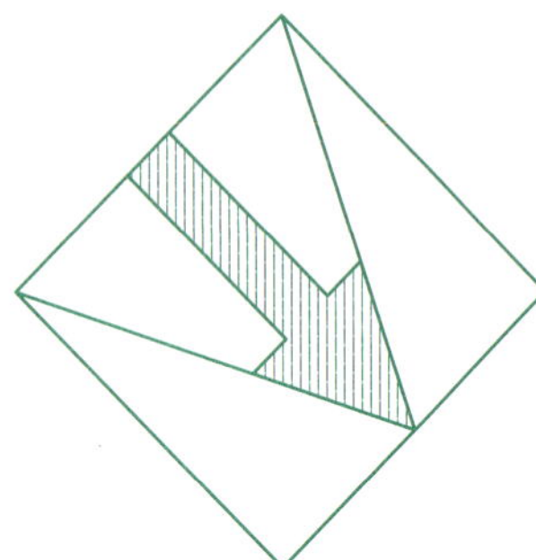

Through what angle has it been rotated?

45°	90°	135°	225°	270°
A	**B**	**C**	**D**	**E**

32 The diagram shows the net of a rectangular prism.

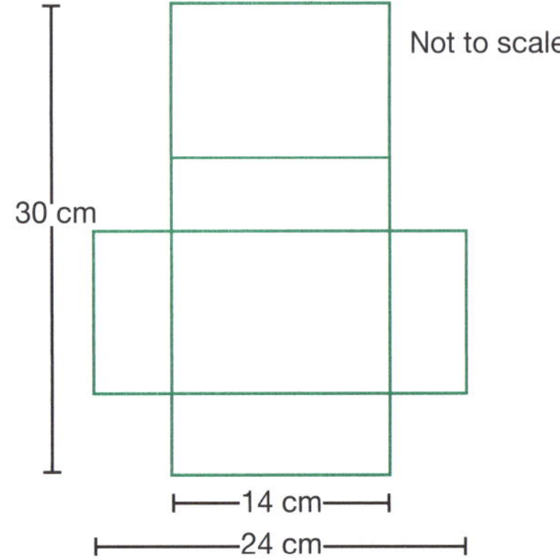

When the prism is formed what is its volume?

A 700 cm^3
B 660 cm^3
C 10 080 cm^3
D 680 cm^3
E 720 cm^3

33 An $8 \times 8 \times 8$ cube is painted. It is then cut into $2 \times 2 \times 2$ cubes. How many of these smaller cubes have exactly two faces painted?

8	12	16	18	24
A	**B**	**C**	**D**	**E**

34 The graph shows the profit made by the operator of a coffee cart in one week. The profit for Thursday is not shown.

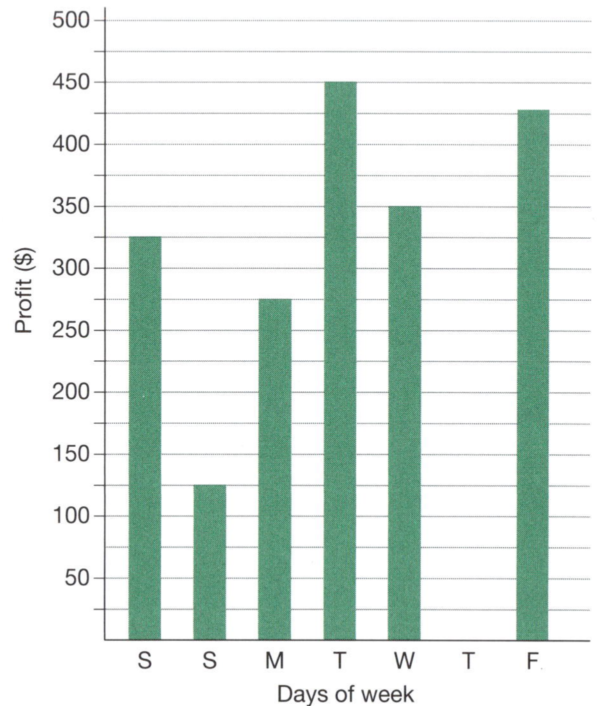

Which of these statements is/are correct?

1 The total profit on the weekend was $450.
2 Twice as much profit was made on Monday than on Sunday.
3 If the total weekly profit was $2325, then $375 was Thursday's profit.

A statement 1 only
B statement 2 only
C statements 1 and 2 only
D statements 1, 2 and 3
E statements 1 and 3 only

Answers and explanations on pages 102–104

SAMPLE TEST 12

35 Penny left Perth at 11:40 pm Tuesday and flew for 4 hours 45 minutes, landing at the Gold Coast. She had to wait 6 hours 10 minutes for a connecting flight to Newcastle. This second flight took 1 hour 10 minutes. If Perth is 2 hours behind Newcastle, at what time did Penny's flight touch down in Newcastle?

A 11:45 am Wednesday
B 10:45 am Wednesday
C 12:45 pm Wednesday
D 2:45 pm Wednesday
E 1:45 pm Wednesday

☞ Answers and explanations on pages 102–104

SELECTIVE SCHOOL-STYLE TEST **Mathematical Reasoning**

SAMPLE TEST 13

1 Here are the times the 721 bus leaves a shopping centre:

9:17 10:23 11:58 1:02 2:49 4:17

If Patty arrives 7 minutes after the 11:58 bus leaves, how long does she have to wait for the next bus?

A 47 minutes
B 52 minutes
C 57 minutes
D 1 hour 2 minutes
E 1 hour 3 minutes

2 Half the sum of 94 and 114 is subtracted from 200. What is the result?

112	39	69	104	96
A	**B**	**C**	**D**	**E**

3 Harriet used her calculator to work out an answer. She entered a two-digit number, multiplied it by 4, subtracted 32 and divided by 2. Her answer was 56. She realised she had made two errors. Starting with the same number, she should have multiplied by 2, subtracted 32 and then divided by 4. What should have been the correct answer?

14	40	10	9	28
A	**B**	**C**	**D**	**E**

4 Four lights flash at intervals of 3, 4, 5 and 9 seconds. If they flash together at midday, what is the next time they flash together again?

A 12:01:08
B 12:00:54
C 12:05:40
D 12:09:00
E 12:03:00

5 Goran scored a mark of 48 for a quiz. He calculated this was a result of 80%. Jaclyn sat the same test and answered every question correctly. What was Jaclyn's mark?

50	54	55	60	64
A	**B**	**C**	**D**	**E**

6 When Connor adds 598 to a number the answer is 1472. What is his answer if he instead subtracts 598 from the number?

A 276 **B** 2668 **C** 874
D 346 **E** 256

7 What is 20% of 30% of $400?

$32	$12	$36	$40	$24
A	**B**	**C**	**D**	**E**

8 What is the value of $8 + 2 \times (9 - 6)^2$?

44	26	54	90	152
A	**B**	**C**	**D**	**E**

9 Today is 24/7/21 and it is Courtney's birthday. Last year her age was a multiple of 4. Next year Courtney's age will be a multiple of 5. If she was born last century, which of these could be Courtney's age today?

9	19	39	49	59
A	**B**	**C**	**D**	**E**

10 Water flows from three taps at the rate of 3.5 L/minute, 4.2 L/minute and 4.3 L/minute. How much water can be collected from the three taps in 2 hours?

A 720 L
B 1.44 kL
C 1.26 kL
D 1.6 kL
E 1.32 kL

11 James and Aly downloaded a movie and started watching it at 8:40. Aly watched all the movie which finished at 10:20. James watched the movie until he went to bed at 9:55. What fraction of the movie had James watched?

$\frac{3}{4}$	$\frac{4}{5}$	$\frac{8}{15}$	$\frac{2}{3}$	$\frac{5}{6}$
A	**B**	**C**	**D**	**E**

Answers and explanations on pages 104–106

SAMPLE TEST 13

12 The number line shows the location of X, which is in the middle of 2.79 and 3.5.

2.79 X 3.5

What decimal is represented by X?

A 3.015 **B** 3.12 **C** 3.145
D 3.15 **E** 3.3

13 The prices of all items in a jewellery store are being reduced by the same percentage. A watch originally priced at \$600 has been reduced to \$480. What will be the total amount paid for a bracelet and a ring if they were originally priced at \$360 and \$1800 respectively?

A \$1620 **B** \$1728 **C** \$1818
D \$1860 **E** \$1920

14 In this magic square, numbers in each row, column and diagonal add to the same number.

	24		8	15
	*		14	16
4		13		22
10	12		21	3
	18	25		9

What is the number represented by *?

5	8	11	17	23
A	**B**	**C**	**D**	**E**

15 Ashley makes a pattern using triangles and squares. If the pattern continues, how many squares are in the shape with 48 triangles?

21	22	23	24	25
A	**B**	**C**	**D**	**E**

16 Michael is participating in a Perth to Newcastle charity ride. Each week he plans to increase his training distance by 50 km. In week 3 he rode 260 km. What distance does Michael hope to ride in his tenth week of training?

A 350 km
B 500 km
C 590 km
D 610 m
E 760 km

17 What same number is used to replace the squares in this number sentence?

$150 - (20 + 4 \times \boxed{?}) = 45 \div 9 + \boxed{?}$

What is the value of the missing number?

5	10	15	20	25
A	**B**	**C**	**D**	**E**

18 The net below forms a cube where opposite faces multiply to the same number.

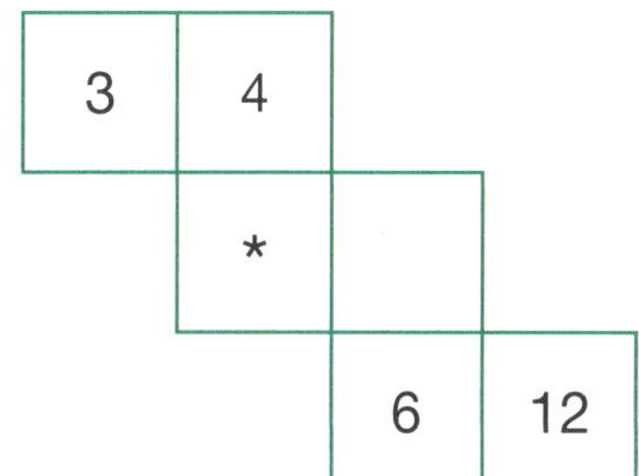

What is the number represented by *?

1	8	9	10	2
A	**B**	**C**	**D**	**E**

19 A right-angled triangle with dimensions 12 cm and 16 cm is drawn inside a rectangle.

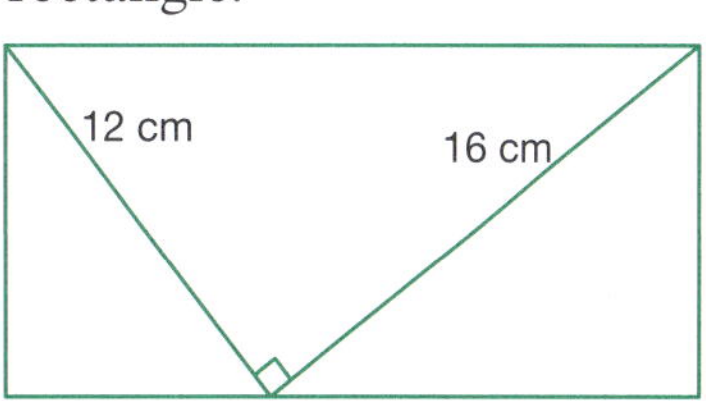

Not to scale

What is the area of the rectangle?

A 192 cm^2 **B** 384 cm^2 **C** 196 cm^2
D 224 cm^2 **E** 180 cm^2

Answers and explanations on pages 104–106

SAMPLE TEST 13

20 A tank is $\frac{5}{12}$ full and holds 240 L of water. How much water needs to be added to fill the tank to $\frac{3}{4}$ full?

A 180 L
B 192 L
C 196 L
D 240 L
E 300 L

21 On a driving trip Justin averaged 90 km/h for 20 minutes. Tamsin travelled the same distance but took 10 minutes longer. What was the difference in their speeds?

A 27 km/h
B 18 km/h
C 24 km/h
D 45 km/h
E 30 km/h

22 Bella drew a rectangle measuring 8 cm by 6 cm. She then shaded two 1-cm wide strips on the rectangle.

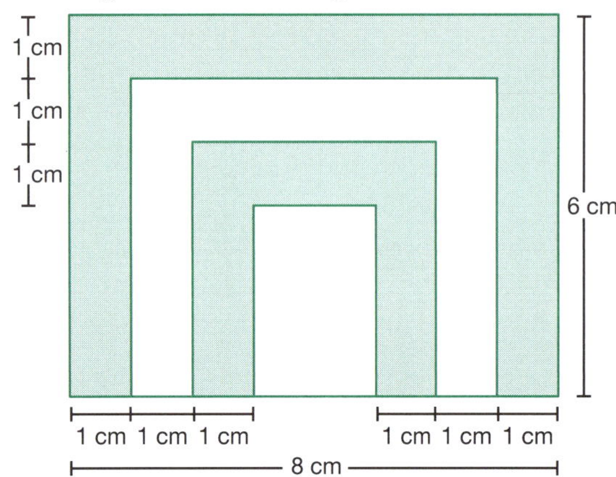

What is the total area shaded?

A 20 cm^2 **B** 24 cm^2 **C** 28 cm^2
D 30 cm^2 **E** 32 cm^2

23 6% of the mass of a truck is 288 kg. What is the mass of the truck?

A 4.8 tonnes
B 5.6 tonnes
C 6.4 tonnes
D 1.728 tonnes
E 17.28 tonnes

24 A photograph has dimensions 15 cm by 10 cm. It is placed on a scanner to be enlarged so that the length and width increase at the same rate. If the width increases by 15 cm, what is the area of the new enlarged photograph?

A 600 cm^2 **B** 750 cm^2 **C** 900 cm^2
D 937.5 cm^2 **E** 945.5 cm^2

25 The diagram shows a small square drawn inside a larger square. The shaded section has a perimeter of 44 cm and an area of 72 cm^2.

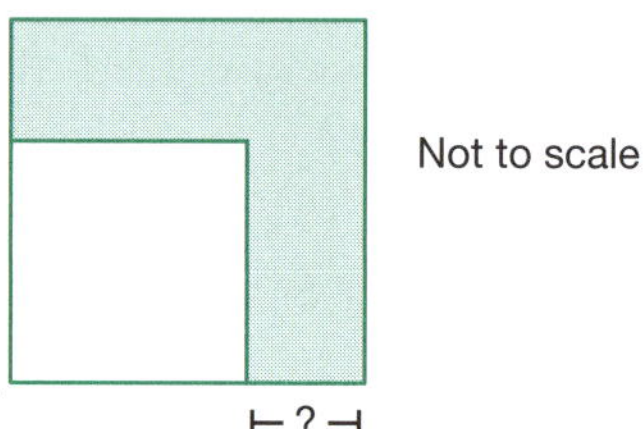

What is the unknown length shown on the diagram?

A 2 cm **B** 3 cm **C** 4 cm
D 5 cm **E** 6 cm

26 When full, a container holds 8 L of juice. It is now $\frac{3}{4}$ full. The juice is used to fill 24 bottles. What is the capacity of each of the bottles?

A 250 mL **B** 200 mL **C** 220 mL
D 325 mL **E** 275 mL

27 The diagram shows a balance.

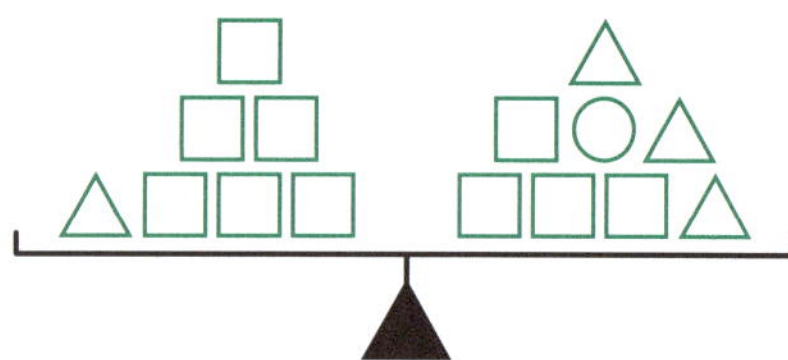

If the square has a value of 8 and the triangle a value of 6, what is the value of the circle?

2	4	5	7	8
A	**B**	**C**	**D**	**E**

Answers and explanations on pages 104–106

SAMPLE TEST 13

28 Aleesha flew from Mumbai to Tokyo arriving at 0620 Wednesday. The flight took 8 hours 10 minutes. What time in Mumbai had the plane taken off if Tokyo is 3 hours 30 minutes ahead of Mumbai?

A 1840 Tuesday
B 1920 Tuesday
C 1940 Tuesday
D 0040 Wednesday
E 0140 Wednesday

29 Vinnie works as a driver for a ride-share company. He works six days a week and the amount he makes each day is recorded in the graph below.

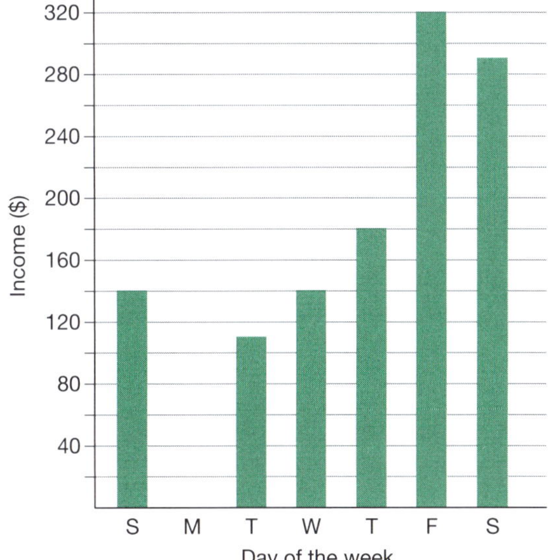

Here are three statements about the graph.

1 Vinnie earned twice as much on Thursday as he earned on Tuesday.
2 On three days Vinnie earned more than $140.
3 Vinnie earned less than $1200 throughout the week.

Which of these statements is/are correct?

A statement 1 only
B statement 2 only
C statements 1 and 2 only
D statements 2 and 3 only
E statements 1, 2 and 3

30 A bag contains white, yellow, blue and red buttons. The probability of choosing a blue button is 0.2 and the probability of selecting a red button is 0.15. The probability of selecting a yellow button is the same as selecting a blue or red button. If there are 18 white buttons, how many yellow buttons are in the bag?

26	24	25	21	20
A	**B**	**C**	**D**	**E**

31 The dotted line is to be a line of symmetry. Which of the following squares will be shaded?

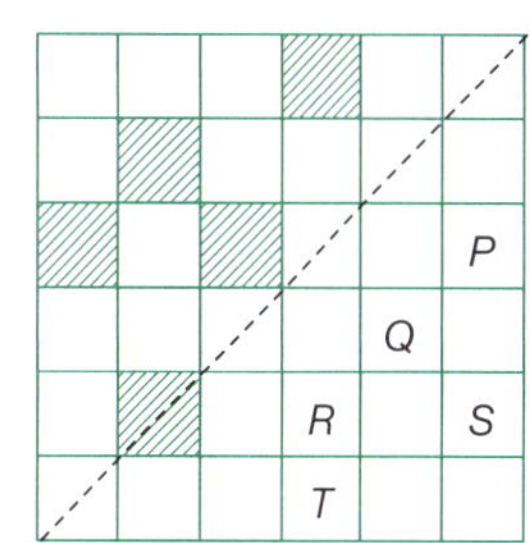

A P and Q
B P and T
C P and S
D Q and R
E T and R

32 What is the value of x?

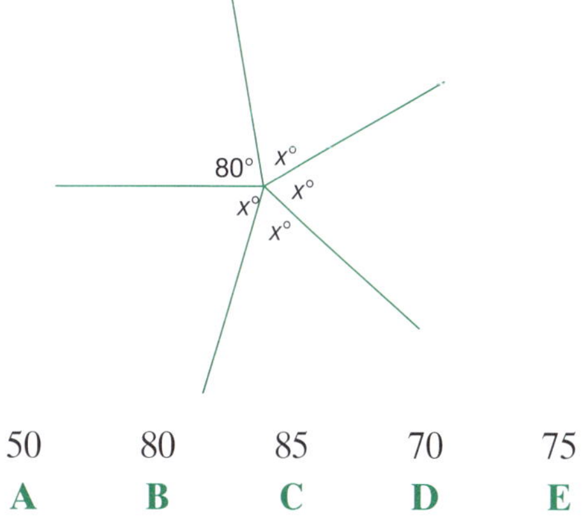

50	80	85	70	75
A	**B**	**C**	**D**	**E**

Answers and explanations on pages 104–106

SAMPLE TEST 13

33 Here is a cube made of 27 small cubes. 24 cubes are white and three are green.

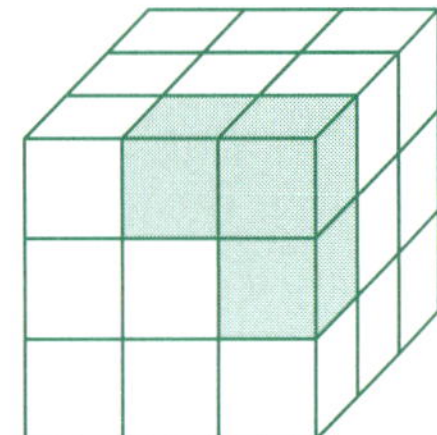

The three green cubes are removed and discarded. Which of these statements is/are correct?

1 The volume has decreased.
2 The surface area has decreased.
3 The surface area is unchanged.

A statement 1 only
B statement 2 only
C statement 3 only
D statements 1 and 2 only
E statements 1 and 3 only

34 A group of students were surveyed to find their country of birth.

	Australia	Overseas
Girls	12	6
Boys	20	12

Which of these statements is/are correct?

1 If a student is chosen at random, the probability that they are a boy born in Australia is 0.4.
2 If a boy is chosen at random, the probability that they were born overseas is $\frac{3}{5}$.
3 If a student born overseas is chosen at random, the probability that they are a girl is $\frac{1}{3}$.

A statement 1 only
B statement 2 only
C statements 1 and 3 only
D statements 1 and 2 only
E statements 1, 2 and 3

35 The number of girls and boys in different year groups who play weekend sport in summer is recorded on the graph below.

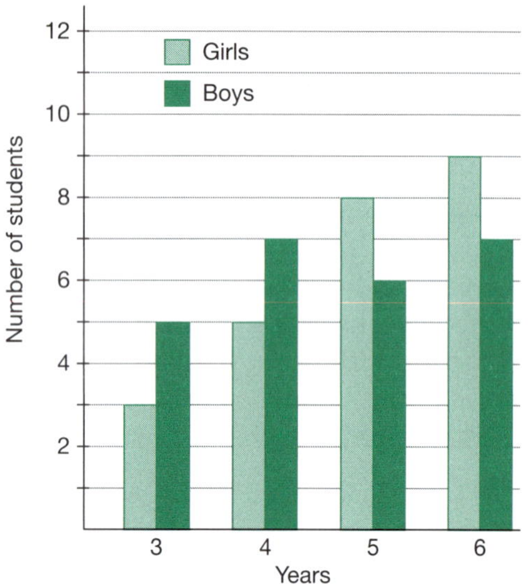

Here are three statements about the graph.

1 24 girls play weekend sport.
2 The same number of boys as girls play weekend sport.
3 Four more students from Year 6 play weekend sport than Year 4.

Which of these statements is/are correct?

A statements 2 and 3 only
B statements 1 and 2 only
C statement 1 only
D statement 2 only
E statement 3 only

Answers and explanations on pages 104–106

SELECTIVE SCHOOL–STYLE TEST **Mathematical Reasoning**

SAMPLE TEST 14

1 A whole number when rounded off to the nearest thousand is 986 000. Which of these is the largest possible value of the whole number?

A 986
B 985 501
C 985 999
D 986 499
E 986 500

2 Jack wrote lots of consecutive numbers starting with 1. When he stopped he had written 240 digits. What was the last number he wrote?

114	115	116	117	120
A	**B**	**C**	**D**	**E**

3 How many multiples of 4 are less than 170, greater than 50 and divisible by 5?

5	6	7	8	9
A	**B**	**C**	**D**	**E**

4 Which of the following nets could be folded to form a square pyramid?

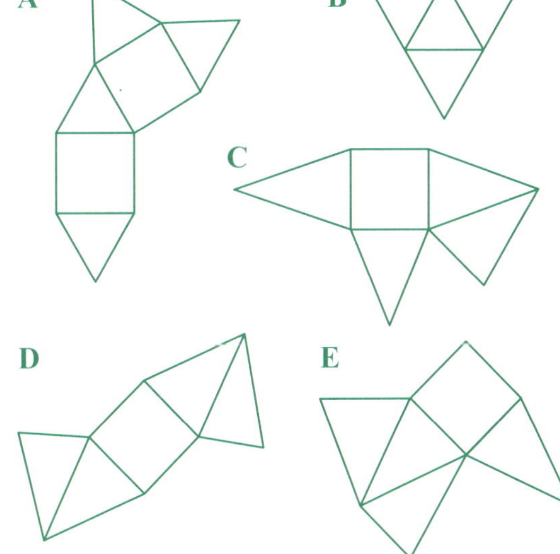

5 Which of these is the smallest number divisible by all the positive integers less than 8?

420	2520	840	210	105
A	**B**	**C**	**D**	**E**

6 A survey of 360 students showed one-quarter had arrived at school this morning by car, three-fifths had caught the bus, 16 students had ridden a bike and the rest had walked. How many students had walked to school this morning?

36	38	40	44	54
A	**B**	**C**	**D**	**E**

7 Ariarne calculated her average for four maths quizzes was 90%. What would be the lowest possible result she could have scored in one of the quizzes?

40%	68%	60%	86%	75%
A	**B**	**C**	**D**	**E**

8 A four-digit number is written using different even numbers. The sum of the digits is 20. The thousands digit is the sum of the tens and ones digits. The ones digit is the quotient of the hundreds and tens digit. There are two possible numbers. What is the difference between these numbers?

A 24 **B** 18 **C** 126
D 128 **E** 96

9 The rows of the table follow rules.

a	1	2	3	4	5
b	1	4	9		
c	1	6	15	28	45
d	4	12	24	40	*

What is the number represented by *?

75	70	65	60	55
A	**B**	**C**	**D**	**E**

10 What same number is used to replace the squares in this number sentence?

$$(16 - 8) \div (\boxed{?} + \boxed{?}) = \boxed{?}$$

What is the value of the missing number?

1	2	4	6	8
A	**B**	**C**	**D**	**E**

☞ Answers and explanations on pages 106–108

SAMPLE TEST 14

11 From his superannuation account Jack receives \$60 000 in the first year of retirement in 2018. This amount is increased by \$5000 each year. He plans to give 10% of all of the money he receives each year to charity. What amount of money will Jack give away in 2028?

A \$6000
B \$6500
C \$10 000
D \$10 500
E \$11 000

12 Haley is organising a party. She expects that each person will eat $\frac{3}{8}$ of a pizza. If each pizza costs \$14 and she spends \$168 on pizzas, how many people will be at the party?

20	16	32	36	24
A	**B**	**C**	**D**	**E**

13 Frida writes a sequence of numbers using the rule 'Starting with 2, double the number, add 4 and halve the result'. What is the result of multiplying the 10th and 110th numbers in the sequence?

A 2200
B 4000
C 4200
D 4400
E 5600

14 The diagram shows a regular octagon. Two parts of the shape are shaded.

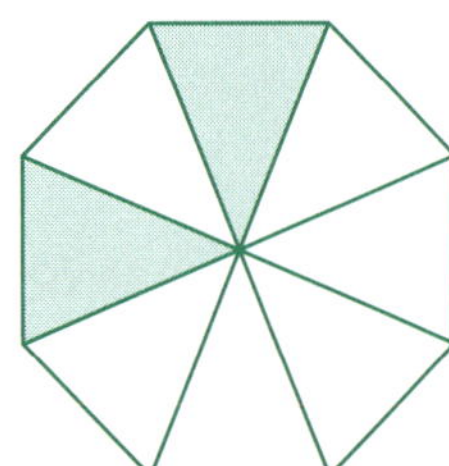

The shape is rotated clockwise into the position shown below.

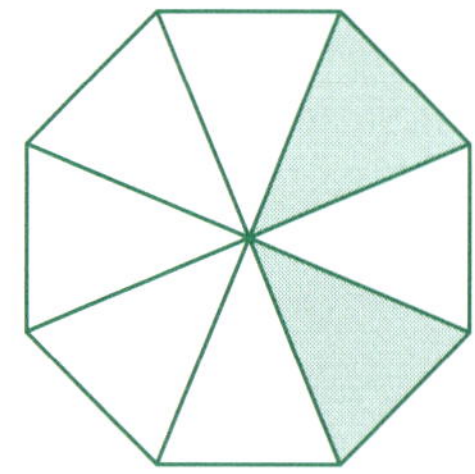

Through what angle has it been rotated?

A 45°
B 90°
C 135°
D 225°
E 270°

15 Andrea hires a ride-on mower to mow a sportsfield. She is paid \$360. The cost of hiring the mower was \$120 and she used \$24 worth of fuel. The job took her 4 hours 45 minutes. Which of these number sentences is used to work out her hourly pay, in dollars?

A $360 - 120 + 24 \div 4.45$
B $360 - (120 + 24) \div 4.45$
C $[360 - (120 + 24)] \div 4.45$
D $360 - (120 + 24) \div 4.75$
E $[360 - (120 + 24)] \div 4.75$

16 Two identical squares overlap to form a shape.

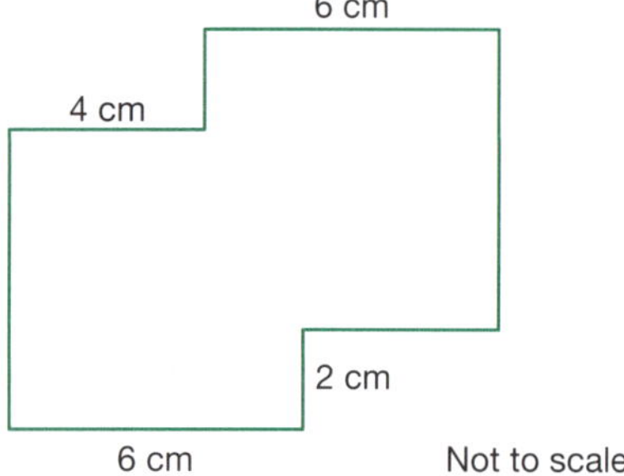

What is the area of the new shape?

A 40 cm^2
B 56 cm^2
C 60 cm^2
D 64 cm^2
E 72 cm^2

Answers and explanations on pages 106–108

SAMPLE TEST 14

17 A tank contains 3600 L of oil when two-thirds full. Later the tank is two-fifths full. How much oil has been removed?

A 1540 L
B 1840 L
C 1660 L
D 1440 L
E 1740 L

18 The diagram shows the dimensions of a net of a rectangular prism.

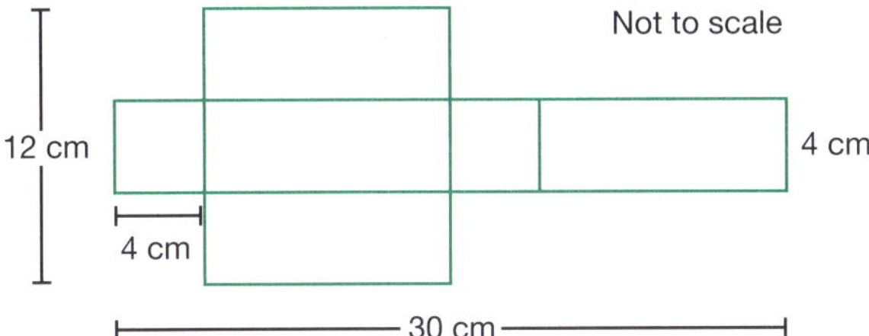

What is the volume when the solid is formed?

A 176 cm^3
B 210 cm^3
C 240 cm^3
D 720 cm^3
E 1440 cm^3

19 A set of five weights are used to weigh objects using a pan balance. The weights are 50 g, 200 g, two 350 g and a 500 g. Which of these weights is not possible to weigh?

A 700 g **B** 750 g **C** 800 g
D 900 g **E** 950 g

20 David can paint 6 m^2 in 12 minutes. How long will it take for him to paint a wall measuring 16 m by 2.5 m?

A 40 minutes
B 1 hour
C 1 hour 10 minutes
D 1 hour 20 minutes
E 2 hours 40 minutes

21 The diagram below represents Helga's speedometer showing her current speed.

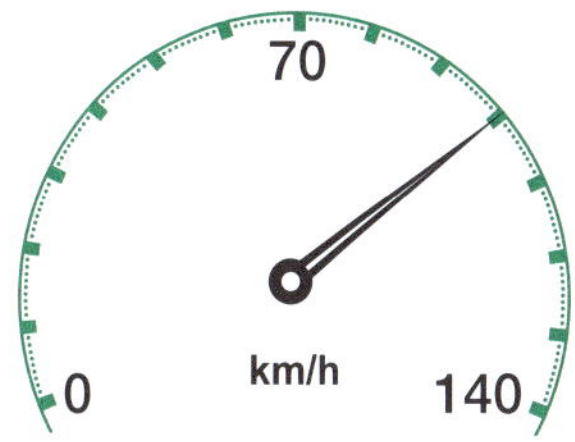

If she maintains this speed for 20 minutes, which of these is the best estimate of the distance travelled?

A 25 km **B** 30 km **C** 33 km
D 35 km **E** 38 km

22 Cate spends $\frac{1}{5}$ of her weekly wage on rent, $\frac{1}{4}$ on bills, $\frac{1}{3}$ on food and fun, and the remaining \$260 is saved. How much is her weekly wage?

A \$1200
B \$960
C \$900
D \$1500
E \$1600

23 Alicia ran from A to B then to C. She used the same route to return to A before finishing at D. Alicia ran a total distance of 14 km. If $BC = DA = 3$ km, how far is it between A and B?

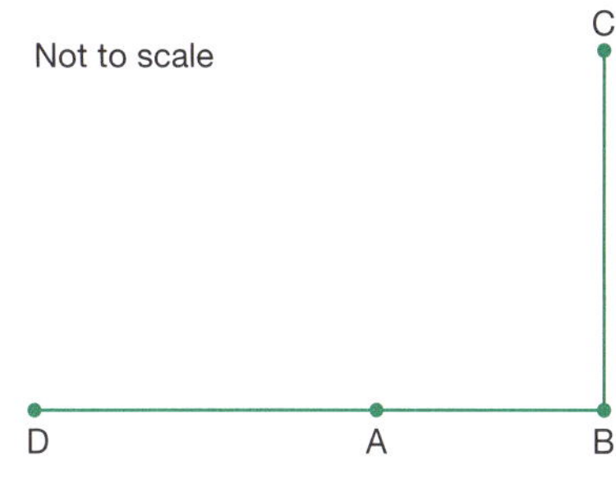

A 2 km
B 2.5 km
C 2.75 km
D 3 km
E 3.5 km

Answers and explanations on pages 106–108

SAMPLE TEST 14

24 The table shows the minimum and maximum temperatures recorded in Alice Springs throughout a week in early August.

Day	Minimum (°C)	Maximum (°C)
Sunday	4	20
Monday	7	21
Tuesday	11	25
Wednesday	16	30
Thursday	10	28
Friday	18	30
Saturday	18	31

Which of these statements is/are correct?

1 Saturday had the greatest difference between the minimum and maximum.

2 The difference between the lowest minimum and the highest maximum was 27 °C.

3 Thursday was the third warmest day during the week.

A statement 1 only
B statement 2 only
C statement 3 only
D statements 1 and 2 only
E statements 1, 2 and 3

25 How many more days were in the winter months than in the summer months in 2020?

0	3	4	2	1
A	**B**	**C**	**D**	**E**

26 Nikki has a spinner made of four coloured sectors. It is equally likely that the arrow will land on a blue, red or green.

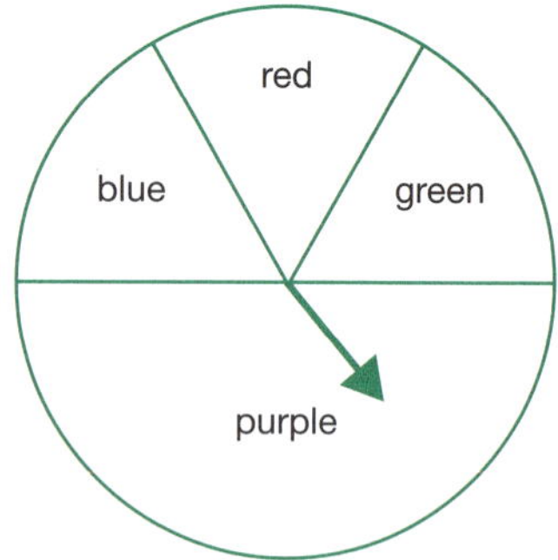

What is the probability that the arrow lands on red?

$\frac{1}{6}$	$\frac{1}{3}$	$\frac{1}{4}$	$\frac{1}{5}$	$\frac{1}{12}$
A	**B**	**C**	**D**	**E**

27 Eliza left home at 7:56 am. She took 0.2 of an hour to walk to the train station. She waited 3 minutes for her train to arrive. The train trip took half an hour and then she walked for 9 minutes to her office. What time did she arrive?

A 8:30 am
B 8:40 am
C 8:44 am
D 8:50 am
E 8:52 am

28 What is the smallest number of squares that need to be shaded if the diagram is to have two lines of symmetry?

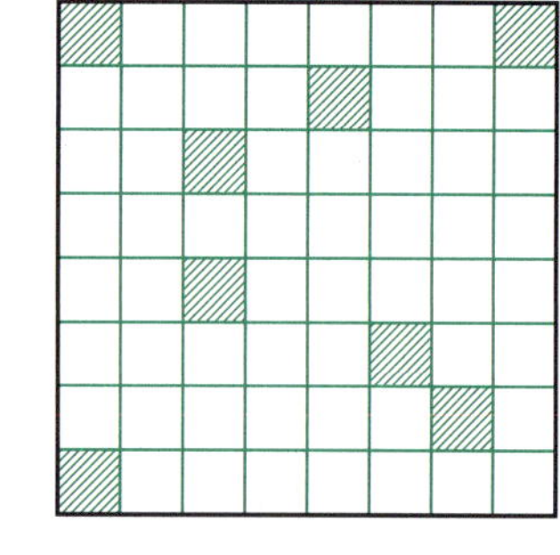

4	6	8	12	10
A	**B**	**C**	**D**	**E**

Answers and explanations on pages 106–108

SAMPLE TEST 14

29 The trip to the beach this morning took Michael 20 minutes at an average speed of 60 km/h. On the trip home, driving the same route, he averaged 40 km/h. What was the average speed for the entire trip?

A 52 km/h
B 50 km/h
C 48 km/h
D 51 km/h
E 54 km/h

30 Luella knows that there is 180° inside a triangle. To find the angle sum of a pentagon she splits the shape into 3 triangles. As 180 × 3 = 540, the angle sum is 540°.

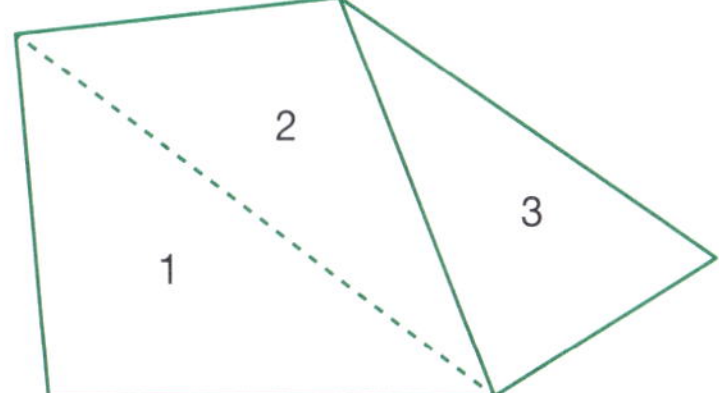

What is the size of each angle in a regular octagon?

40°	80°	110°	120°	135°
A	**B**	**C**	**D**	**E**

31 A rectangle is made up of a row of six squares and a row of eight squares. Squares in each row are identical.

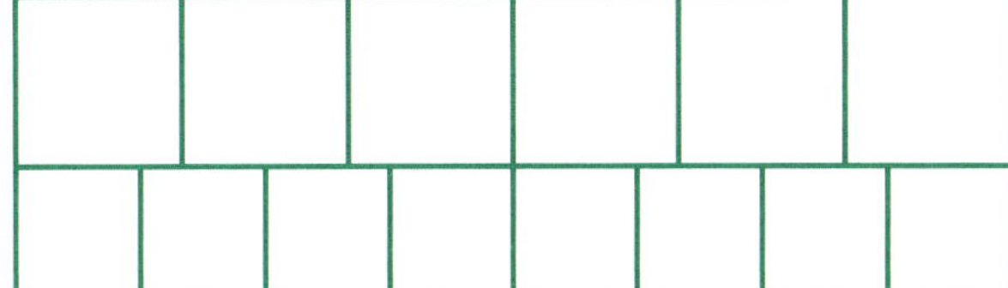

If the area of one square on the top row is 36 cm^2, what is the perimeter of the rectangle?

A 80 cm
B 84 cm
C 93 cm
D 90 cm
E 96 cm

32 There are 40 identical coloured cards in a box. A card is chosen at random. The probability of choosing a blue card is 0.1 and the chance of choosing a red card is twice as likely as choosing a blue card. The chance of choosing a red card is half the chance of choosing a yellow card. The other cards in the box are pink.
Which of these statements is/are correct?

1 The probability of selecting a pink card is 0.3.
2 There are 16 yellow cards in the box.
3 The chance of selecting a blue or pink card is the same as selecting a yellow card.

A statements 1 and 3 only
B statements 1 and 2 only
C statements 1, 2 and 3
D statement 2 only
E statement 3 only

33 Jack and Jill are driving the same 240 km route from Goorangoola to Bernstein. Jill takes 3 hours to complete the journey. Jill's average speed is $\frac{4}{5}$ Jack's average speed. How much longer will Jill take to complete the trip?

A 6 minutes
B 24 minutes
C 30 minutes
D 32 minutes
E 36 minutes

34 The length of a rectangular prism is four times the width and three times the height. If the total length of the edges is 152 cm, what is the volume of the prism?

A 576 cm^3
B 1152 cm^3
C 1200 cm^3
D 1288 cm^3
E 1448 cm^3

Answers and explanations on pages 106–108

35 The travel graph shows the journeys of two brothers, Bill and Ben, who live with their parents.

Both brothers left their home in the morning and arrived back later in the day.

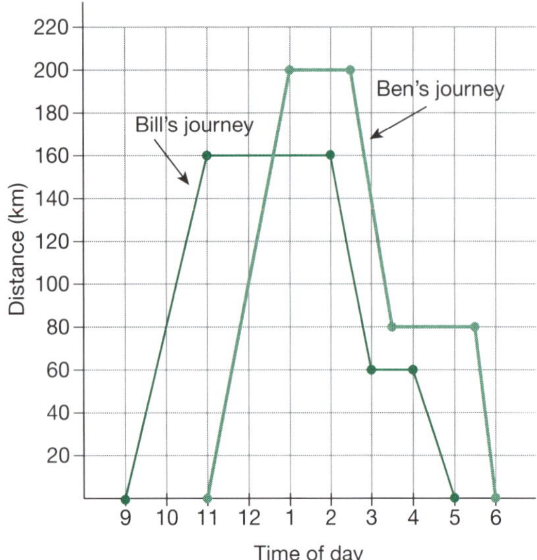

Which of these statements is/are correct?

1 Ben drove 40 km more than Bill.

2 Bill stopped twice as long as Ben.

3 Bill and Ben met up for an afternoon coffee.

A none of the statements

B statement 1 only

C statement 2 only

D statement 3 only

E statements 1, 2 and 3

Answers and explanations on pages 106–108

SELECTIVE SCHOOL–STYLE TEST **Mathematical Reasoning**

SAMPLE TEST 15

1 Louie wrote 11 consecutive odd numbers along a line. If the total of the 7th and 10th numbers is 52, what is the middle number?

21	15	23	17	19
A	**B**	**C**	**D**	**E**

2 Four-digit numbers are made using the digits 4, 2, 8 and 3. What is the difference between the largest even number and the smallest odd number?

A 5481
B 5387
C 5949
D 5762
E 5549

3 A number when divided by 7 leaves a remainder of 3 and when divided by 8 leaves a remainder of 4. What is the smallest possible three-digit number?

102	108	216	220	248
A	**B**	**C**	**D**	**E**

4 A survey was conducted to determine the number of students born in different seasons. A sixth of the group of students were born in summer, a quarter born in autumn, a fifth were born in winter and the remainder in spring. Which of these could be the number of students surveyed?

90	48	72	180	36
A	**B**	**C**	**D**	**E**

5 At Broadmeadow High School, 40% of the females and 50% of the males play weekend sport. 40% of the students at the school are males and the remainder female. What percentage of the entire student population do not play weekend sport?

44%	46%	56%	60%	64%
A	**B**	**C**	**D**	**E**

6 How many two-digit numbers have a remainder of 1 when divided by 3?

28	30	32	31	29
A	**B**	**C**	**D**	**E**

7 Madeline used a roadside stall to sell her pumpkins. She sold one-third of her pumpkins on Saturday and three-quarters of the remaining pumpkins on Sunday. By the end of Sunday, she was left with 12 pumpkins. How many did she start with on Saturday morning?

144	72	108	84	96
A	**B**	**C**	**D**	**E**

8 What number is represented by *?

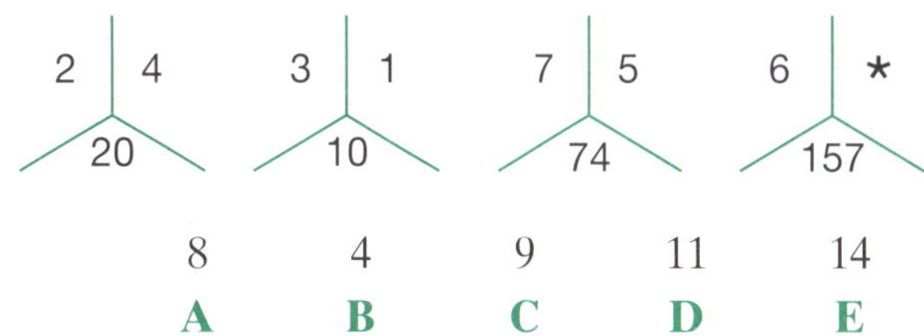

8	4	9	11	14
A	**B**	**C**	**D**	**E**

9 Jorja drew a pattern of rectangles.

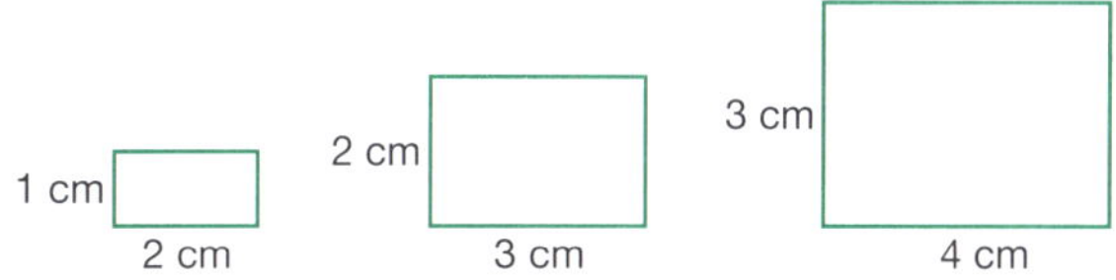

Jorja continues the pattern. One of her rectangles has a perimeter of 82 cm. What is the area of this rectangle?

A 410 cm^2
B 380 cm^2
C 400 cm^2
D 440 cm^2
E 420 cm^2

10 What is the total number of edges and vertices in a hexagonal prism?

28	18	24	20	30
A	**B**	**C**	**D**	**E**

Answers and explanations on pages 108–111

SAMPLE TEST 15

11 A ball is dropped from a height of 36 m. After it hits the ground, it always bounces to a height of $\frac{2}{3}$ its previous height. Through what distance has the ball travelled as it hits the ground a third time?

A 58 m
B 76 m
C 84 m
D 116 m
E 152 m

12 45 + (**?** – 11) × 4 – 36 ÷ 4 = 60.

What is the value of the missing number?

25	15	17	20	12
A	**B**	**C**	**D**	**E**

13 A square of side 12 cm is split into two equal rectangles. A diagonal is drawn on the square.

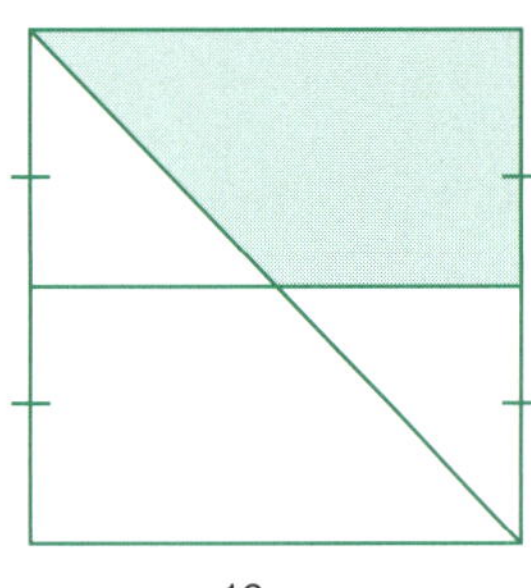

What is the area of the shaded trapezium?

A 54 cm²
B 48 cm²
C 52 cm²
D 60 cm²
E 56 cm²

14 A circle is drawn on a whiteboard. Indiana shades $\frac{1}{4}$ of the circle, Sienna shades $\frac{1}{5}$ and Ava shades $\frac{1}{6}$. What fraction of the original circle has **not** been shaded?

$\frac{3}{8}$	$\frac{1}{3}$	$\frac{5}{12}$	$\frac{21}{60}$	$\frac{23}{60}$
A	**B**	**C**	**D**	**E**

15 Students conducted a survey of the vehicles that passed the school in a 10-minute period. The results are shown on the graph below.

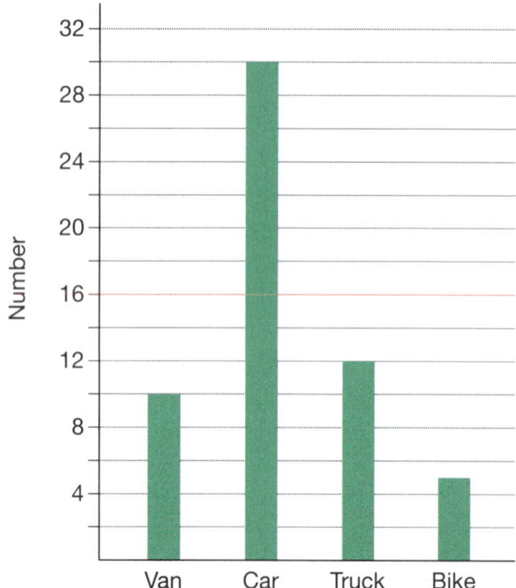

Here are three statements about the graph.

1 Three times as many cars passed the school as vans.

2 The total of vans, trucks and bikes was more than the number of cars.

3 If this pattern continued for an hour, 12 more trucks than vans would pass the school.

Which of these statements is/are correct?

A statement 1 only
B statement 2 only
C statement 3 only
D statements 1 and 3 only
E statements 1, 2 and 3

16 What is the sum of the difference in the place value of the 4s and the difference in the place value of the 7s in the number 479 475?

A 329 670
B 469 530
C 465 480
D 461 110
E 483 240

☞ Answers and explanations on pages 108–111

SAMPLE TEST 15

17 Nine identical squares each have a perimeter of 80 cm. The squares are joined together to make a larger square. What is the area of the large square?

A 3600 cm^2
B 2400 cm^2
C 1600 cm^2
D 8100 cm^2
E 6400 cm^2

18 The total cost of a calculator and a notebook is $27.10. The cost of the calculator is $15.80 more than the cost of the notebook. What is the cost of two notebooks?

A $5.65
B $21.45
C $11.30
D $20.95
E $10.90

19 Kieran is to take 15 mL of medicine every 8 hours from a bottle containing 210 mL. If he has his first dose at 6 am on Wednesday, when does he have his last dose?

A 2 pm Sunday
B 6 am Saturday
C 2 pm Saturday
D 10 pm Saturday
E 6 am Sunday

20 Jessica wrote these statements about the diagonals of a rectangle.

1 The diagonals always bisect each other.
2 The diagonals always divide the rectangle into four identical triangles.
3 The diagonals always meet at right angles.

Which of these statements is/are correct?

A statement 1 only
B statement 2 only
C statement 3 only
D statements 1 and 2 only
E statements 1, 2 and 3

21 Holly and Mia are driving towards each other. Holly left Gunnedah at 7 am and averaged 80 km/h. Mia left Lithgow at the same time and averaged 100 km/h. The distance between Gunnedah and Lithgow is 360 km. Which of these statements is/are correct?

1 The women passed each other at 9 am.
2 Holly arrived in Lithgow at 11:30 am.
3 Mia's trip took 30 minutes less time than Holly's trip.

Which of these statements is/are correct?

A statement 1 only
B statement 2 only
C statement 3 only
D statement 1 and 2 only
E statements 1, 2 and 3

22 Marg uses pan balances to compare the mass of pineapples, oranges and apples.

How many apples have the same mass as two pineapples?

15	8	9	6	12
A	**B**	**C**	**D**	**E**

23 Craig places an empty bowl on a set of digital scales. The readout shows 80 g. He places four potatoes in the bowl and the readout is 1.06 kg. What is the average mass of the potatoes?

A 465 g
B 285 g
C 245 g
D 295 g
E 231.5 g

Answers and explanations on pages 108–111

SAMPLE TEST 15

24 The perimeter of a rectangle with side length 12 cm is 40 cm. The rectangle has been split into four triangles. The area of triangle *A* is 12 cm^2.

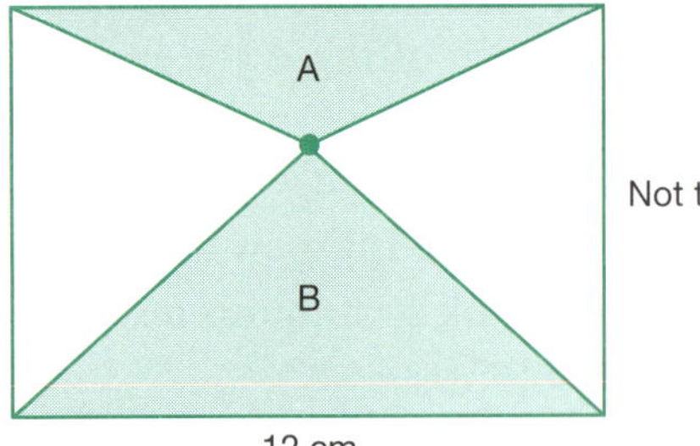

What is the area of triangle *B*?

A 24 cm^2
B 30 cm^2
C 48 cm^2
D 32 cm^2
E 36 cm^2

25 The table shows the number of different coloured cubes contained in a box.

Colour	Number
red	5
blue	9
green	6

A cube is chosen at random.

Which of these statements is/are correct?

1 The probability of choosing a red cube is $\frac{1}{3}$.
2 The probability of choosing a green cube is 0.3.
3 If two green cubes are removed, the probability of choosing a blue cube is 50%.

A statements 2 and 3 only
B statements 1 and 2 only
C statement 1 only
D statement 2 only
E statement 3 only

26 A tank is in the shape of a rectangular prism with dimensions 1.2 m by 80 cm by 70 cm. The empty tank is to be filled with water from a hose. The tank will fill at the rate of 6 L per minute. How long will it take to three-quarters fill the tank? Use 1 cm^3 = 1 mL.

A 1 hour 48 minutes
B 1 hour 12 minutes
C 1 hour 36 minutes
D 1 hour 24 minutes
E 1 hour 52 minutes

27 Fiona's flight takes off from Sydney at 8:45 pm Wednesday. After 8 hours 25 minutes the plane lands in Singapore. After 5 hours 50 minutes, the plane takes off again and lands in London 13 hours 40 minutes later. If London is 9 hours behind Sydney, what is the local time in London when Fiona arrives?

A 2:40 pm Thursday
B 3:40 pm Thursday
C 4:40 pm Thursday
D 5:40 pm Thursday
E 9:40 am Friday

28 Here is a pattern of triangles.
The triangles are white, grey or black.

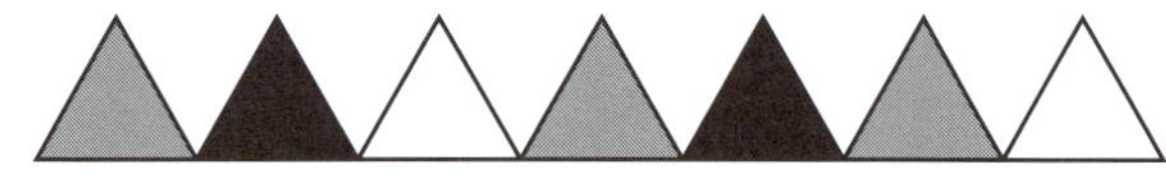

Ingrid wants the pattern to have a line of symmetry.
She adds more triangles to the right of the existing triangles.
How many more triangles will be added?

0	1	2	3	4
A	**B**	**C**	**D**	**E**

Answers and explanations on pages 108–111

29 What is the missing angle in this diagram?

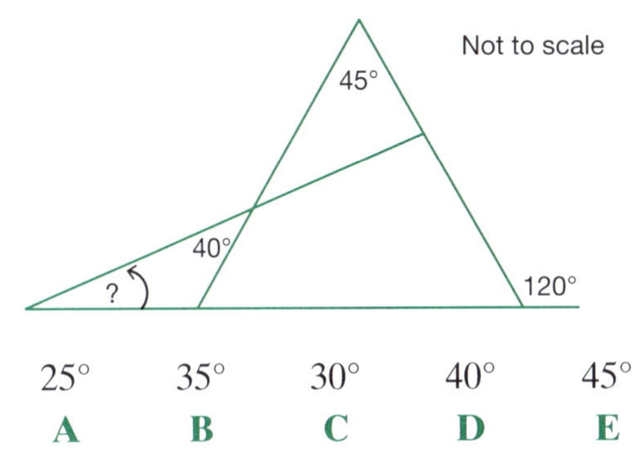

25°	35°	30°	40°	45°
A	**B**	**C**	**D**	**E**

30 Which of these is **not** a net of a triangular prism?

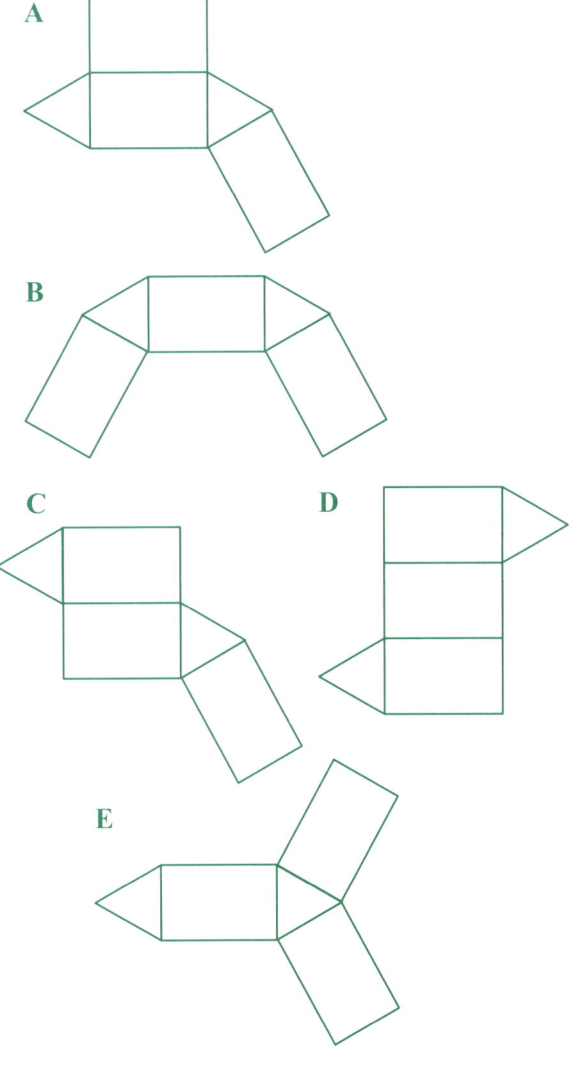

31 A group of 360 students were surveyed to find the brand of toothpaste they use. The survey showed the students use four brands of toothpaste.

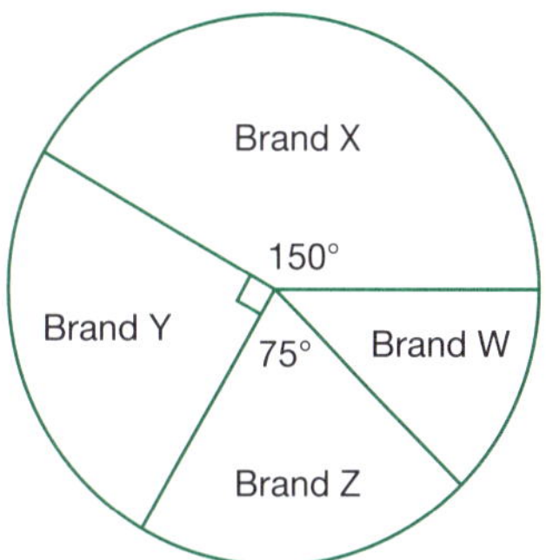

Here are three statements about the graph.

1 Ninety students use Brand *Y*.

2 Twice as many students use Brand *Y* as use Brand *W*.

3 More than half of the students use Brand *X* or Brand *W*.

Which of these statements is/are correct?

A statements 1, 2 and 3
B statement 1 only
C statement 2 only
D statement 3 only
E statements 1 and 3 only

32 On the island of Camphor, locals play a game where points are awarded for goals and outers. In a game between the Cats and the Dogs, the Cats kicked 8 goals and 12 outers. The Dogs kicked 4 goals and 10 outers.

The Cats won the game 64–40.

When the Cats played their next game, they kicked 10 goals and 5 outers. How many points did they score in the second game?

48	50	54	55	60
A	**B**	**C**	**D**	**E**

Answers and explanations on pages 108–111

SAMPLE TEST 15

33 A farmer has a shed which is in the shape of a rectangular prism. The floor dimensions are 12 m by 10 m and it is 3 m high. In a thunderstorm 10 mm of rain fell on his farm. If 1 cm^3 = 1 mL, how much water will run off the roof of the shed and into a water tank?

A 360 L
B 1200 L
C 12 000 L
D 3600 L
E 36 000 L

34 ☆ + ☆ × ☆ = 20.

⃠ ÷ ☆ = 3.

☺ − 2 × (⃠ + ☆) = 8.

If ☆, ⃠ and ☺ represent positive whole numbers, what is the value of ☺ ?

16	32	40	28	24
A	**B**	**C**	**D**	**E**

35 Alyson has a spinner made of three numbered sectors.

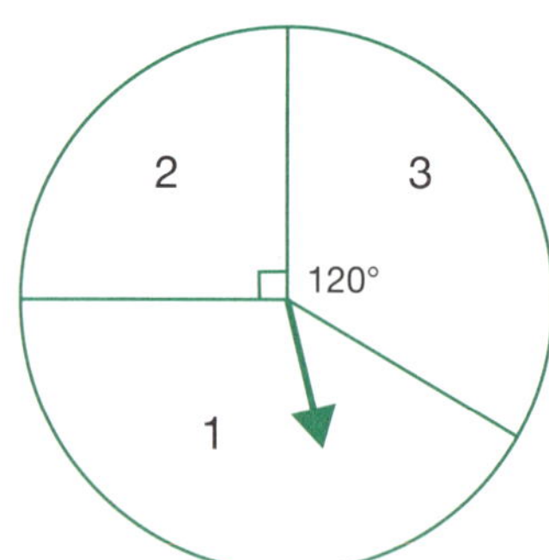

What is the probability that the arrow lands on 1?

$\frac{1}{3}$	$\frac{17}{36}$	$\frac{5}{12}$	$\frac{3}{8}$	$\frac{4}{9}$
A	**B**	**C**	**D**	**E**

☞ Answers and explanations on pages 108–111

SAMPLE TEST 1

Page 1

1 A **2** B **3** E **4** A **5** A **6** D **7** B **8** A **9** B
10 E **11** C **12** C **13** A **14** A **15** A **16** C
17 B **18** C **19** A **20** E **21** A **22** B **23** E
24 D **25** C **26** C **27** B **28** D **29** D **30** C
31 E **32** D **33** D **34** D **35** A

1 As 49 ÷ 6 is 8 with remainder 1, the last positive number is 1.

2 The largest number is 7632 and the second largest is 7623. The smallest number is 2367 and the second smallest is 2376.

$$\begin{array}{r} 7623 \\ -\ 2376 \\ \hline 5247 \end{array}$$

The difference is 5247.

3 $\frac{3}{10}$ = 0.3, which can be written as 0.300. Expressing each of the options with three decimal places, the choices are 0.310, 0.306, 0.400, 3.100 and 0.296. As 296 is closest to 300, the number closest to $\frac{3}{10}$ is 0.296.

4 As 26 × 4 = 104, and 104 – (12 + 16 + 23) = 104 – 51 = 53, Stella has 53 in her collection.

5 The catch in this one is in the 30s. Do not forget to count two 3s for 33 (3, 13, 23, 30, 31, 32, 33, 34, 35, 36, 37, 38, 39, 43, 53, 63).

6 Out of every hundred 71 (or 71%) do not walk. 29% of students must walk. There are 300 students. 29% of 300 = 87

7 As $\frac{2}{3} + \frac{3}{3} = \frac{5}{3}$, then $\frac{5}{3}$ of the larger number is 45. As 45 ÷ 5 × 3 is 27, the larger number is 27.

8 As 2000 ÷ 4 = 500, and 2000 + 500 = 2500, the price increased to \$2500. As 2500 ÷ 4 = 625 and 2500 – 625 = 1875, the final price was \$1875.

9 $P = 19$, $Q = 18$ and $R = 3$.
$P - (Q - R) = 19 - (18 - 3) = 19 - 15 = 4$.

10	7	4	20
5	19	11	6
18	2	9	12
8	13	17	3

10 $A + B + B + C = 48 + 64 = 112$.
$A + B + C = 96$ and 112 – 96 = 16. This means B has a mass of 16 kg. As 48 – 16 = 32, A has a mass of 32 kg. As 32 + 16 + C = 96, the mass of C is 48 kg. As 48 – 16 = 32, the difference is 32 kg.

11 As $\frac{2}{3} - \frac{1}{4} = \frac{8}{12} - \frac{3}{12} = \frac{5}{12}$, Marley used $\frac{5}{12}$ of 60 L. As 60 ÷ 12 × 5 = 25, she used 25 L of petrol.

12 From the 3rd term to the 13th term there are 10 terms. As 138 – 10 × 3 = 108, the 13th term would be 108.

13 As 20 – **?** ÷ 2 × 3 + 5 = 7, then

20 – **?** ÷ 2 × 3 = 2.

This means **?** ÷ 2 × 3 = 18. As 18 ÷ 3 is 6,

then **?** = 12.

14 Let the number be X. This means $X + X + 8 = X + 12$. This can be rewritten as $X + 8 = 12$, which means the number is 4.

15 By drawing lines, the rectangle can be split into identical triangles. There are 16 triangles, and 8 triangles are shaded. This means $\frac{1}{2}$ of the rectangle is shaded.

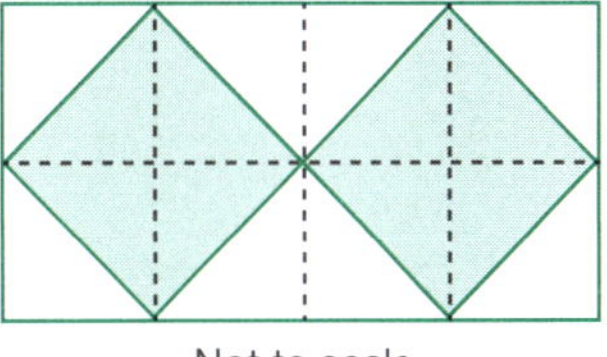

Not to scale

16 As $1 - \frac{1}{5} = \frac{4}{5}$, the container has 120 L when four-fifths full. As 120 ÷ 4 = 30, the container has 30 L of water when $\frac{1}{5}$ full.

17 The lengths of P and Q are the same and as $80 - 64 = 16$, then twice the difference in the width is 16 cm. As $16 \div 2 = 8$, rectangle P is 8 cm wider than rectangle Q.

18 As $175 \div 25$ is 7, and 20×7 is 140, it takes 140 minutes. This is rewritten as 2 hours 20 minutes.

19 The numbers are 12, 15, 18, 21 and 24. This is 5 out of 30, which is a probability of $\frac{5}{30}$, or $\frac{1}{6}$.

20 As $2 \times 5 \times 365 = 3650$, the fish eat for 3650 minutes. As $3650 \div 60 = 365 \div 6 = 60\frac{5}{6}$, her fish eat for about 60 hours a year.

21 Aubrey: Multiplying by 2 gives 6 apples and 4 bananas cost \$7.30. As Sarah's 2 apples and 4 bananas cost \$4.30, then 4 apples cost \$7.30 – \$4.30 = \$3. This means 1 apple costs 75 cents. As 2 × 75c = \$1.50, 4 bananas cost \$4.30 – \$1.50 = \$2.80, and 1 banana costs 70 cents. Michaela paid 75c + 70c = \$1.45.

22 As 1 can = 7 eggs, then 5 cans = 35 eggs. This means 5 cans = 3 loaves. Multiplying by 4 gives: the mass of 20 cans = mass of 12 loaves.

23 Suppose there are 100 people originally vaccinated. After 3 months the number is 200, after 6 months it is 400, after 9 months it is 800 and after 12 months it is 1600.
As $100 \times 16 = 1600$, the number vaccinated is 16 times the original number.

24 The shape becomes a six-sided 3D shape. It is a little like a 'misshapen cube'.

25 The steepest section of the graph is between 2:15 and 2:45. As $140 - 90 = 50$, in this half hour Darcy travelled 50 km. This means his fastest average speed was 100 km/h.

26 There are two lines of symmetry.

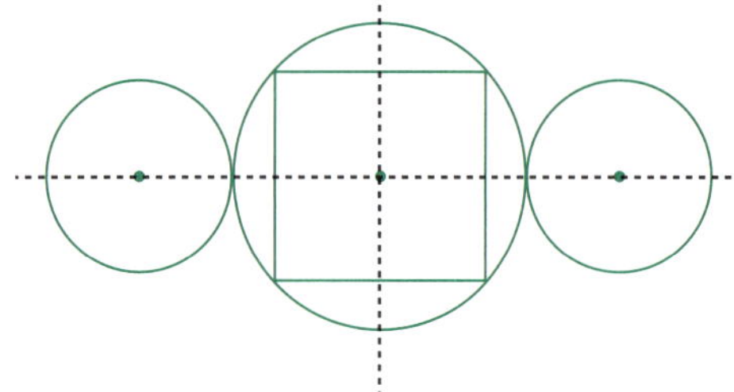

27 Rotate each of the hands a quarter turn in an anticlockwise direction. The minute hand was pointing to 2 and now points to 11. The hour hand was pointing to 11 and now points to 8. The time will be 5 minutes to 8.

28 There are 360° in a revolution. As $\frac{60}{360} = \frac{1}{6}$, and $240 \div 6 = 40$, the area not shaded is 40 cm². As $240 - 40 = 200$, the shaded area is 200 cm².

29 The net is made from 4 triangles and a square. As $48 \times 4 + 36 = 192 + 36 = 228$, the area is 228 cm².

30 As 20 minutes is $\frac{1}{3}$ of an hour, and $15 \div 3 = 5$, Max lives 5 km from school. As $20 - 5 = 15$, Max needs to take 15 minutes, which is $\frac{1}{4}$ of an hour. As $5 \div \frac{1}{4}$ is $5 \times 4 = 20$, Max needs to ride at 20 km/h.

31 As $360 - (90 + 90 + 60) = 120$, the angle for 'red' is 120°. As $60 \times 2 = 120$, the probability of spinning a red is twice as likely as spinning a blue. Statement X is correct. As $\frac{90}{360} = \frac{1}{4} = 0.25$, the probability of spinning a pink is 0.25. Statement Y is correct. As $90 + 60 = 150$, and $\frac{150}{260} = \frac{5}{12}$, the probability of spinning a yellow or a blue is $\frac{5}{12}$. Statement Z is correct.
Statements X, Y and Z are correct.

32 The side length of square P is 3 cm. The side length of square Q is 7 cm. As $7 - 3 = 4$, the height of the triangle is 4 cm. As $\frac{1}{2} \times 3 \times 4$ is 6, the area of the triangle is 6 cm².

33 As $6 - 2 = 4$, there were 4 more students who liked purple than yellow. Statement 1 is not correct. As $4 + 6 = 10$ and $4 + 3 + 6 + 5 + 2 = 20$, then half of the students liked red or purple. Statement 2 is correct. As 3 out of 20 is $\frac{3}{20} = \frac{15}{100} = 15\%$, Statement 3 is correct.
Statements 2 and 3 are correct.

34 Consider a rectangle with dimensions 12 cm and 3 cm and a square of side 6 cm. The perimeter of the rectangle is 30 cm and the square is 24 cm. Statement 1 is not correct but statement 3 is correct.
As $12 \times 3 = 6 \times 6 = 36$, the area is 36 cm². Statement 2 is correct. This means statements 2 and 3 are correct.

35 You need to find the height if $40 \times 30 \times \text{height} = 3600$. As $1200 \times \text{height} = 3600$, the height is 3 cm. As $10 + 3 = 13$, the height of the water is now 13 cm.

SAMPLE TEST 2

Page 6

1 A **2** B **3** A **4** E **5** E **6** D **7** D **8** C **9** C
10 C **11** A **12** E **13** A **14** A **15** D **16** B
17 D **18** A **19** E **20** B **21** A **22** A **23** B
24 D **25** A **26** B **27** B **28** C **29** C **30** E
31 E **32** C **33** C **34** E **35** B

1 As $9 + 4 + 7 + 12 = 32$, and $32 \div 4 = 8$, Dane needs 8 balls in each box. He needs to move 1 ball from the first box to the third box, and 4 balls from the fourth box to the second box. As $1 + 4 = 5$, Dane should move a total of 5 balls.

2 As $48 - 16 = 32$, half the square of a number is 32. As $32 \times 2 = 64$, the square of a number is 64. This means the number is 8.

3 There will be only one line of symmetry.

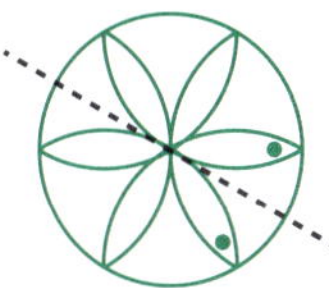

4 There are 12 white tiles and 12 grey tiles. As $9 + 2 = 11$, each grey tile costs \$11. The cost is $12 \times 9 + 12 \times 11 = 12 \times 20 = 240$, which is \$240.

5 As $6 + 1 + 8 = 15$, each row has 15 chairs. As $7 + 1 + 12 = 20$, there are 20 rows of chairs. As $20 \times 15 = 300$, there are 300 chairs in the hall.

6 You could trial the possible answers. You could list all the numbers that fit the conditions for $\div 6$ with remainder 3 (e.g. 9, 15, 21 … 57). Do the same with $\div 5$ with remainder 2 (e.g. 7, 12, 17 … 57) and then $\div 4$ with remainder of 1. This means the number is 57.

7 Jason gives 25% of \$8 to Scott, which is \$2. Scott then has \$10. He gives Jason 25% which is \$2.50. Jason now has \$6 + \$2.50 = \$8.50.

8 As $387 + 46 = 433$, Liam earned \$433. As $433 + 87 = 520$, Jacob earned \$520.

$$\begin{array}{r} 433 \\ 387 \\ +\ 520 \\ \hline 1340 \end{array}$$

The total amount was \$1340.

9 You need to work out $6 \div \frac{3}{4}$. $\frac{3}{4} + \frac{3}{4} = 1\frac{1}{2}$. This means four lots of $\frac{3}{4}$ is 3 and so eight lots of $\frac{3}{4}$ is 6. Eden can make 8 cakes.

10 $999 \times 100 = 99\,900$.

$$\begin{array}{r} 1\,000\,000 \\ -\ \ 99\,900 \\ \hline 900\,100 \end{array}$$

The answer is 900 100.

11 As $(44 - 32) \div 6 = 2$, the mass of each box is 2 kg. As $44 - 12 \times 2 = 20$, the mass is 20 kg.

12 $2 + \frac{1}{2} + \frac{1}{2} + \frac{1}{2} + \frac{1}{2} = 4$, and $72 \div 4 = 18$. The cost of an adult ticket is \$18 and a child's ticket is \$9. As $18 + 9 = 27$, Tom and his daughter pay \$27.

13 The magic number is $12.25 + 7.25 + 11.25 + 0.25 = 31$. The number replacing the * is 8.25.

15.25	1.25	2.25	12.25
4.25	10.25	9.25	7.25
8.25	6.25	5.25	11.25
3.25	13.25	14.25	0.25

14 The rule is the number of matches = 2 × number of triangles + 1. This means 2 × number of triangles + 1 = 191, which is 2 × number of triangles = 190. As $190 \div 2 = 95$, Alice will have 95 triangles in the shape.

15

16 As $5 + 5 \times 4 = 25$ then $(\boxed{?} + 5)^2 - 4 \times 6 = 25$. As $4 \times 6 = 24$, and $25 + 24 = 49$, then $(\boxed{?} + 5)^2 = 49$. As $7^2 = 49$, then $\boxed{?} = 2$.

17 Let the number be X. This means $20 - 4 \times X = X + 10$. Look at each of the options: as $20 - 4 \times 2 = 2 + 10$, the number is 2.

18 The squares have side lengths 1 cm, 2 cm, 4 cm and 8 cm. As 1 + 2 + 4 + 8 = 15 and 2 × (15 + 8) = 46, the perimeter is 46 cm.

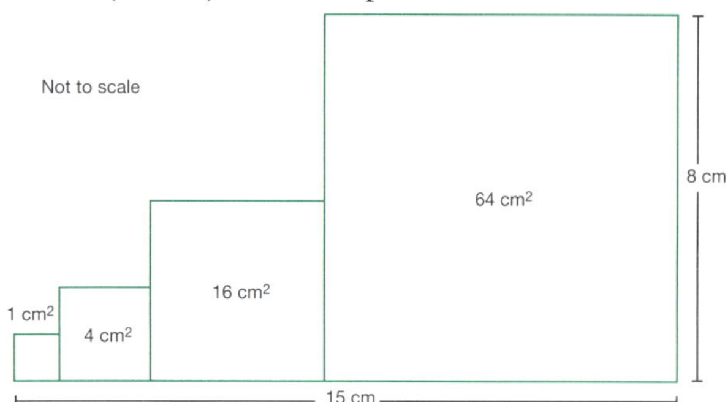

19 The last digits in the numbers are in the pattern 2, 4, 8, 6, 2, 4, 8, … The four numbers (2, 4, 8, 6) are repeated. As 24 ÷ 4 = 6, the fourth digit in the pattern, 6, will be the last digit in 2^{24}. (2^{24} = 16 777 216)

20 The two middle blocks on the top and bottom. There are 4 blocks.

21 As 70 – 55 = 15, Aaron scored 15 marks more than Drew. Statement 1 is correct. As (50 + 80) ÷ 2 = 130 ÷ 2 = 65, the average of Sophie's mark and Leo's mark is 65. Statement 2 is correct. As 80 ÷ 2 = 40, which is not 35, Taya did not score half as many marks as Leo. Statement 3 is not correct. Statements 1 and 2 are the only correct statements.

22 As 1000 ÷ 5 = 200 and 20 × 10 = 200, each rectangle measures 20 cm by 10 cm. As 6 × (20 + 10) = 180, the perimeter is 180 cm.

23 As 10 × 10 × 20 = 2000, the volume of Container *P* is 2000 cm^3. As 25 × 20 × 12 = 500 × 12 = 6000, the volume of Container *Q* is 6000 cm^3. The fraction is $\frac{2000}{6000}$, which is $\frac{1}{3}$.

24 As 12 ÷ 4 = 3 and 3 × 3 × 3 = 27, there are 27 small cubes.

25 As 15 minutes is $\frac{1}{4}$ of an hour, Oscar drove at 80 km/h for $1\frac{1}{4}$ hours. $80 \times 1\frac{1}{4} = 80 + 80 \div 4 = 100$, so Oscar drove 100 km at the start of his trip. As 100 + 70 = 170, the entire trip was 170 km. As 170 ÷ 85 = 2, the whole trip took 2 hours.

26 1 hour 12 minutes is 72 minutes. As 72 ÷ 9 = 8, it takes 8 minutes to paint $\frac{1}{20}$ of the wall. As $1 - \frac{9}{20} = \frac{11}{20}$ and 8 × 11 = 88, it takes another 88 minutes, which is 1 hour 28 minutes.

27 Subtract 31 minutes from 3 hours 14 minutes. As 31 – 14 = 17, and 60 – 17 = 43, Edward took 2 hours 43 minutes. From 11:47 am, add 2 hours to get 1:47 pm, then adding 13 gives 2:00 pm and finally 30 minutes gives 2:30 pm.

28 As half of 72 is 36, the sum of the length and width is 36 cm. As 36 – 20 = 16 the width is 16 cm. As (20 – 2) ÷ 2 is 9, the dimensions of the triangles are 16 cm and 9 cm. The shaded area is the rectangle minus 2 triangles.
As $20 \times 16 - 2 \times \frac{1}{2} \times 16 \times 9 = 176$, the area is 176 cm^2.

29 A square has 4 equal sides which makes it a rhombus. Conclusion 1 is correct. A rhombus has pairs of adjacent sides equal which makes it a kite. Conclusion 2 is correct. A rectangle is a special type of parallelogram with right angles. Not all parallelograms are rectangles. Conclusion 3 is not correct.

30 As $\frac{3}{4}$ of the spinner is red and yellow, 360 ÷ 4 × 3 = 270, and so the total angle size for red and yellow is 270°. As 4 + 1 = 5, then $\frac{1}{5}$ of the spinner is yellow. As 270 ÷ 5 = 54, the angle is 54°.

31 As $\frac{1}{2}$ × base × 12 = 108, then 6 × base = 108 and so the base of the triangle is 18 cm. The net has 2 triangles and 3 rectangles. The dimensions of the rectangles are 10 cm by 18 cm, 20 cm by 15 cm and 20 cm by 15 cm.
As 2 × 108 + 20 × 18 + 2 × 20 × 15 = 216 + 360 + 600 = 1176, the area is 1176 cm^2.

32 The three angles in a triangle add to 180°. As 180 – 56 = 124, the third angle is 124°.

33 As 280 – 220 = 60, the price dropped $60 during week 7. Statement 1 is not correct. The highest price was $400 at the end of week 4. Statement 2 is correct. As 360 – 280 = 80, the greatest change was during week 6. Statement 3 is correct. Statements 2 and 3 are correct statements.

34 As 15 ÷ 3 = 5, one-third of the distance is 5 km. Darcie has walked for one hour. As 15 – 5 = 10, Darcie completes the remaining 10 km in one hour. This means her running speed was 10 km/h.

35 There are 2 red marbles, 6 green marbles and 4 blue marbles in the bag. As $\frac{2}{12} = \frac{1}{6}$, the probability of choosing a red marble is $\frac{1}{6}$. Statement 1 is not correct. As $\frac{6}{12} = \frac{1}{2}$, the probability of choosing a green marble is $\frac{1}{2}$. Statement 2 is correct. As 3 out of 11 marbles are blue, the probability of choosing a blue marble is $\frac{3}{11}$. Statement 3 is not correct. This means Statement 2 is the only correct statement.

SAMPLE TEST 3

Page 12

1 B **2** C **3** D **4** B **5** C **6** B **7** B **8** D **9** E **10** E **11** B **12** B **13** A **14** C **15** C **16** A **17** C **18** D **19** C **20** B **21** A **22** D **23** C **24** B **25** A **26** B **27** E **28** A **29** A **30** B **31** A **32** C **33** A **34** B **35** E

1 A would round down to 19 million.
B would round up to 20 million.
C would round up to 21 million.
D would round up to 21 million.
E would round down to 19 million.

2 The sequence is 5, –2, –9, –16, –23 … The fifth number is –23.

3 To get an average of 8 correct in five weeks she needs a total of 40. After 4 weeks her total is 30 (4 × 7.5). She must get all 10 correct.

4 1 pineapple = 2 apples in price. With the same money you could buy 5 apples.
$3.25 ÷ 5 = 65c

5 First you need all the odd numbers (31, 33, 35, 37, 39). Now look for the number that is 2 more than the multiples of 3 (30, 33, 36, 39). The number of ducks is 35.

6 $\frac{3}{6} = \frac{1}{2}, \frac{6}{3} = 2$. The difference is $1\frac{1}{2}$.

7 36 ÷ 2 × 3 = 54

8 As 45 ÷ 3 = 15, the softball costs $15. As 15 + 3 = 18, the soccer ball costs $18.

9 10 student fares = 5 adult fares,. As 5 + 2 = 7, then 7 adult fares = $42. As 42 ÷ 7 = 6, the adult fare is $6.

10 The magic number is 5 + 15 + 16 + 2 = 38. The number replacing the * is 17.

17	3	4	14
6	12	11	9
10	8	7	13
5	15	16	2

11 You could count but it would be better to find the pattern
Stack 1: 2 + (2 × 3) = 8
Stack 2: 2 + (2 × 3) + (3 × 4) = 20
Stack 3: 2 + (2 × 3) + (3 × 4) + (4 × 5) = 40
Stack 4: (Stack 3) 40 + (5 × 6) = 70

12 The sequence is ?, 11, ?, 25, ?, 39 …
As 25 – 11 = 39 – 25 = 14, the numbers in the sequence are increasing by 7. Adding multiples of 7 to an existing number will give other numbers in the sequence. Adding 70 to 39 will give 109 so 109 is in the sequence.

13 The total cannot be over 200.
As 91 + 9 = 100, BCC = 100

14 As 6480 × 3600 = 23 328 000, then 648 × 36 = 23 328. This means 23 328 ÷ 648 = 36.

15 2 × (12 + 6) = 2 × 18 = 36, or 10 + 4 + 2 + 2 + 4 + 2 + 4 + 2 + 4 + 2 = 36. The perimeter is 36 cm.

16 First ignore the small, unshaded square. The length of the diagonal of the shaded square is 8 cm. As the square is made of 2 identical triangles each with area $\frac{1}{2} \times 8 \times 4 = 16$, the square has an area of 32 cm^2. Now deduct the area of the small unshaded square. You can see it is 4 half-squares or 2 full squares. As 32 – 2 = 30, the area of the shaded part is 30 cm^2.

17 Area of the door: 1 m × 1.75 m (1.75 m^2); area of window: 0.5 m × 0.5 m (0.25 m^2).
1.75 m^2 – 0.25 m^2 = 1.5 m^2
Note: The position of the window does not change the area to be painted.

18 As 1 m^3 = 1000 L, a volume of 20 m^3 will hold 20 000 L. As 2 × 2 × 5 = 20, the tank is 5 m long.

19 The front of the prism is a triangle with base 4 cm and height of 4 cm. As $\frac{1}{2} \times 4 \times 4 = 8$, the area is 8 cm^2. As the solid is 3 cm deep, and 8 × 3 = 24, the volume is 24 cm^3.

20 As $36 \div 2 = 18$, then $360 \div 20 = 18$. There are 18 lots of 20-g serves in the jar. Now 18×1.5 is $18 \times 3 \div 2$. This is $54 \div 2 = 27$. There is 27 g of sugar. The protein information is not used.

21 First work out the distance travelled in 20 minutes. As $96 \div 2 = 48$, the train travels 48 km in 20 minutes. As $48 \times 3 = 144$, the train travels at a speed of 144 km/h.

22 If you take equal amounts from each side of the balance, you do not upset the balance. You would have • + 4 = 7. The • must equal 3.

It can be solved using algebra.

$$(2 \times \bullet) + 4 = (1 \times \bullet) + 5 + 2$$
$$2\bullet + 4 = 1\bullet + 7$$
$$2\bullet - 1\bullet = 7 - 4$$
$$\bullet = 3$$

23 The real time will be 1.30 pm. You must then add 4×5.5 min (22 min) to 1.30 pm = 1.52 pm.

24 The dimensions are 12 cm by 8 cm.
$12 \text{ cm} \times 8 \text{ cm} = 96 \text{ cm}^2$

25 Reflection in a mirror is like reflecting across a vertical line of symmetry.

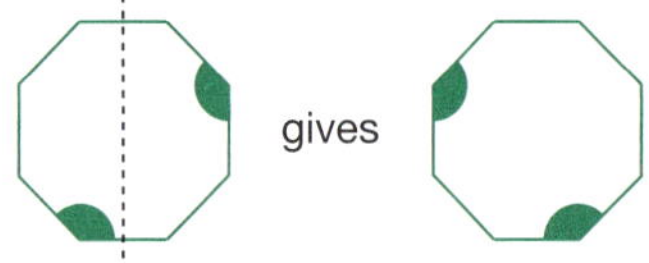

26 The image will complete the letter M.

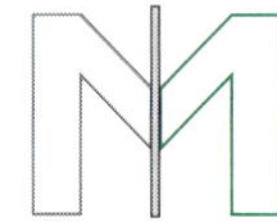

27 As $37 - 21 = 16$, the extra cost is $16.

28 The probability does not change just because Mrs Nour has had more girls than boys. The probability of a girl is $\frac{1}{2}$.

29 The time difference is four and a half hours. (When it is late one morning on Pirate Island it is early afternoon on Tui Island.) Tui Island's time is ahead of Pirate Island's time (Pirate Island is further west). Four and a half hours behind 3.30 am Tuesday is 11 pm Monday.

30 There are 6 numbers divisible by 3. Chances are 6 out of 20 or 3 chances out of 10.

31 This shape has rotational symmetry of degree 4. This means the shape is repeated every 90°. The shape would still be the same after rotating through 180°.

32 There are 360° in a circle.
$360° \div 12 = 30°$

33 You need to be able to imagine the shapes folded. In A, no triangular side will fold onto the top of the square base.

34 There will be 12 cubes with only 2 sides painted.

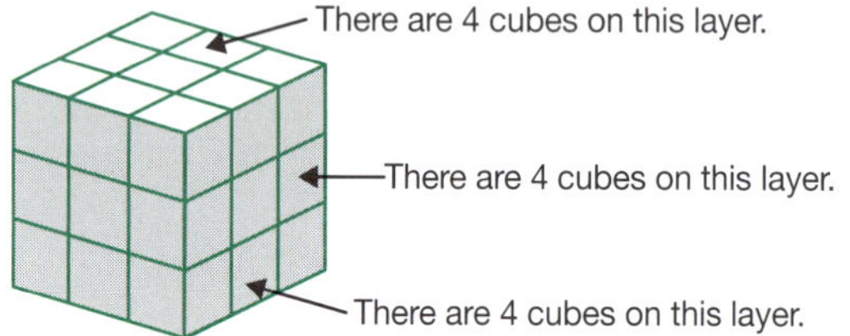

35 Only 5 students were absent for 4 days compared to 7 students absent on 1 day. Statement 1 is not correct. As $4 + 7 + 4 + 4 + 5 + 1 + 2 + 1 = 28$, there are 28 students in the class. Statement 2 is correct. As $7 + 4 + 4 = 15$ and 15 is more than half of 28, statement 3 is correct. Statements 2 and 3 are correct.

SAMPLE TEST 4

Page 17

1 A **2** D **3** D **4** A **5** A **6** D **7** C **8** A **9** E
10 D **11** E **12** C **13** D **14** C **15** D **16** D
17 C **18** D **19** D **20** C **21** D **22** C **23** B
24 B **25** C **26** B **27** D **28** C **29** B **30** C
31 E **32** D **33** A **34** E **35** E

1 Reverse operations.

$7085 - 2878 - 679 - 3025 = 503$.
Some students might prefer to calculate a column at a time by adding.

2 Greg's total number of runs is 105 (3×35). If Greg scored x runs in his first innings, he would get $2x$ (twice x) in the second innings and $2x$ in the third innings. He has scored $5x$ runs. In the first innings he got 21 runs ($105 \div 5$).

3 $3 \times 20 \times 20 \times 200 = 240\,000$

4 Numbers divisible by 8 and 5 are 40, 80 and 120. The answer is 3.

5 As $75 - 60 = 15$, Bill answered 15% more questions correctly than Tony. As 15% is $\frac{15}{100}$ or $\frac{3}{20}$, Bill answered 3 more questions correctly.

6 \$5.96 is close to \$6. As $25 \times 6 = 150$, Mrs Moon will need 8 \$20 notes.

7 The supervisor is paid 2 × contractor. Suppose there were 5 contractors paid. As $460 \div 5 = 92$, and $92 \times 2 = 184$, the supervisor is paid \$184.

8 Here is the hexagon divided into 6 equal triangles:

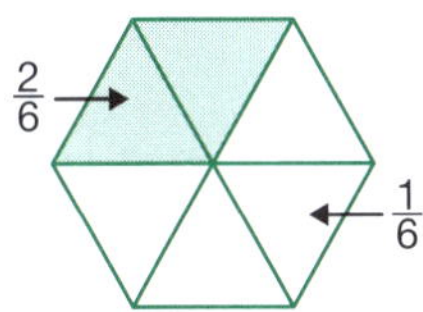

Each triangle is $\frac{1}{6}$ of the hexagon. The section shaded here is $\frac{2}{6}$ of the hexagon. In the question, half of this area is $\frac{1}{6}$ and there are 2 shaded areas so the fraction shaded is $\frac{2}{6}$, which is $\frac{1}{3}$ of the hexagon.

9 As $d + d + d + d = 20$, then $d = 5$.
As $b + d + d + b = 24$, then $b + 5 + 5 + b = 24$, and so $b = 7$. As $c + c + d + d = 26$, then $c + c + 5 + 5 = 26$, and so $c = 8$.
As $a + a + d + d = 18$, then $a + a + 5 + 5 = 18$, and so $a = 4$. As $a + b + c + d = X$, and $4 + 7 + 8 + 5 = 24$, then $X = 24$.

10 Stack 1: $1 + 3^2$

Stack 2: $1 + 3^2 + 5^2$

Stack 3: $1 + 3^2 + 5^2 + 7^2$

Stack 3: $1 + 3^2 + 5^2 + 7^2 + 9^2 = 165$

11 Since [?] + 23 – 4 + 2 × 5 = 31 can be rewritten as [?] + 23 – 4 + 10 = 31, which is [?] + 29 = 31, the missing number is 2.

12 As product means to multiply and quotient means to divide, the number sentence is $2 \times (5 + 3 \times 2) > 20 - 12 \div 4$.

13 The shape is symmetrical.

(9 cm × 16 cm) – (6 cm × 4 cm)
= 144 cm² – 24 cm² = 120 cm²

14 There is one axis for each pair of points (3) and one for each pair of dips (3).

15 There are 13 small squares. Each square is 4 cm² (56 cm² ÷ 13 = 4 cm²).

Each square has side length of 2 cm. There are 4 squares with 3 sides on edge of shape and 4 squares with 2 sides on edge of shape. As $4 \times 3 + 4 \times 2 = 20$ and $20 \times 2 = 40$, the perimeter is 40 cm.

16 20 m ÷ 10 (the number of outer edges) = 2 m
Each small table has a perimeter of 8 m.
4 × 8 m = 32 m

17 Find one quarter first.

(24 ÷ 3) × 4 = 32 L

18 100 ÷ 7 (days in a week) = 14 r 2. Two days after Saturday is Monday.

19 There are 26 black cards in the pack. If the first card is black, there are 25 remaining black cards out of 51. The chance of a second black card is $\frac{25}{51}$.

20 As $0.75 = \frac{3}{4}$, then $5.60 \div 4 \times 3 = 4.2$. The cost is \$5.60 + \$4.20 = \$9.80.

21 The shape is a pentagonal prism. It has 15 edges, 7 faces and 10 vertices.

22 If he cycled 8 km per hour, he would take 30 minutes to cycle 4 km. He has 5 minutes to cycle the fifth kilometre, which means he must cycle at 12 km/h.

23 Take two • boxes from each side:
(2 × •) + 7 = 19, (2 × •) = 12, • = 6

24 England is behind Melbourne by 10 hours. When it is 9 pm Friday (night) in England it is 10 hours 'ahead' in Melbourne—Saturday morning, 7 am.

25 There are 12 lots of 5 minutes in an hour.

As $12 \times 4 = 48$, his speed is 48 km/h.

26 Experiment with lines to see how the shapes fit.

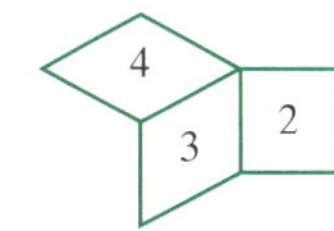

27 The shape has been rotated more than 180°. From the options it has been rotated through 225°.

28 Break the problem up into small parts.

Single angles	=	4
Double angles	=	3
Triple angles	=	2
Quadruple angles	=	1
TOTAL	=	10

29 $1200 has to be shared. The extra amount that goes to the players that the bass player doesn't share in is $600 ($100 + $200 +$300). Deduct this from $1200 which has to be shared evenly ($600 ÷ 4 = $150). You could also try each of the options.

30 An enclosed space has the same number of posts as it has spaces between them. For one paddock the farmer would need 400 ÷ 5 = 80. The second paddock has one side completed. The farmer needs 300 ÷ 5 = 60. But the farmer already has a starting post (or finishing post) so he only needs 59 for the second paddock.
Solution: 80 + 60 – 1 = 139

31 From 9:00 to 10:00 Jack travelled 60 km, which is at 60 km/h. From 10:00 to 10:30 Jack travelled 40 km, which is at 80 km/h. From 11:00 to 11:30 Jack travelled 30 km, which is at 60 km/h. Jack's fastest speed was 80 km/h.

32 You may get 2 the same after two tries but you may have four different ones after four tries. The fifth try must give a second one of one of the four colours. To be **sure** you need to take 5 marbles.

33 There are 6 faces of the prism. As $2 \times 8 \times 6 + 2 \times 6 \times 4 + 2 \times 8 \times 4 = 96 + 48 + 64 = 208$, the area would be 208 cm^2.

34 40 times a minute is every 1.5 seconds. This means a sequence of 0, 1.5, 3, 4.5, 6, 7.5, 9, 10.5, 12 … 15 times a minute is every 4 seconds. This means a sequence of 0, 4, 8, 12 … Every 12 seconds the lights flash simultaneously. As 60 ÷ 12 = 5, this means 5 times a minute. As 60 × 5 = 300, the lights flash simultaneously 300 times.

35 As 8 + 11 + 4 + 2 = 25, there were 25 students surveyed. Statement 1 is correct.
As 11 + 4 + 2 = 17, there are 17 students who are in a family of at least 2 children. Statement 2 is correct.
As 8 × 1 + 11 × 2 + 4 × 3 + 2 × 4 = 8 + 22 + 12 + 8 = 50, and 50 ÷ 25 = 2, the average number of children per family is 2. Statement 3 is correct. Statements 1, 2 and 3 are correct.

SAMPLE TEST 5

Page 22

1 B **2** A **3** B **4** C **5** C **6** C **7** B **8** B **9** C **10** A **11** E **12** E **13** C **14** D **15** A **16** B **17** D **18** A **19** B **20** A **21** C **22** D **23** B **24** A **25** D **26** B **27** B **28** D **29** C **30** E **31** E **32** B **33** E **34** C **35** B

1 The simplest way is to keep adding the next even number until you get to 90. The last number is 18.

2 As 9 × (7 + □) – 10 = 98, then 9 × (7 + □) = 108. As 108 divided by 9 is 12, then 7 + □ = 12. This means the missing number is 5.

3 Consider the sequence starting with 33 and adding 25: 33, 58, 83, 108, 133, 158, 183 … Jody is sitting in the 2nd row. Emily is sitting in the 8th row, which is 6 rows behind Jody.

4 From 23° to 0° is a drop of 23°. Another drop of 4 degrees means 23 + 4 = 27. There is a difference of 27°.

5 Find the lowest common multiple of all three numbers and add 1. You could trial each option. The number is 60 + 1 = 61.

6 Eliminate the answers that cannot be right. The motorcyclist will go a little under 100 km on 5 L. D and E are much too far. A is nowhere near far enough. B is not sensible (on about twice as much fuel he is only going a little over half as far again!). C is about right. On about twice as much fuel the motorcycle will go almost twice the distance. The answer is 182 km.

7 Add in the other diagonal. A quarter (25%) of the square is shaded.

8 You could start with each of the 5 options so that increasing by one-quarter would give 10 (A), 15 (B), 20 (C), 30 (D) and 25 (E). Decreasing these answers by two-thirds means finding one-third. Now, 15 and 30 are the multiples of 3. As 15 ÷ 3 = 5, the starting number was 12. Another method was to use algebra.

9 There are 3 lines of symmetry.

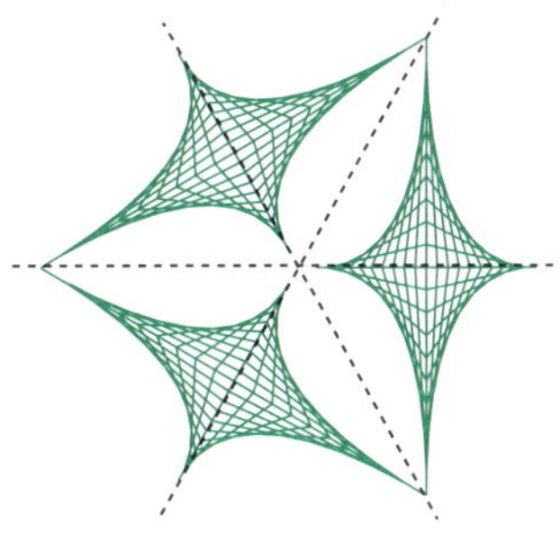

10 You need to find three-quarters of 72. As $72 \div 4 = 18$, and $18 \times 3 = 54$, the distance is 54 km.

11

	1	2	3	4	5	6	7	8	9
1	1	2	3	4	5	6	7	8	9
2	2	4	6	8	1	3	5	7	9
3	3	6	9	3					
4	4	8					**1**	5	
5	5	1							
6	6	3			**3**				
7	7								
8	8								**9**
9	9								

For X: $7 \times 4 = 28$, and $2 + 8 = 10$, which means $1 + 0 = 1$. For Y: $5 \times 6 = 30$, and $3 + 0 = 3$. For Z: $9 \times 8 = 72$, and $7 + 2 = 9$. Now, $X + Y \times Z = 1 + 3 \times 9 = 28$.

12 $2 + 1 + 2 + 1 + 1 = 7$. This means 7 balls are repeated. As $45 \div 7 = 6$ and remainder 3, the 45th ball is the same as the 3rd ball, which is green.

13 He has thirteen 5c, twice as many 10c (26), which gives a total of 39 five and ten cent coins. This is half his coins. The other half are 50c coins.

Toby has (13 × 5c) + (26 × 10c) + (39 × 50c) = 65c + \$2.60 + \$19.50 = \$22.75.

14 If 10 – (▲ – 15 ÷ 5) = 4, then 10 – (▲ – 3) = 4. This means ▲ – 3 = 6, and so ▲ = 9.

15 It helps if you can imagine the shape in your mind but you can eliminate the cubes on either end. That only leaves the middle set of 'steps' to think about. The top middle cube is exposed. Those along the underneath are exposed.

In the middle row only one cube is completely hidden from view.

16 Each side must be 300 m. The area is then 300 × 300 (90 000 m^2 or 9 ha).

17 The large, shaded triangle is half of the square because a line of symmetry cuts the square into two equal rectangles and then each rectangle can be cut into two equal triangles.

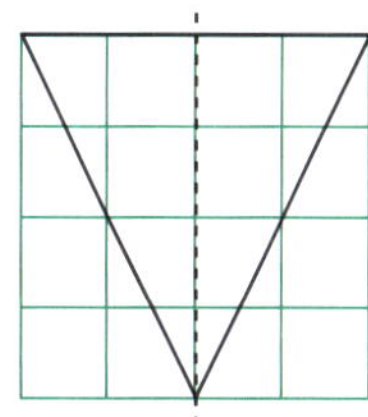

This means the area of the large triangle is half the area of the square.

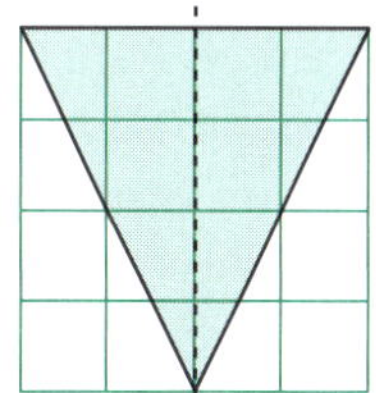

The two small triangles make up half of the remaining area. As half of a half is a quarter, the shaded area is $\frac{1}{2} + \frac{1}{4} = \frac{3}{4} = 75\%$ of the original square.

18 UP is a 2-digit number and TUB is a 3-digit number. There are no 'thousands' digits in the question so the only possible value for B in BOOT is 1. This means that T must be 9 as adding U and U would have given 10. BOOT must be 1009. Here is the sum again.

$$\begin{array}{r} 58 \\ +\ 951 \\ \hline 1009 \end{array}$$

19 As $6 \times 3 = 18$, the equilateral triangle has a perimeter of 18 cm. As $18 \times 2 = 36$, the isosceles triangle has a perimeter of 36 cm. The isosceles triangle could have dimensions 13 cm, 13 cm and 10 cm, or 14 cm, 11 cm and 11 cm.

20 Convert 750 mL to quarter litres (÷ by 3). (750 mL ÷ 3) × 5 = 1.25 L. 447 ÷ 3 × 5 = 149 × 5 = 745. The cost is \$7.45.

21 As $10 \times 10 \times 10 = 1000$, the original cube had a volume of 1000 cm^3. As $5 \times 5 \times 5 = 125$, the removed cube had a volume of 125 cm^3. As $125 \times 8 = 1000$, the removed cube was one-eighth of the original cube.

22 The Boeing flies 50 km in 5 minutes. $(250 \div 5)$. It will fly 600 km in one hour and 900 km in one and a half hours.

23 There are only 4 gaps between the chimes, each a gap of 1 second. If the clock chimed 10, there would be 9 one-second gaps.

24 As $2 \div 4 = \frac{1}{2}$, the length of each side is $\frac{1}{2}$ m.

As $\frac{1}{2} \times \frac{1}{2} = \frac{1}{4}$, the area is 0.25 m^2.

25 31 July is a Thursday. $31 \div 7 = 4$ r 3.

Three days before Thursday is Monday.

26 6 students had 2 cars at their household. Statement 1 is not correct. 4 students had 1 car and 2 students had 0 cars. As $2 \times 2 = 4$, statement 2 is correct. As $2 \times 0 + 4 \times 1 + 6 \times 2 + 3 \times 3 + 1 \times 4 = 0 + 4 + 12 + 9 + 4 = 29$, there was a total of 29 cars. Statement 3 is not correct. Statement 2 is the only correct statement.

27 If you have difficulty with this type of question, draw a quick diagram.

The directions are starting at north, then south-east, north-west, north-east then south-west.

28 20 minutes is one-third of an hour. $3 \times 7 = 21$

The speed is 21 km/h.

29 The angle between the numbers on the clock face is 30° (360° ÷ 12). At 6.30 the minute hand is at 6 and the hour hand is midway between 6 and 7. The angle is 15°.

30 As $24 + 20 + 16 = 60$, the chance of choosing a yellow ball is $\frac{16}{60}$, which is $\frac{4}{15}$.

31 There are 5 squares that make up the net. As $80 \div 5 = 16$, the area of each square is 16 cm^2. This means the side length is 4 cm. As $4 \times 4 \times 4 = 64$, the volume is 64 cm^3.

32 Look at the pattern. For $4^2 - 2^2$, the middle of 4 and 2 is 3 and then $3 \times 4 = 12$. This means for $121^2 - 119^2$, the middle of 121 and 119 is 120 and then $120 \times 4 = 480$.

33 As $5 + 7 + 9 + 6 + 1 = 28$, there were 28 students surveyed. Statement 1 is correct. As $7 + 9 = 16$, the majority of students spent between 9 and 24 hours on screen time. Statement 2 is correct. $5 + 7 = 12$, which is 3 more than 9. Statement 3 is correct. Statements 1, 2 and 3 are correct.

34 As $4 + 3 = 7$, $3 + 4 = 7$ and $4 + 4 = 8$, a score of at least 7 occurs 3 different ways. As $4 \times 4 = 16$, there are 16 possible scores. The probability is $\frac{3}{16}$.

35 The sequence is $1^2 = 1$, $2^2 = 4$, $3^2 = 9$, $4^2 = 16$, and so on. A feature of the list of square numbers is the difference that can be calculated using the sum of consecutive terms. The difference between the sixth and seventh terms is 13 and $6 + 7 = 13$. As $20 + 21 = 41$, you need to find $20^2 + 21^2$. As $20^2 = 400$ and $21^2 = 441$, then $400 + 441 = 841$.

SAMPLE TEST 6

Page 27

1 C **2** D **3** D **4** D **5** E **6** C **7** D **8** C **9** B
10 D **11** B **12** B **13** C **14** A **15** C **16** D
17 B **18** D **19** B **20** C **21** B **22** E **23** B
24 C **25** C **26** E **27** E **28** D **29** A **30** D
31 A **32** E **33** C **34** C **35** D

1 As $78 \div 3 = 26$, the middle number will be 26. This means the numbers are 24, 26 and 28. The next three consecutive even numbers are 30, 32 and 34. The sum is 96.

2 As $3^3 = 3 \times 3 \times 3 = 27$, $2^3 = 2 \times 2 \times 2 = 8$, then $(3^3 + 2^3) = 27 + 8 = 35$. As $5^3 = 5 \times 5 \times 5 = 125$, and $125 - 35 = 90$, the difference is 90.

3 Try each of the options. If $\square = 0$, then $4 \times (0 + 9) = 36$, which is equal to $3 \times (0 + 11) + 3 = 36$.

4 The numbers are 543 and 345.

$$\begin{array}{r} 543 \\ -\ 345 \\ \hline 198 \end{array}$$

The difference is 198.

5 As $20 + 10 - 8 = 22$, Layla has \$22, and so each girl has \$22. As $22 + 10 = 32$, Elena started with \$32. As $22 - 8 = 14$, Avery started with \$14. As $32 - 14 = 18$, Elena had \$18 more than Avery.

6 There are 12 edges to a rectangular prism. $(4 \times 5 \text{ cm}) + (4 \times 4 \text{ cm}) + (4 \times 3 \text{ cm}) = 48$ cm It may help to draw a quick diagram.

7 As $28 - 20 = 8$, and $8 \div 2 = 4$, the width of each rectangle is 4 cm. 3 lengths + 1 width = 28, means 3 lengths = 24, and so the length of each rectangle is 8 cm. As $8 \times 4 = 32$, the area of each rectangle is 32 cm^2.

8 The lowest common multiple (LCM) of 2, 3, 4, 5, and 6 is 60.

9 If 30% = 12 then 10% = 4. There are ten lots of 10% in 100%. 10 × 4 = 40

10 To find $\frac{2}{3}$ of 12, use 12 ÷ 3 × 2. As the perimeter is twice the sum of the length and width, the number sentence is 2 × (12 + 12 ÷ 3 × 2).

11 Simplify the amount read:

$\frac{1}{4} + \frac{1}{3} = \frac{3}{12} + \frac{4}{12} = \frac{7}{12}$

There is $\frac{5}{12}$ (or 50 pages) to be read.

$\frac{1}{12}$ = 10 pages. Total pages = 120.

12 Split the first square into quarters.

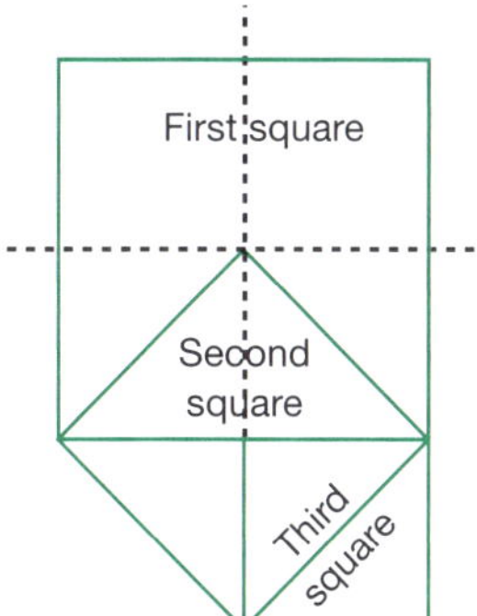

The area of the third square is one-quarter the area of the first square.

13 There are 7 lines of symmetry.

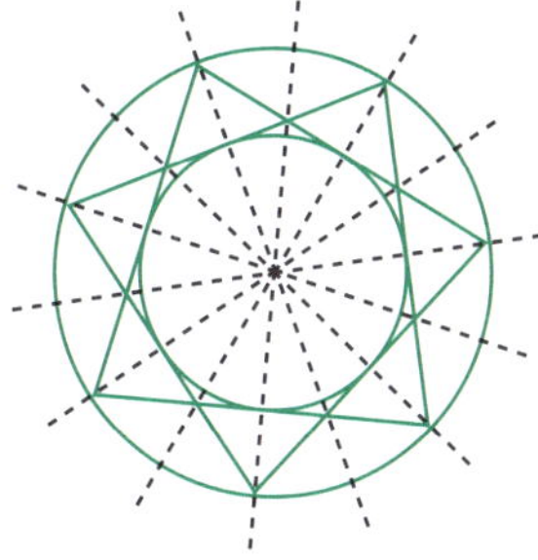

14 The magic number is 3 + 10 + 8 + 13 = 34. The number replacing the * is 1.

9	6	3	16
4	15	10	5
14	1	8	11
7	12	13	2

15 The six digits 7, 1, 4, 2, 8 and 5 repeat. 101 ÷ 6 = 16 with a remainder of 5. As 8 is the 5th digit it must also be the 101st digit.

16 18 × 2 gives the cost of the adult tickets. (18 × 3) ÷ 2 gives the cost of the children's tickets. 5 × 4 gives the cost of the ice creams. The number sentence is
18 × 2 + (18 × 3) ÷ 2 + 5 × 4.

17 As 10 × 10 = 100, the area of the large square is 100 cm². As 4 × 4 = 16, the area of each small square is 16 cm².
As 100 – 4 × 16 = 100 – 64 = 36, the remaining area is 36 cm². This means 36% of the original square remains.

18 As 250 ÷ 2 = 125, the volume of a cube is 125 cm³. As 5 × 5 × 5 = 125, the cube has a side length of 5 cm. Each square face has an area of 5 × 5 = 25, and there are 6 faces.
As 25 × 6 = 150, the total area on each cube is 150cm². As there are 2 cubes, the total area is 300 cm².

19 In your mind, slide one cardboard shape across the other. The only part common to both squares is the small square in the middle.

20 As $1 - \frac{1}{4} = \frac{3}{4}$, 180 pages is $\frac{3}{4}$ of the book. As 180 ÷ 3 × 4 = 240, there are 240 pages in the book. As Lincoln has $\frac{1}{3}$ of the book remaining, and 240 ÷ 3 = 80, Lincoln has 80 pages to read.

21 As 63 – 49 = 14, the mass of 10 L of olive oil is 14 kg. As 14 × 4 = 56 and 63 – 56 = 7, the empty container has a mass of 7 kg.

22 3 hours 30 minutes is $3\frac{1}{2}$. As 90 × 3 = 270 and $\frac{1}{2}$ of 90 is 45, 270 + 45 = 315. Marin has driven 315 km.

$$\begin{array}{r} 198\,761 \\ +\quad 315 \\ \hline 199\,076 \end{array}$$

The odometer shows 199076.

23 It may be best to list the multiples of 2 and 2.5. You will find they beep together every ten minutes (2, 4, 6, 8, 10/ 2.5, 5, 7.5, 10). This means they will beep together 6 times every hour and on the hour. The first time after 12 noon will be 12.10.

24 2 and 3 are factors of 6. The hot tap can fill 2 containers in 6 minutes. The cold tap can fill

3 containers in 6 minutes. This means 5 containers are filled in 6 minutes, or 360 seconds. As $360 \div 5 = 72$, it will take 1 minute 12 seconds.

25 As $3 \times 4 = 12$ there are 12 possible products. An odd multiplied by an odd gives an odd number. This means 5 & 3, 5 & 5 and 5 & 7 will give odd answers. The probability is $\frac{3}{12}$, which is $\frac{1}{4}$.

26 As $145 + x = 180$, then $x = 35$. Also, $y = 90$. As $90 + 35 = 125$, the sum is 125.

27 Distance is Speed × Time. As $80 \times 3 = 240$, the distance is 240 km. As $80 - 20 = 60$, her new average speed would be 60 km/h. As Time = Distance ÷ Speed, and $240 \div 60 = 4$, it would then take 4 hours. This means the trip would be longer by 1 hour, or 60 minutes.

28 As $\frac{1}{5}$ of 20 is $20 \div 5 = 4$, the width is 4 cm. As the perimeter is 20 cm, the sum of the length and width is 10 cm. As $10 - 4 = 6$, the length is 6 cm. As $6 \times 4 = 24$, the area is 24 cm^2.

29 Here is the net of the cube. W is opposite Y.

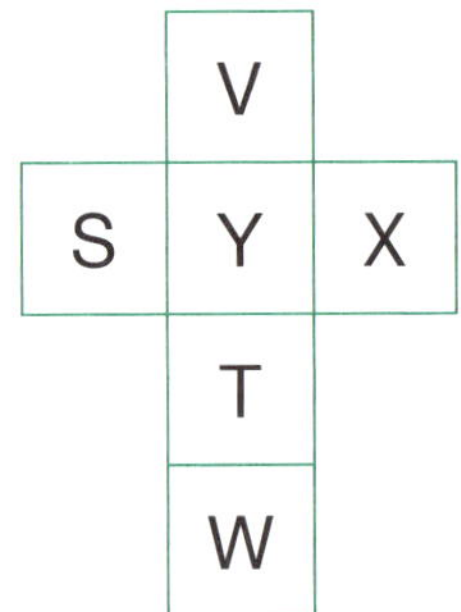

30 As $25 \times 3 = 75$ and $75 \times 2 = 150$, Theo needs to paint an area of 150 m^2. Also 6 m^2 per 500 mL is a coverage of 12 m^2 per L. As $150 \div 12 = 12\frac{1}{2}$, Theo will use $12\frac{1}{2}$ L of paint. He needs to buy 4 cans of paint.

31 As $18 + 32 + 28 + 22 = 100$, then 28 out of the 100 students (28%) live outside Sydney and have a driver's licence. Statement 1 is correct. As $32 + 22 = 54$ and 54 out of 100 is 54%, then 54% of the students surveyed do not have a driver's licence. Statement 2 is correct. As $18 + 32 = 50$, and $\frac{18}{50} = 36\%$, then 36% of the students surveyed who live in Sydney have a driver's licence. Statements 1, 2 and 3 are correct.

32 As square P has an area of 16 cm^2, each side is 4 cm. Square Q has side length 5 cm. As $4 + 5 = 9$, square R has side length 9 cm. As $4^2 + 5^2 + 9^2 = 16 + 25 + 81 = 122$, the combined area is 122 cm^2.

33 As $36 \div 2 = 18$, the first half of the competition had 18 games. Tigers had won 7 games and Kangaroos 14 games. As one-third of 18 is 6, and $14 + 6 = 20$, the Kangaroos win a total of 20 games. As $20 - 7 = 13$, the Tigers need to win 13 more games.

34 As $\frac{3}{4}$ of 8 is $8 \div 4 \times 3 = 6$, there are originally 6 red balls in the bag. After the 2 red balls are removed, there are 4 red balls in the bag of 6 balls. This is a probability of $\frac{4}{6}$, which is $\frac{2}{3}$.

35 As the entire graph (360°) represents 36 students, then 120° represents 12 students. Statement 1 is correct. As $360 - (150 + 120) = 360 - 270 = 90$, and $\frac{90}{360} = \frac{1}{4} = 25\%$, then 25% of the students had either red or black hair. Statement 2 is correct. Blonde + Black > Brown as $120 + 70 > 150$. Statement 3 is not correct. Statements 1 and 2 are correct.

SAMPLE TEST 7

Page 32

1 E **2** A **3** B **4** B **5** D **6** C **7** A **8** A **9** A
10 B **11** E **12** D **13** A **14** C **15** A **16** C
17 A **18** A **19** C **20** A **21** C **22** A **23** A
24 E **25** C **26** E **27** A **28** D **29** D **30** E
31 B **32** C **33** E **34** B **35** E

1 As $84 \times 3 = 252$, his total after 3 tests was 252. As $(84 + 3) \times 5 = 87 \times 5 = 435$, his total after 5 tests was 435. As $435 - 252 - 88 = 95$, Marco scored 95 in his fifth test.

2 The number sentence is $75 + 25 \times 5 - 80$ which is $75 + 125 - 80 = 200 - 80 = 120$.

3 There are 31 days in May, 30 in June and 31 in July. Tuesdays are 18 and 25 May, also, 1, 8, 15, 22 and 29 June and finally 6, 13, 20 and 27 July. If 27 July is a Tuesday, then 1 August is a Sunday.

4 As $8 \times 4 = 32$, the sum of the original numbers is 32. As $32 - 4 - 4 = 24$, the new sum is 24. As $24 \div 4 = 6$, the new average is 6. The average has decreased by 2.

5 Total possible number of points is 50 (5×10). Incorrect answers mean a loss of 7 points.

(5 for not getting it right and 2 for the incorrect answer).

9 right would give $9 \times 5 - 1 \times 2 = 43$
8 right would give $8 \times 5 - 2 \times 2 = 36$
7 right would give $7 \times 5 - 3 \times 2 = 29$
7 right means 3 wrong.

6 Consider each of the options. 50% is half so $6.50 ÷ 2 = $3.25. As 10% of $8.40 is 84 cents, and $84 \times 4 = 336$, then 40% is $3.36.
As $14 \div 4 = 7 \div 2 = 3.5$, then 25% is $3.50.
100% is the whole amount of $3.10. 200% of $1.70 is 2 × $1.70 = $3.40. The greatest amount is $3.50, which is 25% of $14.00.

7 If you look at all the small squares you will discover that half of each one is shaded. Half of the whole square is shaded.

8 As $1 + \frac{2}{3} = \frac{5}{3}$ then $\frac{5}{3}$ of the number of days to read the first half equals 30 days. You need to find $\frac{2}{3}$ which is $30 \div 5 \times 2 = 12$. It took 12 days to read the second half of the book.

9 $13 = 2^2 + 3^2$, $25 = 3^2 + 4^2$, and so on.
As $5^2 + 6^2 = 25 + 36 = 61$, the missing number is 61.

10 As $8 + 2 \times 2 = 8 + 4 = 12$, then
[?] – 12 = [?] ÷ 4. This means [?] = 16.

11 Two more squares need to be shaded.

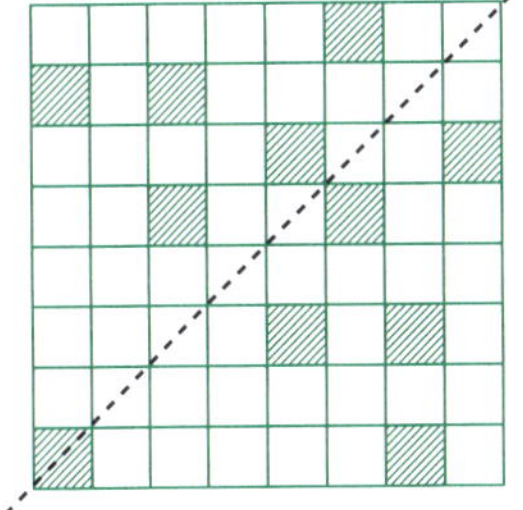

12 Consider each of the options.
As $17 \times 3 - 3 \times 2 = 51 - 6 = 45$, Ashleigh answered 17 questions correctly.

13 The sequence of temperatures, in Celsius, is 4, 2, 0, –2 … At 6 am the temperature was –2 °C.

14 Representing a post as X, the fence is
X 4 m X 4 m X 4 m X 4 m X 4 m X.
This means there must be 4 m between posts. As there are 39 spaces between the 40 posts, and $39 \times 4 = 156$, the length of the fence is 156 m.

15 As $12 \times 12 \div 3$ is $144 \div 3 = 48$, the area of the rectangle at the top of the square is 48 cm². The trapezium is the rectangle minus 2 triangles. As $48 - 2 \times \frac{1}{2} \times 4 \times 4 = 48 - 16 = 32$, the area is 32 cm².

16 As $Y = 24 \div 3 = 8$, and $Z = 8 \div 2 = 4$, then
$\frac{24}{8 + 4} = 24 \div (8 + 4) = 24 \div 12 = 2$.

17 Year 1 $600 + ($600 × 0.05) = $630.
Year 2 $630 + ($630 × 0.05) = $661.50.

18 As $1500 \times 4 = 6000$, the tank holds 6000 L when full. As $6000 \div 3 \times 2 = 4000$, there is now 4000 L of water in the tank.
As $4000 - 1500 = 2500$, another 2500 L of water has been added to the tank.

19 As $64 \div 8 = 8$, each of the small cubes has a volume of 8 m³. As $2 \times 2 \times 2 = 8$, each side of the small cubes is 2 m. As $8 \times 2 = 16$, these small cubes will make a stack 16 m high.

20 As $18 \div 3 \times 2 = 12$, Jonah has cycled 12 km. As $18 - 12 = 6$, Jonah has 6 km to cycle in 40 minutes. This is 3 km in 20 minutes, or 9 km in an hour, which is written as 9 km/h.

21 As $30 - 24 = 6$ and $30 - 12 = 18$, the shaded rectangle has side lengths 18 cm and 6 cm. As $18 \times 6 = 108$, the area is 108 cm².

22 From the graph the mass is 150 g when there is no water in the container. Statement 1 is correct. Half of 800 mL is 400 mL and the mass is 550 g. Statement 2 is not correct. The mass of the container with 600 mL is 750 g.
As $1 - \frac{2}{3} = \frac{1}{3}$, and $600 \div 3 = 200$, the container now holds 200 mL and has a mass of 350 g.
From $750 - 350 = 400$, so the mass has decreased by more than 50%. Statement 3 is not correct. Statement 1 is the only correct statement.

23 As $8 \times 5 = 40$, the fractions could be rewritten as $\frac{3}{8} = \frac{15}{40}$ and $\frac{3}{5} = \frac{24}{40}$. This means there could be 15 red balls and 24 blue balls.
As $40 - (15 + 24) = 1$, there could be 1 green ball.

24 The third bus leaves Luskintyre at 10:55 and arrives in Dalwood at 12:20. After this time the next bus leaves Dalwood at 14:45 and arrives in Luskintyre at 16:10. The time difference between 10:55 and 16:10 is 5 hours 15 minutes.

25 As $1 - (0.3 + 0.2 + 0.3) = 1 - 0.8 = 0.2$, the probability of choosing a blue box is 0.2. As there are 40 boxes, and $0.2 \times 40 = 8$, there are 8 blue boxes in the crate.

26 As $6 + 3 = 9$, the height of the large triangle is 9 cm.

As $\frac{1}{2} \times 6 \times 9 - \frac{1}{2} \times 4 \times 6 = 27 - 12 = 15$, the area is 15 cm^2.

27 As $4 \times 4 \times 4 = 64$, and $128 \div 64 = 2$, the metal has a mass of 2 kg per cm^3. As $1200 \div 2 = 600$, the square prism has a volume of 600 cm^3. As $10 \times 10 \times \text{edge} = 600$, then the length of the edge is 6 cm.

28 From 9 am to 3 pm is 6 hours.

As $24 + 9 \times 4 = 24 + 36 = 60$, the cost of Friday's parking is \$60. As $18 + 7 \times 2 = 18 + 14 = 32$, the cost for each weekend day is \$32. As $60 + 32 + 32 = 124$, the total cost is \$124.

29 Mark each one you can see on the front (2). It will be the same number for the back. The middle section is the hardest: 1 on the side, 1 on the top, 2 on the second level and 4 underneath.

There are 12 cubes with only one face painted.

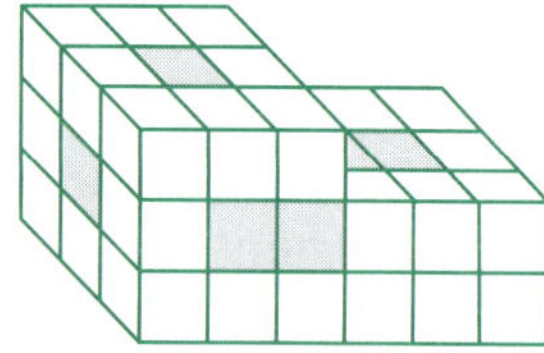

30 There are 4 lines of symmetry.

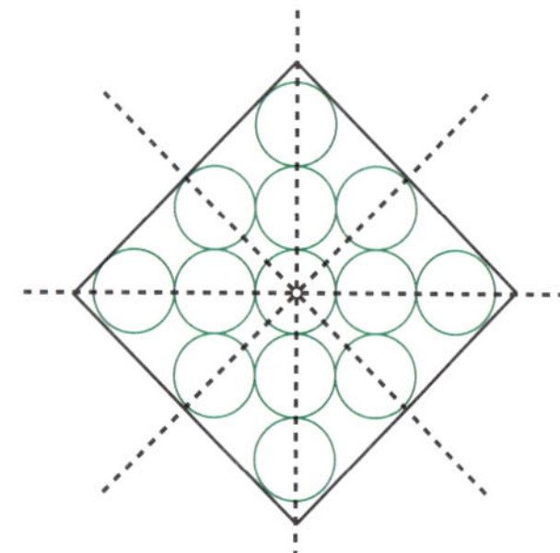

31 Each of the four angles in a square measures 90°. Each of the three angles in an equilateral triangle measures 60°. As $(90 - 60) \div 2 = 15$, the angles measure 15° each.

32 There are 360° in a revolution so 120° is one-third of a revolution. As $12 \div 3 = 4$, Karen was in the city for 4 hours. This means she left at 3 o'clock.

33 As $3 + 4 + 8 + 7 + 2 = 24$, there were 24 students who took the quiz. Statement 1 is correct. As $4 + 8 = 12$, and 12 out of 24 is 50%, then 50% of the students scored 6 or 7. Statement 2 is correct. As $7 + 2 = 9$ and 8 out of 10 is 80%, then 9 students scored at least 80% on the quiz. Statement 3 is correct. Statements 1, 2 and 3 are correct.

34 Suppose the dimensions of rectangle P are 2 cm by 1 cm. The area of rectangle P is 2 cm^2. As $2 \times 2 \times 2 = 8$, the dimensions of rectangle R are 8 cm by 1 cm. The area of rectangle R is 8 cm^2. As $8 \div 2 = 4$, there are 4 rectangle Ps that will cover rectangle R.

35 Use letters to represent the boys' mass: $B + E = 100$, $E + N = 125$ and $B + N = 141$. Adding the first two pairs gives $B + E + E + N = 100 + 125 = 225$. But as $B + N = 141$, then $141 + E + E = 225$. This means $E + E = 84$, and so $E = 42$. Eli has a mass of 42 kg.

SAMPLE TEST 8

Page 38

1 C **2** A **3** D **4** C **5** A **6** D **7** C **8** E **9** C
10 C **11** B **12** D **13** C **14** E **15** A **16** D
17 B **18** A **19** E **20** C **21** C **22** B **23** A
24 C **25** D **26** E **27** E **28** D **29** C **30** D
31 E **32** E **33** B **34** D **35** B

1 As $51 \times 3 = 153$ and $153 - 110 = 43$, the third boy has a mass of 43 kg.

2 Start by choosing squares that are close to 15 and 150.

$\sqrt{16} = 4$ and $\sqrt{144} = 12$. Listing 4, 5, 6 … 12 is 9 numbers.

3

4 Count backwards by 5s from 71 until you find a multiple of 4. The sequence is 66, 61, 56, … As 56 is a multiple of 4, Halle will have 3 groups of 5 and the rest are groups of 4.

5 As $168 \div 4 - 168 \div 6 = 42 - 28 = 14$, there will be 14 more teams.

6

7 I have $2 \times \$4.80 = \$9.60$.
Kevin has $\$4.80 \div 2 \times 5 = \$12$ (40% is two-fifths). $\$9.60 + \$12.00 = \$21.60$

8 As $1280 \div 2 = 640$, then one-third of the amount is \$640. As $640 \times 3 = 1920$, the whole amount is \$1920. Now, $1920 \div 4 \times 3 = 480 \times 3 = 1440$, so three-quarters of the amount is \$1440.

9 The shape has a top section and bottom section. None of the cubes in the top section are hidden. The 4 cubes under the top section are hidden from view.

10 As $6000 - 2000 = 4000$, the price increased by 4000. Increasing by \$2000 would be increasing by 100%. But the price increased by twice this amount, so the price increased by 200%.

11 Theo: As 4 wins + 1 draw = 22, then 8 wins + 2 draws = 44. Cleo: 3 wins + 2 draws = 19. As $44 - 19 = 25$, then 5 wins = 25 points. This means 1 win = 5 points. Also, 4×5 + 1 draw = 22 means 1 draw is 2 points.
For Leo, as $2 \times 5 + 3 \times 2 = 16$, he has 16 points.

12 The factors of 12 are 1, 2, 3, 4, 6 and 12. The factors of 18 are 1, 2, 3, 6, 9 and 18. This means the highest common factor is 6. The multiples of 12 are 12, 24, 36 … and the multiples of 18 are 18, 36 … This means the lowest common multiple is 36. As $36 + 6 = 42$, Lucinda's answer is 42.

13 $\frac{2}{5}$ of 40 is $40 \div 5 \times 2 = 16$. Originally there were 16 dark and 24 milk chocolates. Subtracting the eaten chocolates, 15 dark and 20 milk chocolates remain. This means $\frac{20}{35}$, or $\frac{4}{7}$, are milk chocolates.

14 Double \$12.50 is \$25 and $4 \times 25 = 100$. This means $\$12.50 \times 8 = \$100$. As $22 + 8 = 30$, Sarah's baggage had a weight of 30 kg.

15 $32 = 8 \times (5 - 1)$, $60 = 10 \times (7 - 1)$, and so on. As $14 \times (11 - 1) = 14 \times 10 = 140$, the missing number is 140.

16 The sequence is 6, 8, 10, 12 … As $8 - 6 = 2$, the rule is 'start with 6 and add 2'. The 25th term in the sequence would be $6 + 24 \times 2 = 6 + 48 = 54$. Adrian would need 54 grey squares.

17 Ella charges \$20 for the first hour and \$12 for each of 3 more hours. The number sentence is $20 + 12 \times (4 - 1)$.

18 The sum of the length and width is 50 cm. The two numbers that add to 50 where the larger is $1\frac{1}{2}$ times the smaller are 30 and 20. As $30 \times 20 = 600$, the area is 600 cm^2.

19 The numbers are increasing by 8.
As $13 + 20 \times 8 = 173$, the 21st number is 173.

20 As $8 + 2 + 2 = 12$ and $4 + 2 + 2 = 8$, the dimensions of the fence are 12 m by 8 m. As $2 \times (12 + 8) = 40$, the length of the fence is 40 m. As $300 \times 40 = 12000$, the cost is \$12000.

21 6 + 6 + 6 + 6 + ■ + ■ = 40 means
■ + ■ = 40 − 24 = 16. This means ■ = 8.
● + ■ × ● = 6 + 8 × 6 = 6 + 48 = 54.

22 As $13 - 9 = 4$, $9 + 15 = 24$, $13 + 15 = 28$ and $9 + 13 + 15 = 37$, the only impossible measurement is 23 cm.

23 If the average of 3 numbers is 10, the sum is 30. This means the perimeter is 30 cm.
As $13 - 8 = 5$, the shortest side is 5 cm.
As $30 - 13 - 5 = 12$, the other side is 12 cm.
The longest side is opposite the right angle and is not used to find the area. As $\frac{1}{2} \times 5 \times 12 = 30$, the area is 30 cm^2.

24 As $\frac{4}{5}$ of $250 = 250 \div 5 \times 4 = 200$, each glass will have 200 mL of juice. As 2 L = 2000 mL, and $2000 \div 200 = 10$, Morgan will use 10 glasses. As $12 - 10 = 2$, he will have 2 glasses empty.

25 A rotation of 180° around O:

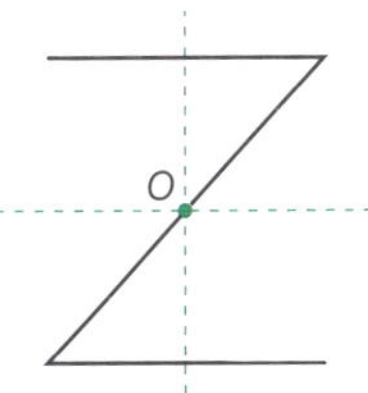

26 From the graph 60 km is covered in a time of 45 minutes. Statement 1 is correct. The motorist travels 80 km in 1 hour and so the speed is 80 km/h. Statement 2 is correct. From the graph the motorist travels 200 km in 150 minutes, and so 50 km in 37.5 minutes. This is 250 km in 187.5 minutes, which is 3 hours 7.5 minutes. Statement 3 is not correct.

Statements 1 and 2 are the only correct statements.

27 As $50 \times 30 \times 40 = 60000$, the volume is 60000 cm^3, which is 60 L. As 15 L is poured into the tank, and $\frac{15}{60} = \frac{1}{4}$, the tank is one-quarter full. As $40 \div 4 = 10$, the depth of the water is 10 cm.

28 From 9:20 pm 3 hours is 12:20 am Thursday, plus 5 hours is 5:20 am Thursday and then add 15 minutes gives 5:35 am Thursday. Now, adding the time difference gives 9:35 am Thursday.

29 As $5 + 4 + 7 + 4 = 20$, and 4 out of 20 like purple, the probability is $\frac{4}{20} = \frac{2}{10} = 0.2$.

30 As $480 \div 4 = 120$, and $120 \div 60 = 2$, the first quarter of the trip took 2 hours. As $60 + 20 = 80$ and $120 \div 80 = 1.5$, the second quarter took 1.5 hours. As $2 + 1.5 + 2.5 = 6$, the journey took 6 hours.

31 Change each to m/min. 0.3 km/h = 300 m/h = **5 m/min**. **6 m /min**. 160 cm/min = **1.6 m/min**. 12 mm/sec = 720 mm/min = **0.72 m/min.** 480 m/h = **8 m/min**. The fastest speed is 480 m/h.

32 The small hand is halfway between 12 and 1. As there are 60 minutes on the clock and 360° in a revolution, every 1 minute = 6°. As $180 - 2.5 \times 6 = 180 - 15 = 165$, the angle is 165°.

33 As $60 \div 20 = 3$, Michael can dig 3 trenches in an hour. Together they can dig 4 trenches in an hour. As $60 \div 4 = 15$, it will take 15 minutes to dig the trench.

34 As $5 \times 4 = 20$, there are 20 different pairs of cards that can be chosen. Odd scores occur when 2 odd numbers are chosen: (1, 3), (1, 5), (3, 1), (3, 5), (5, 1) and (5, 3). This is 6 times out of 20 which is $\frac{6}{20}$ or $\frac{3}{10}$.

35 29 out of 42 students scored at least 7 out of 10. This is $\frac{29}{42}$. If 8 students scored 9, this fraction would change to $\frac{37}{50}$, which is $\frac{74}{100} = 74\%$.

SAMPLE TEST 9

Page 43

1 D **2** B **3** C **4** E **5** C **6** D **7** A **8** A **9** C **10** B **11** C **12** A **13** C **14** A **15** E **16** D **17** B **18** C **19** C **20** A **21** D **22** C **23** E **24** A **25** C **26** D **27** B **28** B **29** E **30** C **31** D **32** A **33** C **34** D **35** E

1 There are 6 lines of symmetry.

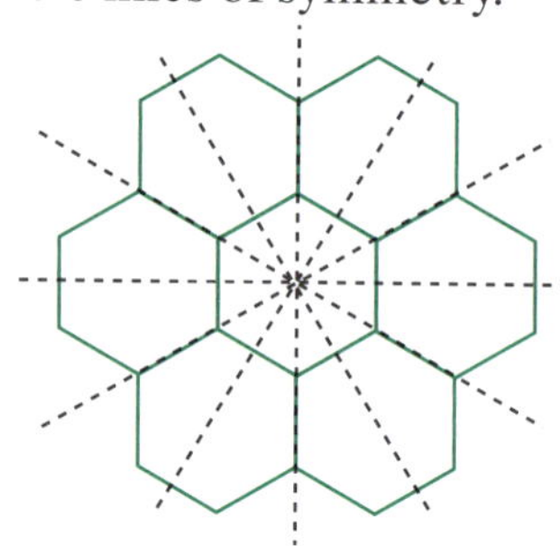

2 Try some numbers. Two years ago: Jesse was 30 and Freya 6. Now, Jesse would be 32 and Freya 8. In 4 years Jesse would be 36 and Freya 12.

3 Lauren's list should contain the numbers 1 to 7 and a large number. As $10 \times 8 = 80$, the sum of the 8 numbers will be 80. As $1 + 2 + 3 + 4 + 5 + 6 + 7 = 28$ and $80 - 28 = 52$, the largest number is 52.

4 16: 1, 2, 4, 8, 16 (5 factors).
24: 1, 2, 3, 4, 6, 8, 12, 24 (8 factors).
36: 1, 2, 3, 4, 6, 9, 12, 18, 36 (9 factors).
50: 1, 2, 5, 10, 25, 50 (6 factors).
64: 1, 2, 4, 8, 16, 32, 64 (7 factors).
In order, the numbers are 16, 50, 64, 24, 36.
The middle number is 64.

5 Using the rules for order of operations, $36 - 12 \div 3 \times 2 + 1$ is $36 - 8 + 1 = 29$.

6

7 Kate needs to add five more tiles.

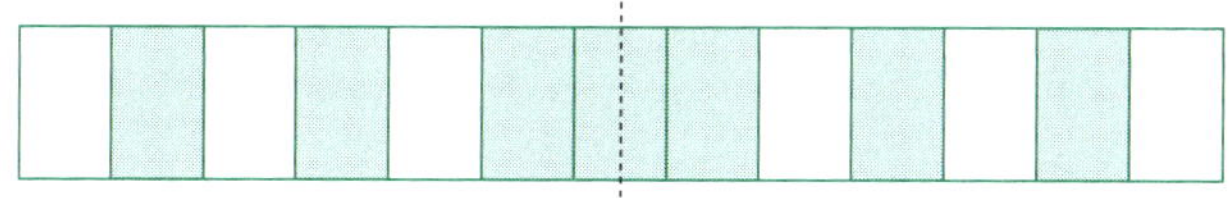

8 As $3 + 5 + 8 + 24 + 10 = 50$, and 24 out of 50 were born in Asia, the probability is $\frac{24}{50} = \frac{48}{100} = 0.48$.

9 Suppose Kate has X dollars. This means Lara has $X + 50$ and Jannah has $X + X$. Now $X + X + 50 + X + X = 290$, then $4 \times X + 50 = 290$. This means $4 \times X = 240$ and $X = 60$. If Kate has \$60, then Lara has \$110.

10 $4\#8 = 8 + 4 \times 8 \div (8 - 4) = 8 + 32 \div 4 = 8 + 8 = 16$ This means $4\#8 = 16$.

11 One and a half minutes is 90 seconds. As $90 \div 2 = 45$ and $45 \times 5 = 225$, the balloon has travelled 225 m in height. As $225 + 2 = 227$, the balloon is 227 m high.

12 If there are 5 people (A, B, C, D, E) the handshakes are $AB, AC, AD, AE, BC, BD, BE, CD, CE, DE$. This means there are 10 handshakes. The number of handshakes is the sequence of the triangular numbers: 1, 3, 6, 10, 15, 21, 28, 36, 45. There will be 45 handshakes.

13 Try each of the options. As $\frac{1}{2}$ of $8 = 4$ and $\frac{1}{3}$ of $(8 + 4) = 4$, then ▲ $= 4$.

14 As $72 \div 12 = 6$, the width of the rectangle (and the height of the triangle) is 6 cm. As $72 \div 3 = 24$, the area of the triangle is 24 cm^2. As $\frac{1}{2} \times \text{base} \times 6 = 24$, then $3 \times \text{base} = 24$, and so the base is 8. The missing length is 8 cm.

15 As $8\overline{)54.00}$ = 6.75, Emily will travel 6.75 lots of 100 km. As $6.75 \times 100 = 675$, Emily will travel 675 km.

16 As $\frac{1}{2}$ of $\frac{1}{2}$ is $\frac{1}{4}$, you need to halve two of Jenna's dimensions (or $\frac{1}{4}$ of one of the dimensions). Leilani's dimensions could be 40 cm by 40 cm by 10 cm.

17 As $30 \times 1\frac{1}{2} = 45$, Symon visits the petrol station $1\frac{1}{2}$ times every week, which is 3 times every 2 weeks. As $26 \times 3 = 78$, Symon bought petrol about 78 times last year.

18 As $4.9 \times 2 = 9.8$ and $9.8 - 8.2 = 1.6$, the empty container has a mass of 1.6 kg. As $4.9 - 1.6 = 3.3$, and $3.3 \times 4 = 13.2$, the mass of liquid in a full container is 13.2 kg. As $13.2 + 1.6 = 14.8$, the mass is 14.8 kg.

19 As 11:00 to 11:15 is 15 minutes, or quarter of an hour, the distance is a quarter of 80 km, which is 20 km. As $80 + 10 = 90$, Charlie drives at 90 km/h for 20 minutes. As 20 minutes is a third of an hour, and $90 \div 3 = 30$, Charlie drives for another 30 km. As $20 + 30 = 50$, Charlie drives a total of 50 km.

20 As $A + C + C = 24$ and $B + C + C = 17$, then A is 7 kg heavier than B. As $A + B = 25$, then $A = 16$ and $B = 9$. This also means that $C = 4$. As $A + B + C = 16 + 9 + 4 = 29$, the unknown mass is 29 kg.

21 As $23 + R = 50$, then $R = 27$. Also, as $27 - P = 11$, then $P = 16$. Finally, $16 + Q + 27 = 50$ means $Q = 7$. Now, $Q + (R - P) = 7 + (27 - 16) = 7 + 11 = 18$.

22 As $12 \times 10 = 120$, the area of the rectangle was 120 cm^2. As $120 - 56 = 64$, the area of the square is 64 cm^2. This means the side length of the square is 8 cm. As $8 \times 4 = 32$, the perimeter is 32 cm.

23 P is north-east of T.

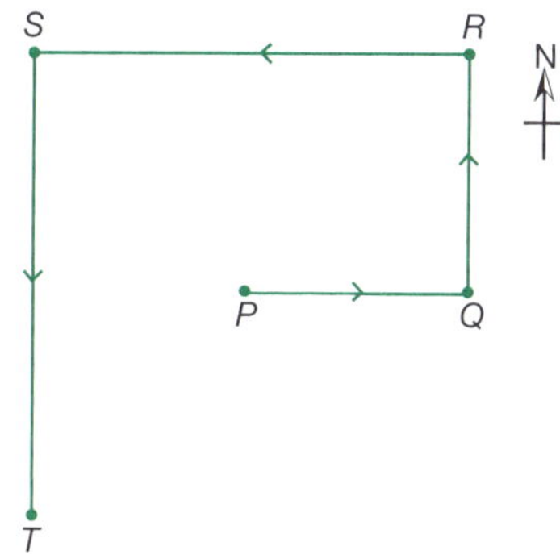

24 As $14 - 6 = 8$, Melbourne is 8 hours ahead of Paris. As 11:30 pm plus 8 hours = 7:30 am, it is 7:30 am Thursday in Melbourne.

25 As 16 hours before midday is 8 pm, then 16 hours before 12:16 pm is 8:16 pm. This is rewritten as 2016.

26 Suppose 52% means a result of 52. As $52 \times 4 = 208$, Elle's total mark is 208. As $60 \times 5 = 300$, and $300 - 208 = 92$, Elle needs a result of 92%. As $92\% = \frac{92}{100} = \frac{23}{25}$, Elle needs to get 23 questions correct.

Here is another solution: As $4 \times 25 = 100$, Elle has answered 52 questions correctly out of 100. As $0.6 \times 125 = 75$, after the fifth test Elle will have answered 75 questions correctly. As $75 - 52 = 23$, she has to answer 23 questions correctly in the fifth test.

27 Third place receives \$2000. As $2000 \times 3 = 6000$, second place receives \$6000. As $6000 + 2000 = 8000$, then one-third of the prizemoney is \$8000. As $8000 \times 3 = 24000$, three-thirds of the total prizemoney was \$24000.

28 The shaded section has numbers that are between 1 and 60, are multiples of both 3 and 4, but not multiples of 5. Numbers that are multiples of both 3 and 4 are 12, 24, 36, 48 and 60. But 60 is a multiple of 5, so the only numbers in the shaded section are 12, 24, 36 and 48. There are 4 numbers.

29 Double the tickets bought by the Harvey family: 2 adults + 4 children = \$136. Now, compare this to the Henderson family: 2 adults + 3 children = \$118. As $136 - 118 = 18$, the cost of a child ticket is \$18.
As adult + \$36 = \$68, then an adult ticket is \$32. As $2 \times 32 + 18 = 64 + 18 = 82$, the Dann family pay \$82.

30 There are 12 letters around the spinner. From *T* to *V* is 4 letters. This is one-third of a revolution. As $360 \div 3 = 120$, the angle is 120°.

31 The octahedron has 12 edges, 6 vertices and 8 faces.

32 There are 360° in a revolution. As $\frac{120}{360} = \frac{1}{3}$, one-third of the cars were white. As $48 \div 3 = 16$, there were 16 white cars in the car park. Statement 1 is not correct. As $\frac{90}{360} = \frac{1}{4} = 25\%$, then 25% of the cars were grey. Statement 2 is correct. As $\frac{60}{360} = \frac{1}{6}$ and $48 \div 6 = 8$, there were 8 red cars. As $48 - 8 = 40$, there were 40 cars that were not red. Statement 3 is correct. Statements 2 and 3 are correct.

33 Olivia's temperature was at least 39.6 °C from 5 pm to 8 pm which is 3 hours. Statement 1 is correct. Olivia's temperature was taken 11 times. Statement 2 is not correct. Olivia's temperature was recorded from 4:30 pm to 2 am which is 9 hours 30 minutes. Statement 3 is not correct. Statement 1 is the only correct statement.

34 Rolling a 3 is $\frac{1}{6}$. Rolling a 6 is $\frac{1}{6}$. Rolling a prime number (2, 3, 5) is $\frac{3}{6} = \frac{1}{2}$. Rolling a factor of 18 (1, 2, 3, 6) is $\frac{4}{6} = \frac{2}{3}$. Rolling at least a 5 (5, 6) is $\frac{2}{6} = \frac{1}{3}$. The most likely is rolling a factor of 18.

35 Look for pairs of factors. As $20 = 5 \times 4$, $10 = 5 \times 2$ and $18 = (4 + 2) \times 3$, the dimensions of the large rectangle are 8 cm by 6 cm. As $2 \times (8 + 6) = 28$, the perimeter is 28 cm.

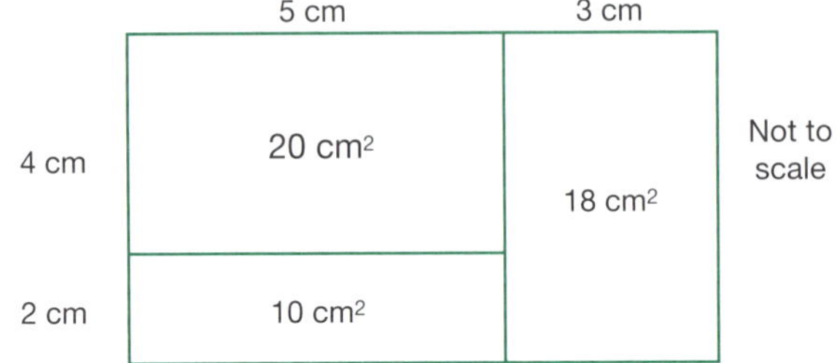

SAMPLE TEST 10

Page 48

1 B **2** A **3** C **4** D **5** D **6** A **7** C **8** B **9** C **10** E **11** C **12** A **13** A **14** E **15** C **16** B **17** A **18** A **19** C **20** C **21** A **22** D **23** C **24** D **25** D **26** B **27** A **28** C **29** E **30** D **31** C **32** E **33** A **34** C **35** E

1 As $4 + 1 = 5$, the total number of spectators will be divisible by 5. 22 785 has a last digit of 5 and so the number of spectators is 22 785.

2 As $X + Y = 60$ and $X - Y = 36$, then X is the middle of 60 and 36. As $(60 + 36) \div 2 = 48$, the value of X is 48. As $48 - Y = 36$, then $Y = 12$. $\frac{X}{Y} = \frac{48}{12} = 4$.

3 As $3 \times 4 \times 5 = 60$, so 62 has a remainder of 2 when divided by either 3, 4 or 5.

4 As 45% is $\frac{45}{100} = \frac{9}{20}$, then $\frac{9}{20}$ of the number is 27. As $27 \div 9 = 3$ and $3 \times 20 = 60$, the number is 60.

5 10% is the same as $\frac{1}{10}$. As $100 \div 10 = 10$, and $100 + 10 = 110$, Holly will deposit \$110 in the second month. As $110 \div 10 = 11$, and $110 + 11 = 121$, Holly will deposit \$121 in the third month. As $100 + 110 + 121 = 331$, Holly will have saved \$331.

6 As $4 + 16 \times 2 + 2 \times 1.5 = 4 + 32 + 3 = 39$, the cost is \$39.

7 $6.2 - 3.4$ is 2.8.

8 Here is the completed grid:

1	2	3	4
2	4	6	8
4	8	12	16
8	16	24	32
16	32	48	64

$a = 8$, $b = 24$ and $c = 64$. This means $c - (b - a) = 64 - (24 - 8)$. This is $64 - 16 = 48$.

9 The number of grey squares is the total number of squares minus 1 and then half the result.

Total squares	1	5	9	13
Grey squares	0	2	4	6

As $(37 - 1) \div 2 = 18$, there will be 18 grey squares.

10 The total height of the women is 172×3 and the total height of the men is 175×5. The average is found by adding these quantities and dividing by the total number of people. The number sentence is $(172 \times 3 + 175 \times 5) \div 8$.

11 6 balls + 4 cubes = 3 balls + 8 cubes
Removing 3 balls and 4 cubes from both sides gives 3 balls = 4 cubes. This means 6 balls balance 8 cubes.

12 Suppose Eve's number is X. Multiplying by 4 and then dividing by 2 is like doubling. She has $X + X + 8 - 5 - X + 3 - X$, which is 6.

13 The rectangle has dimensions 4 square sides and 1 square side. As 10 square sides = 40 cm, then the side length of the square is 4 cm. The rectangle is 16 cm long by 4 cm wide. As $16 \times 4 = 64$, the area is 64 cm^2.

14 A square has 4 lines of symmetry, a rectangle has 2, a parallelogram has 0, a rhombus has 2 and a kite has 1. This means a rectangle and a rhombus have exactly two lines of symmetry.

15 Each triangle has a base of 12 cm and a height of 5 cm. As $2 \times \frac{1}{2} \times 12 \times 5 = 60$, the area of the kite is 60 cm^2.

16 Men (m) + women (w) = 184, $w + c = 250$ and $m + c = 286$. Adding all three gives $m + w + w + c + m + c = 184 + 250 + 286 = 720$. As twice the total of men, women and children = 720, the total number of Saturday visitors was 360.

17 As $6 \times 6 = 36$, the side length of the large square is 6 cm. As $4 \times 6 = 24$, the perimeter of the large square is 24 cm. As $6 \div 3 = 2$, the side length of the small square is 2 cm. As $4 \times 2 = 8$, the perimeter of the small square is 8 cm. As $\frac{8}{24} = \frac{1}{3}$, the perimeter of the small square is $\frac{1}{3}$ the perimeter of the large square.

18 1 m = 100 cm. $120 \div 15 = 240 \div 30 = 8$, $100 \div 25 = 4$ and $90 \div 10 = 9$. As $9 \times 8 \times 4 = 288$, Payne can fit 288 boxes into the carton.

19 5 L /15 seconds is 20 L/minute.
As $6000 \div 20 = 600 \div 2 = 300$, it will take 300 minutes. As $300 \div 60 = 5$, it will take 5 hours. 11:30 am plus 5 hours is 4:30 pm.

20 As $100 \div 40 = 10 \div 4 = 2\frac{1}{2}$ hours.
As $160 \div 2\frac{1}{2} = 320 \div 5 = 64$, the average speed of the motorist is 64 km/h.

21 Adrienne needs to add 3 more tiles.

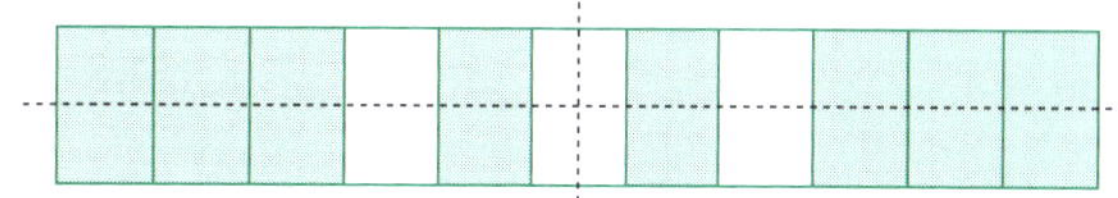

22 From 3 pm to midnight is 9 hours, and then to 7:30 am is another $7\frac{1}{2}$, which is a total of $16\frac{1}{2}$ hours. As $16\frac{1}{2} \times 2 = 33$, the clock will show 6:57 am. This is 3 minutes to 7.

23

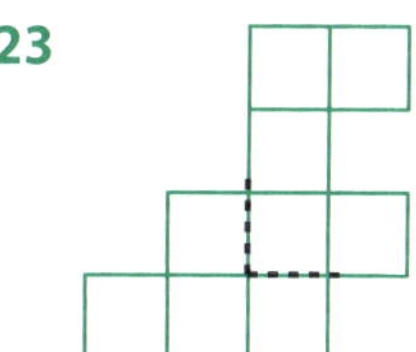

24 As $120 \div 3 = 40$, Ben and Claire are 40 metres apart. Now, Claire and Daphne are also 40 metres apart. As $220 - (120 + 40) = 60$, Daphne and Eddie are 60 metres apart.

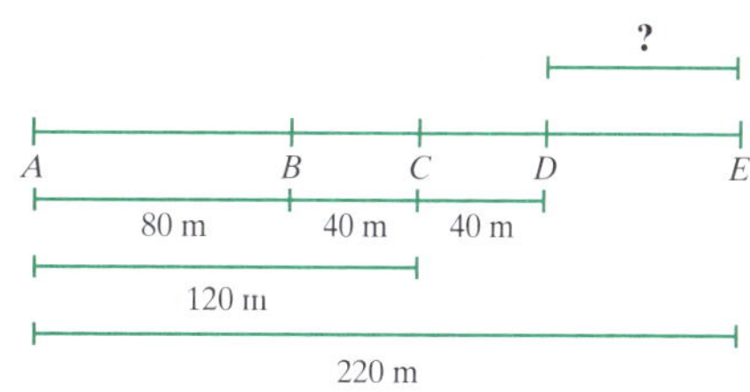

25 The hexagonal prism has 18 edges, 12 vertices and 8 faces.

26 As 90° is one-quarter of 360°, and $15 \times 4 = 60$ there are 60 spectators at the game. Statement 1 is correct. As 150° out of 360° is written as $\frac{150}{360} = \frac{5}{12}$, and $60 \div 12 \times 5 = 25$, there are 25 women at the game. Statement 2 is correct. As $360 - (150 + 90) = 120$ and $\frac{120}{360} = \frac{1}{3}$, a third of the spectators are men. Statement 3 is correct. Statements 1, 2 and 3 are correct.

27 Joel needs to spin a number greater than 1. There are 9 out of 12 numbers greater than 1. This is a probability of $\frac{9}{12}$, which is the same as $\frac{3}{4}$.

28 As $55 - 8 - 8 = 39$, the distance around $\frac{3}{4}$ of the circle is 39 cm. As $39 \div 3$ is 13, the distance around $\frac{1}{4}$ of the circle is about 13 cm.

29 As $1 + 3 = 4$, and $116 \div 4 = 29$, the smallest angle is 29°. As $29 \times 3 = 87$, the largest angle is 87°.

30 As 9 am to 2 pm is 5 hours, Chicago is 5 hours ahead of Honolulu. The plane leaves Chicago at 9:45 am Sunday Honolulu time. Adding 8 hours 30 minutes is 6:15 pm Sunday.

31 $1 - (\frac{2}{5} + \frac{1}{2}) = 1 - (\frac{4}{10} + \frac{5}{10}) = \frac{1}{10}$. At 10:00 am Emma has $\frac{1}{10}$ of the journey to complete. As $200 \div 10 = 20$, Emma drives 20 km in quarter of an hour. As $20 \times 4 = 80$, she averages 80 km/h for the final 15 minutes.

32 As $60 \div 5 = 12$, the middle number is 12. This means the first five numbers are 10, 11, 12, 13 and 14. The 25 numbers are 10, 11, 12 … 34. The middle number is $(34 + 10) \div 2 = 22$. As 25×22 is $25 \times 20 + 25 \times 2 = 500 + 50 = 550$, the sum is 550.

33 As $0.4 + 0.2 = 0.6$ the probability of choosing a red or blue ball is 0.6, or $\frac{3}{5}$. This means there are 20 balls that are either purple or yellow. As $20 - 8 = 12$, there are 12 yellow balls in the box.

34 As half of 28 is 14, and only 12 students in Year 4 can swim the distance, then fewer than half of the students in Year 4 can swim 50 m. Statement 1 is correct. As $22 \div 2 = 11$, which is not 10, statement 2 is not correct. $10 + 12 + 16 + 22 = 60$. As $28 \times 4 = 112$, and 60 is more than half of 112, more than 50% of the students in Years 3 to 6 can swim 50 m. Statement 3 is correct. Statements 1 and 3 are correct.

35 As $224 \div 8 = 28$, the tower has 28 cubes. Counting the cubes in each of the towers, the pattern is 1, 3, 6, 10 … This is a pattern of triangular numbers. The list is 1, 3, 6, 10, 15, 21, 28 … The seventh tower is 7 cubes high and as each cube has a side length of 2 cm, the height is 14 cm.

SAMPLE TEST 11

Page 53

1 D **2** B **3** C **4** A **5** E **6** A **7** C **8** D **9** E
10 B **11** C **12** D **13** A **14** B **15** A **16** C
17 D **18** E **19** D **20** A **21** D **22** B **23** C
24 D **25** B **26** A **27** E **28** C **29** A **30** B
31 C **32** A **33** C **34** A **35** E

1 As $(10 + 4 + 6 + 7 + 8) \div 5 = 35$ and $35 \div 5 = 7$, the average is 7. If Scott removes 7, the average remains the same.

2 Multiples of 5 and 8 are 40, 80, 120 … Now, $387 \div 40$ is about $380 \div 40 = 38 \div 4 = 9$ and remainder 2. As $90 \times 4 = 360$, the largest multiple is 360. As $387 - 360 = 27$, the smallest number is 27.

3 The multiples of 2, 3 and 5 are multiples of 30. Numbers that are 1 more than multiples of 30 are 31, 61, 91, and so on. From the options, Grandpa is 61 years old.

4 As $45 + 90 = 135$, Cooper turned through 135°.

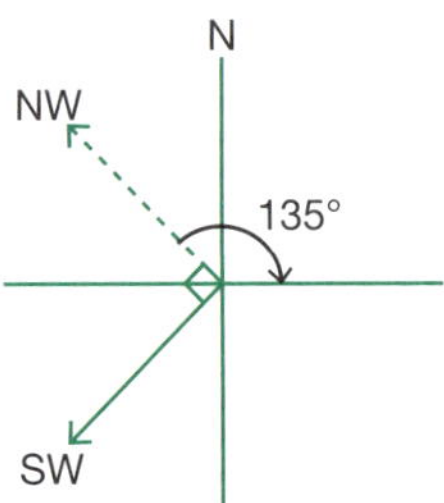

5 The circle, pentagon, hexagon and octagon: there are 4 shapes.

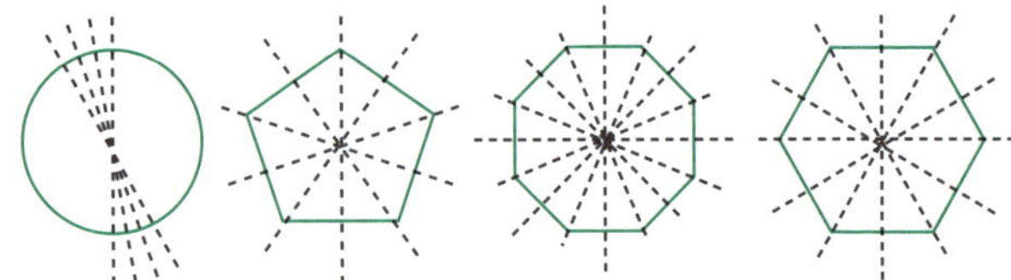

6 As $100 - 20 = 80$, Katherine still has 80% of the book to read. As $80 \div 20 = 4$ and $136 \div 4 = 34$, 20% of the book is 34 pages. Katherine has read 34 pages.

7 Besides Phoebe's team there are 9 other teams. As $9 \times 2 = 18$, her team played 18 games. As $18 \div 3 = 6$, Phoebe's team won 6 games. As $18 - (6 + 4) = 8$, her team lost 8 games.

8 The odd numbers from largest to smallest are 54 321, 54 231, **54 213** … **12 453**, 12 435, 12 345. The third largest is 54 213 and the third smallest is 12 453.

$$\begin{array}{r} 54\,213 \\ -\ 12\,453 \\ \hline 41\,760 \end{array}$$

The difference is 41 760.

9 As $290 - 60 \times 4 = 290 - 240 = 50$, the call out fee is \$50. As $50 + 60 \times 6 = 50 + 360 = 410$, Mrs Roberts was charged \$410.

10 Numbers that have factors of 3, 4 and 5 are multiples of 60. The number must end in a 1. The first 2 digits must be divisible by 6. As 96 is divisible by 6, the number is 961.

11 The small triangle is half the large triangle, which is half the square, which is half the rectangle. As $\frac{1}{2}$ of $\frac{1}{2}$ of $\frac{1}{2}$ is $\frac{1}{8}$, the small triangle is one-eighth of the original rectangle.

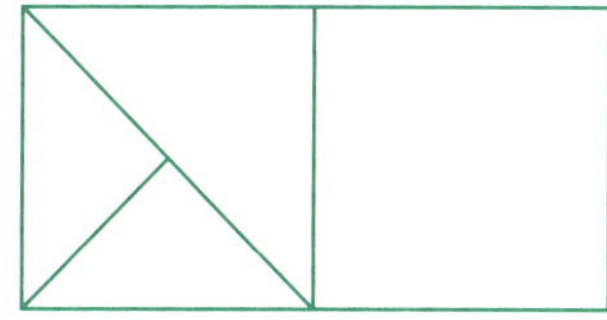

12 $(3 + 5) \div 4 = 2$, $(8 + 7) \div 3 = 5$, and so on. As $(15 + 21) \div 4 = 9$, the missing number is 9.

13 After the white ball is removed there are 6 black balls out of 9. The probability is $\frac{6}{9} = \frac{2}{3}$.

14 The diagram shows the net of a cone.

15 The fraction shaded forms the sequence $\frac{2}{3}$, $\frac{2}{5}$, $\frac{2}{7}$ … Look at the denominators: 3, 5, 7 … The 12th number will be $3 + 11 \times 2 = 25$. This means the 12th shape will have $\frac{2}{25}$ shaded.

16 As $2 + 1 + 2 + 1 + 2 + 1 + 2 + 1 = 12$, and $100 \div 12 = 8$, remainder 4, there are eight full patterns and four extra beads. The fourth bead in the pattern is blue and so the 100th bead is blue.

17 More means to add, difference is to subtract, product is to multiply and increased is to add. The number sentence is $9 + 24 - 4 \times 3 + 2$.

18 Consider integer lengths. Look for two numbers that multiply to give 126 and have a difference of 5. As $14 \times 9 = 126$, and $14 - 9 = 5$, the dimensions of the rectangle are 14 cm by 9 cm. As $2 \times (14 + 9) = 46$, the perimeter is 46 cm. (The square had side length of 11 cm.)

19 For James to multiply the number by 6 his possible answers are $4 \times 6 = 24$, $5 \times 6 = 30$, $6 \times 6 = 36$, $7 \times 6 = 42$, and so on. For Amelia to multiply the number by 8 her possible answers are $1 \times 8 = 8$, $2 \times 8 = 16$, $3 \times 8 = 24$, $4 \times 8 = 32$, $5 \times 8 = 40$ and $6 \times 8 = 48$. The numbers that are common to both are 4, 5 and 6. As $4 + 5 + 6 = 15$, the sum is 15.

20 The perimeter of the large rectangle is 4 lengths + 5 widths = 44 cm. Also, as 2 lengths = 3 widths, then 4 lengths = 6 widths. This means 11 widths = 44, and so width = 4 cm. This means length = 6 cm. As $2 \times (6 + 4) = 20$, the perimeter is 20 cm.

21 As $2 \times 2 \times 2 = 8$, each of these cubes has a volume of 8 cm^3. As $1000 \div 8 = 125$, Gareth can make 125 cubes.

22 Suppose the square had side length of 10 cm. As $10 \times 10 = 100$, the area is 100 cm^2. Now, increasing 10 cm by 50% (or $\frac{1}{2}$) means the length becomes 15 cm. Also, decreasing 10 cm by 20% (or $\frac{1}{5}$) means the width becomes 8 cm. As $15 \times 8 = 120$, and $120 - 100 = 20$, the area has increased by 20 cm^2. As 20 out of 100 is 20%, the area has increased by 20%.

23 As $60 \div 5 = 12$ and $12 \times 2 = 24$, the tap drips 24 times a minute. As $24 \times 0.25 = 6 \times 1 = 6$, the tap drips 6 mL every minute. As $6 \times 60 = 360$, the tap drips 360 mL every hour. As $360 \times 24 = 720 \times 12 = 8640$, the tap drips 8640 mL, or 8.604 L every day. This is about 9 L per day.

24 $\boxed{?} - 4 \times (3 + 2) - 12 \div 2 = \frac{18 - 4 \div 2}{2} + 2$ can be rewritten as $\boxed{?} - 4 \times 5 - 6 = \frac{18 - 2}{2} + 2$. $\boxed{?} - 20 - 6 = \frac{16}{2} + 2$ is $\boxed{?} - 26 = 8 + 2$ which means $\boxed{?} = 36$.

25 As $8 \div 4 = 2$, Graham took 2 hours to walk up the hill, and 1 hour to jog down. As $8 + 8 = 16$, he took 3 hours to travel 16 km. As $16 \div 3 = 5\frac{1}{3}$, the average speed was $5\frac{1}{3}$ km/h.

26 You need to find 2 numbers that multiply to give 60 where the bigger number is 3 more than 3 times the smaller number. Try the small number = 4. As $3 \times 4 + 3$ is 15, and $15 \times 4 = 60$, the dimensions are 15 cm and 4 cm. As $2 \times (15 + 4) = 38$, the perimeter is 38 cm.

27 As $410 - 80 = 330$, the mass of 270 mL is 330 g. When full the mass of the 540 mL liquid is 660 g. As $660 \div 3 \times 2 = 440$ the mass of the liquid when two-thirds full is 440 g.
As $440 + 80 = 520$, the bottle when two-thirds full has a mass of 520 g.

28 2340 to 2400 is 40 minutes, plus 14 hours 25 minutes is 14 hours 45 minutes. As Perth is 4 hours ahead of Dubai, the flight time was 10 hours 45 minutes.

29 Less rain fell on Sunday than on Wednesday. Statement 1 is not correct. $39 + 28 = 67$ and $15 + 8 + 10 + 26 = 59$. More rain fell on Thursday and Friday than on the first four days. Statement 2 is correct.
As $59 + 67 + 4 = 130$, the total amount of rain that fell throughout the week was less than 140 mm. Statement 3 is correct. Statements 2 and 3 are correct.

30 As $64 \div 4 = 16$, and add 1 for the starting post, there are 17 holes to dig. For Kiah, 3 holes in 40 minutes is 9 holes in 2 hours. Matthew can dig 8 holes in 2 hours. As $9 + 8 = 17$, Kiah and Matthew can dig 17 holes in 2 hours.

31 Look for the factors of 30, 24 and 20.
As $5 \times 4 = 20$, $6 \times 5 = 30$ and $6 \times 4 = 24$, the dimensions of the prism are 6 cm by 5 cm by 4 cm. The height is 5 cm.

32 As 2 hours 30 minutes is $2\frac{1}{2}$ hours, and $80 \times 2\frac{1}{2} = 80 \times 2 + 80 \times \frac{1}{2} = 160 + 40 = 200$, the journey was 200 km. As $200 \div 100 = 2$, the journey could be completed in 2 hours, which is 30 minutes earlier.

33 From 10:40 am to 1:40 pm is 3 hours and then to 2:05 pm is another 25 minutes. As one hour is one revolution = 360°, and $360 \times 3 = 1080$, the hand has travelled through 1080° in 3 hours. As $360 \div 60 = 6$, one minute is 6°. As $25 \times 6 = 150$ and $1080 + 150 = 1230$, the minute hand moves through 1230°.

34 Angelfish is represented by an angle of 90° which is a quarter of the graph. As $72 \div 4 = 18$, there are 18 angelfish. Statement 1 is correct. $120 - 110 = 10$ and 10° is $\frac{1}{36}$ of the graph. As $72 \div 36 = 2$, there are 2 more guppy fish than goldfish. Statement 2 is not correct.
$360 - (120 + 90 + 110) = 360 - 320 = 40$ and 40° is $\frac{40}{360} = \frac{1}{9}$. As $72 \div 9 = 8$, there are 8 tetra. Statement 3 is not correct. Statement 1 is the only correct statement.

35 As there are three 2s out of 8, the probability is $\frac{3}{8}$. Statement 1 is correct. As there are 3 odd numbers, the probability is $\frac{3}{8}$. Statement 2 is not correct. As there are 6 sectors that are numbered 2, 3 or 5, the probability is $\frac{6}{8}$, which is $\frac{3}{4}$. Statement 3 is correct. This means statements 1 and 3 are correct.

SAMPLE TEST 12

Page 58

1 D **2** E **3** B **4** D **5** C **6** B **7** A **8** D **9** A
10 C **11** C **12** D **13** E **14** E **15** B **16** C
17 D **18** C **19** E **20** B **21** E **22** B **23** A
24 D **25** A **26** C **27** B **28** D **29** B **30** B
31 D **32** A **33** E **34** E **35** E

1 The number is 9:

10	3	8
5	7	9
6	11	4

2 Tristan's shape has 4 lines of symmetry. This shape has 2 lines of symmetry.

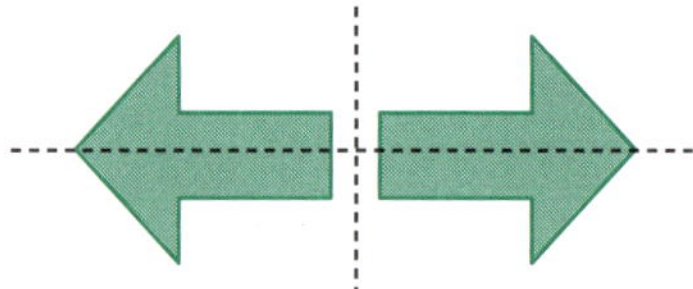

3 Each person buys 4 presents. As $5 \times 4 = 20$, there are 20 presents purchased. $160 \div 20 = 8$, so the average cost is $8.

4 3 over when divided by 5 means the number ends in a 3 or 8. 2 over when divided by 6 means the number is even. 68 is the only correct number between 40 and 80, as $68 \div 5 = 13$, remainder 3 and $68 \div 6 = 11$, remainder 2.

(58 and 78 do not give a remainder of 2 when divided by 6.)

5 As $47 - 6 = 41$ and $47 + 6 = 53$, count the integers between 41 and 53. There are 11 integers.

6 From 10 to 100 there are 8. From 100 to 1000 there are 7 (123, 234, 345, 456, 567, 678, 789). From 1000 to 10 000 there are 6 (1234, 2345, 3456, 4567, 5678, 6789). As $8 + 7 + 6 = 21$, there are 21 numbers.

7 As $3 \times 4 \times 5 = 60$, look for a multiple of 60. The number is 180.

8 $18 \times 45 = 3 \times 6 \times 9 \times 5$. This means $\boxed{?} = 6 \times 9 = 54$.

9 As $15\,200 - 2700 = 12\,500$, the amount of \$12 500 was to be distributed. As $100 - 80 = 20$, Ronald McDonald House receives 20%, or one-fifth of \$12 500. As $12\,500 \div 5 = 2500$, Ronald McDonald House was given \$2500.

10 As $22 - 17 = 5$, and $1000 \div 5 = 200$, the school sold 200 calculators. As $250 - 200 = 50$, the school still had 50 calculators remaining.

11 As $1 - \frac{3}{5} = \frac{2}{5}$, then $\frac{2}{5}$ equals 30. This means $\frac{1}{5}$ equals $30 \div 2 = 15$, and $\frac{3}{5}$ is $15 \times 3 = 45$.

12 $3 + 5 + 7 + 9 + 11 + 13 = 48$. As $48 \times 1.5 = 48 + \frac{1}{2}$ of $48 = 72$, Tyson has cycled a total of 72 km.

13 $2 \times [(30 - 3 \times 6) + 16 \div 2] - (3 + 3)$
$= 2 \times [(30 - 18) + 16 \div 2] - 6$
$= 2 \times [12 + 8] - 6 = 40 - 6$
$= 34$

14 The shape is made up of a square and a triangle. As $5 \times 5 + \frac{1}{2} \times 5 \times 2 = 25 + 5 = 30$, and $30 \times 4 = 120$, the area of the shape is 120 cm^2.

15 As $60 - 18 = 42$, Shyla had 42 oranges remaining after giving some to her sister. As $1 - \frac{2}{3} = \frac{1}{3}$, and $42 \div 3 = 14$, Shyla has 14 oranges remaining.

16 As $360 \div 12 = 30$, the hand sweeps 30° as every hour of time passes. As 2:30 pm to 5:00 pm is $2\frac{1}{2}$ hours and $30 \times 2 + \frac{1}{2}$ of $30 = 60 + 15 = 75$, the hour hand moves through 75°.

17 As 2 m = 200 cm, and $200 \div 20 = 10$, Ella can fit 10 by 10 pieces of cardboard. This means she can fit a maximum of 100 pieces on a concrete square. As Ella is doubling, she needs to stop at 64 because the next number, 128, is too many. As $1 + 2 + 4 + 8 + 16 + 32 + 64 = 127$, Ella will use 127 pieces.

18 The hexagon is a rectangle minus 2 triangles. The rectangle has dimensions 14 cm by 10 cm.
$14 \times 10 - 2 \times \frac{1}{2} \times 4 \times 6 = 140 - 24 = 116$.
The area of the shaded hexagon is 116 cm^2.

19 As 5 L = 5000 mL and $5000 - 200 = 4800$, the directions say to mix 200 mL of oil and 4800 mL of petrol. This is the same as 1 mL of oil to 24 mL of petrol. As $24 \times 120 = 2880$, Carl should use 2880 mL, or 2.88 L, of petrol.

20
$$\begin{array}{r} 80\,018 \\ -79\,568 \\ \hline 450 \\ \hline \end{array}$$
Aastha used 36 L of petrol and drove 450 km. This is a rate of 72 L for 900 km. Dividing both numbers by 9 gives 8 L/100 km.

21 As $1 - \frac{3}{8} = \frac{5}{8}$, the probability of rolling a 1, 2, 3, 4 or 5 is $\frac{5}{8}$. Statement 1 is correct. The probability of rolling a 1, 2, 3, 4 or 5 is each $\frac{1}{8}$. This means the probability of an odd number is $\frac{3}{8}$ which is the same as rolling a 6.
Statement 2 is correct. The factors of 6 are 1, 2, 3 and 6. $\frac{1}{8} + \frac{1}{8} + \frac{1}{8} + \frac{3}{8} = \frac{6}{8}$, which is $\frac{3}{4} = 75\%$.
Statement 3 is correct. This means statements 1, 2 and 3 are correct.

22 The pentagon is a rectangle with a triangle removed. As $24 \times 20 - \frac{1}{2} \times 7 \times 8 = 480 - 28 = 452$, the area is 452 cm^2.

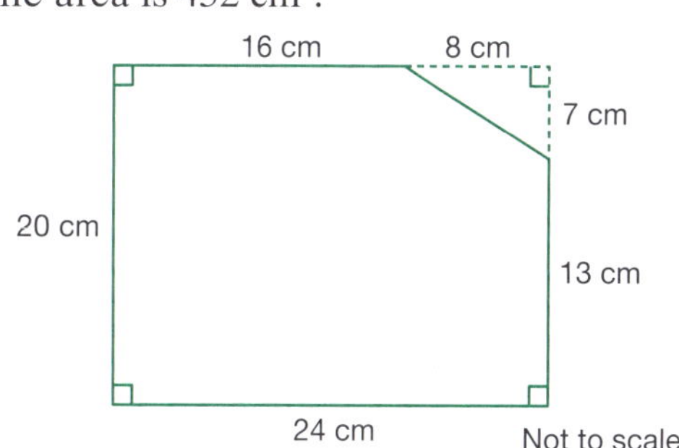

23 $\frac{1}{2}$ of $(1 - \frac{1}{3}) = \frac{1}{2}$ of $\frac{2}{3} = \frac{1}{3}$. The probability is $\frac{1}{3}$.

24 As ○ + ○ + ○ + ○ = □ then ○ × 4 = □. This means △ = 4.
As □ − 4 = 4, then □ = 8, and so ○ = 2.
□ + ○ × △ = 8 + 2 × 4 = 8 + 8 = 16.

25 As $40 + 20 = 60$, you need to find out how long it takes to ride 180 km at a speed of 60 km/h. As $180 \div 60 = 3$, Michael and Jenny meet after 3 hours, which is at 1:15 pm.

26 As $9.05 \times 5 - 8.6 \times 4 = 45.25 - 34.4 = 10.85$, the mass is 10.85 kg.

27 Dividing by 4, Ellie drives 4 km in 3 minutes. As $3 \times 15 = 45$ and $15 \times 4 = 60$, Ellie will travel 60 km.

28 Suppose X stands for the side length of the square. The side length of the triangle is $X + 6$. This means $X + X + X + X = X + 6 + X + 6 + X + 6$, and so $X = 18$. If the square has a side length of 18 cm, and $18 \times 4 = 72$, the length of each piece is 72 cm. As $72 \times 2 = 144$, the original piece was 144 cm.

29 As the lowest common multiple of 10, 15 and 25 is 150, it will take 150 seconds, or $2\frac{1}{2}$ minutes.

30 As $36 - 10 = 26$, the difference between the highest and lowest temperatures was 26°. Statement 1 is correct. At 8 am on Monday the temperature was 16°. At 8 am on Tuesday the temperature was 15°. As $16 - 15 = 1$, the difference was 1°. Statement 2 is not correct. At 4 pm on Monday the temperature was 36°. At 2 am on Tuesday the temperature was 18°. As half of 36 is 18, the temperature halved. Statement 3 is correct. Statements 1 and 3 are correct statements.

31 The object has been rotated 135° clockwise, which is 225° anticlockwise.

32 The length of the prism is 14 cm. As $(24 - 14) \div 2 = 5$, the height is 5 cm. As width + 5 + width + 5 = 30, and $2 \times$ width = 20, the width is 10 cm. As $14 \times 10 \times 5 = 700$, the volume is 700 cm^3.

33 There will be 64 small cubes. The front face has 8 cubes with 2 painted faces and the back face has 8 cubes. Also there are 4 cubes on each of the top and bottom faces as well. This is a total of 24 cubes.

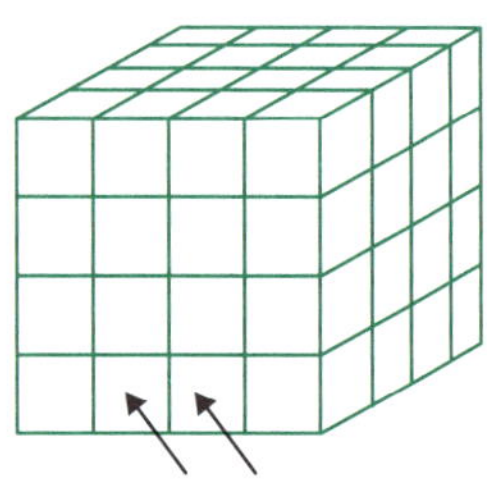

34 As $325 + 125 = 450$, the total profit on the weekend was \$450. Statement 1 is correct. As 275 is not twice 125, statement 2 is not correct. As $2325 - (325 + 125 + 275 + 450 + 350 + 425) = 2325 - 1950 = 375$, the profit was \$375. Statement 3 is correct. Statements 1 and 3 are correct statements.

35 11:40 pm Tuesday Perth time is 1:40 am Wednesday Newcastle time. Adding 4 h 45 min is 5:40 am plus 45 min = 6:25 am. Adding 6 h 10 min is 12:35 pm. Adding 1 h 10 min is 1:45 pm (Wednesday).

SAMPLE TEST 13

Page 64

1 C **2** E **3** C **4** E **5** D **6** A **7** E **8** B **9** D
10 B **11** A **12** C **13** B **14** A **15** C **16** D
17 E **18** E **19** A **20** B **21** E **22** C **23** A
24 D **25** C **26** A **27** B **28** A **29** D **30** D
31 B **32** D **33** E **34** C **35** A

1 7 minutes after 11:58 is 12:05. There are 55 minutes until 1:00 and another 2 minutes gives 57 minutes.

2 $114 + 94 = 208$. Also, $208 \div 2 = 104$, and $200 - 104 = 96$, so the result is 96.

3 Starting with 56, use inverse operations. 56×2 is 112. Adding 32 gives 144 and then dividing by 4 gives 36. Harriet started with 36. Now 36×2 is 72. Subtract 32 to get 40 and divide by 4 to get an answer of 10.

4 As 9 is a multiple of 3, you need to find the product of 4, 5 and 9. $4 \times 5 \times 9 = 180$, and 180 seconds = 3 minutes. The next time will be 12:03:00.

5 80% is 48 marks. As $48 \div 8 \times 10 = 60$, then Goran scored 48 out of 60. Jaclyn's mark was 60 (out of 60).

6 The answer is $1472 - 2 \times 598 = 1472 - 1196$.

$$\begin{array}{r} 1472 \\ -\ 1196 \\ \hline 276 \end{array}$$

The answer is 276.

7 As 30% is $\frac{3}{10}$, then 30% of 400 is $400 \div 10 \times 3 = 120$. Also as 20% is $\frac{2}{10}$, then 20% of 120 is $120 \div 10 \times 2 = 24$. The answer is \$24.

8 $8 + 2 \times (9 - 6)^2 = 8 + 2 \times 3^2$
$= 8 + 2 \times 9 = 8 + 18$
$= 26$

9 As (49 – 1) is a multiple of 4 and (49 + 1) is a multiple of 5, then Courtney is 49 years old. (Courtney could not be 9 years old because she was born last century and so is at least 22 years old.)

10 As 3.5 + 4.2 + 4.3 = 12, water can be collected at 12 L/minute. As 12 × 60 × 2 = 720 × 2 = 1440, the amount of water is 1440 L, or 1.44 kL.

11 From 8:40 to 10:20 is 1 hour 40 minutes, which is 100 minutes. From 8:40 to 9:55 is 1 hour 15 minutes, which is 75 minutes. James watched 75 minutes out of 100 minutes, which is $\frac{75}{100} = \frac{3}{4}$.

12 As 3.5 = 3.50, you need to find the average of 2.79 and 3.50.
As (3.50 + 2.79) ÷ 2 = 6.29 ÷ 2 = 3.145, the value of X is 3.145.

13 600 – 480 = 120, and $\frac{120}{600} = \frac{1}{5}$, which is 20%.
As 1800 + 360 = 2160, and 2160 ÷ 5 = 432, the total price will be reduced by $432.
As 2160 – 432 = 1728, the two items will cost $1728.

14 The number is 5.

17	24	1	8	15
23	5	7	14	16
4	6	13	20	22
10	12	19	21	3
11	18	25	2	9

15 The rule used is triangles = 2 × squares + 2. This means 48 = 2 × squares + 2, which is 2 × squares = 46. There are 23 squares.

squares	1	2	3
triangles	4	6	8

16 10 – 3 = 7 and 260 + 7 × 50 = 260 + 350 = 610, so Michael plans to ride 610 km.

17 150 – (20 + 4 × [?]) = 45 ÷ 9 + [?] is the same as 150 – (20 + 4 × [?]) = 5 + [?].
Consider the options: as 150 – (20 + 4 × 25) = 5 + 25, the missing number is 25.

18 4 and 6 are on opposite faces. As 4 × 6 = 24 then * × 12 = 24. This means * = 2.

19 Drawing a vertical line through the right angle shows that the area of the triangle is exactly half the area of the rectangle.
As $2 \times \frac{1}{2} \times 12 \times 16 = 192$, the area is 192 cm^2.

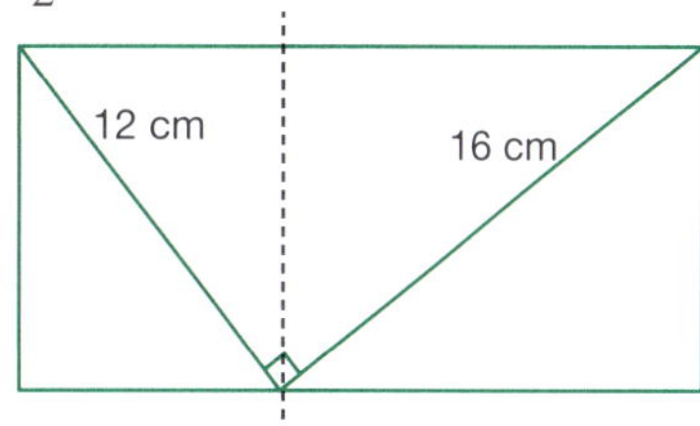

20 As 240 ÷ 5 × 12 = 48 × 12 = 576, the tank holds 576 L when full. As 576 ÷ 4 × 3 = 144 × 3 = 432, the tank holds 432 L when $\frac{3}{4}$ full.
As 432 – 240 = 192, it needs 192 L to be $\frac{3}{4}$ full.

21 As 20 minutes = $\frac{1}{3}$ hour, and 90 ÷ 3 = 30, the distance is 30 km. As 20 + 10 = 30, Tamsin took 30 minutes, or $\frac{1}{2}$ hour. 30 km in $\frac{1}{2}$ hour is 60 km/h. As 90 – 60 = 30, the difference in their speeds is 30 km/h.

22 Four rectangles can be seen on the diagram where the rectangles are inside others. These rectangles measure 8 cm by 6 cm, 6 cm by 5 cm, 4 cm by 4 cm and 2 cm by 3 cm. As 8 × 6 – 6 × 5 + 4 × 4 – 2 × 3 = 48 – 30 + 16 – 6 = 28, the area is 28 cm^2.

23 As 288 ÷ 6 = 48, and 48 × 100 = 4800, the mass is 4800 kg, or 4.8 tonne.

24 As 10 + 15 = 25, and 10 × 2.5 is 25, the dimensions have been enlarged by a factor of 2.5. Also, 15 × 2.5 is 15 × 2 plus half of 15 = 37.5. The new dimensions are 37.5 cm by 25 cm. As 37.5 × 25 = 37.5 × 100 ÷ 4 = 3750 ÷ 4 = 937.5, the new area is 937.5 cm^2.

25 The perimeter of the shaded section is the same as the perimeter of the large square. As 44 ÷ 4 = 11, the large square has a side length of 11 cm and an area of 121 cm^2.
As 121 – 72 = 49, the area of the small square is 49 cm^2. This means the small square has a side length of 7 cm and as 11 – 7 = 4, the unknown length is 4 cm.

26 As $8 \div 4 \times 3 = 6$, there is 6 L of juice in the container. As 6 L = 6000 mL, and $6000 \div 24 = 1000 \div 4 = 250$, each bottle has a capacity of 250 mL.

27 First ignore the symbols that are on both sides of the balance (4 squares and 1 triangle). This means 2 squares = 2 triangles + 1 circle. As $2 \times 8 = 2 \times 6$ + circle, then a circle = $16 - 12 = 4$.

28 0620 Wednesday minus 8 hours 10 minutes is 2210 Tuesday. Subtracting another 3 hours 30 minutes is 1840 Tuesday.

29 Thursday ($180) is not twice as much as Tuesday ($110). Statement 1 is not correct. On Thursday ($180), Friday ($320) and Saturday ($290) Vinnie earned more than $140. Statement 2 is correct.
As $140 + 110 + 140 + 180 + 320 + 290 = 1180$ which is less than 1200, Statement 3 is correct. Statements 2 and 3 are correct.

30 As $1 - (0.2 + 0.15 + 0.35) = 1 - 0.7 = 0.3$, the probability of choosing a white button is 0.3, or $\frac{6}{20}$. As $\frac{6}{20}$ of the total = 18, and $\frac{1}{20}$ of the total = 3, then $0.35 = \frac{7}{20}$ of the total $= 7 \times 3 = 21$. There are 21 yellow buttons.

31 There will be 4 squares shaded, including *P* and *T*.

32 As $360 - 80 = 280$, the 4 equal angles add to 280°. As $280 \div 4 = 70$, the value of x is 70.

33 The number of small cubes has decreased, which means the volume has decreased. Statement 1 is correct. The surface area is unchanged (there are still $9 \times 6 = 54$ small cube faces). Statement 2 is incorrect but statement 3 is correct. Statements 1 and 3 are correct.

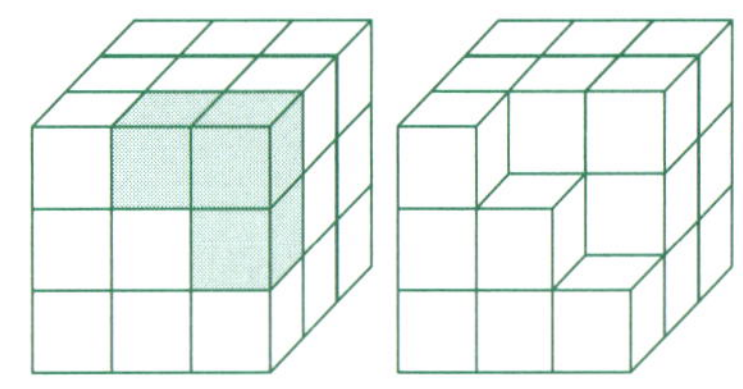

34 As $12 + 6 + 20 + 12 = 50$, a total of 50 students were surveyed. The probability that they are a boy born in Australia is $\frac{20}{50} = \frac{4}{10}$, which is 0.4. Statement 1 is correct.
As $20 + 12 = 32$ there were 32 boys.
As $\frac{12}{32}$ is not $\frac{3}{5}$, statement 2 is not correct.
As $6 + 12 = 18$, there were 18 students born overseas. As there were 6 girls born overseas, and $\frac{6}{18} = \frac{1}{3}$, statement 3 is correct. This means statements 1 and 3 are correct.

35 As $3 + 5 + 8 + 9 = 25$, then 25 girls play. Statement 1 is not correct. As $5 + 7 + 6 + 7 = 25$, the same number of boys as girls play weekend sport. Statement 2 is correct.
As $(9 + 7) - (5 + 7) = 4$, then four more students from Year 6 play weekend sport than Year 4. Statement 3 is correct.
Statements 2 and 3 are correct statements.

SAMPLE TEST 14

Page 69

1 D **2** C **3** B **4** D **5** A **6** B **7** C **8** B **9** D
10 B **11** E **12** C **13** D **14** C **15** E **16** D
17 D **18** A **19** C **20** D **21** C **22** A **23** B
24 B **25** E **26** A **27** D **28** D **29** C **30** E
31 C **32** C **33** E **34** B **35** A

1 The largest whole number is 986 499, as 986 500 will round to 987 000.

2 1 to 9 is 9 digits. 10 to 99 is $90 \times 2 = 180$ digits. As $9 + 180 = 189$, Jack has used 189 digits. As $(240 - 189) \div 3 = 51 \div 3 = 17$, Jack will write 17 three-digit numbers. The last number will be 116.

3 Numbers which are multiples of 4 and divisible by 5 are multiples of 20. These numbers are 60, 80, 100, 120, 140 and 160. There are 6 numbers.

4

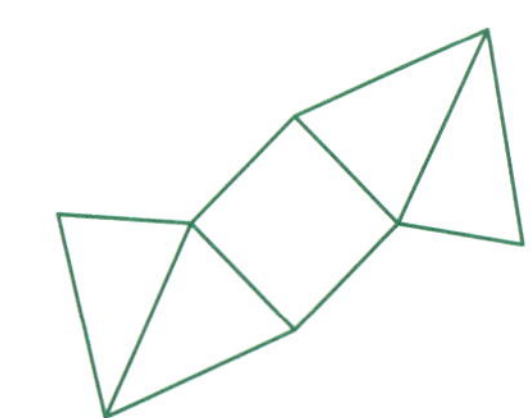

5 60 is a common multiple of 1, 2, 3, 4, 5, and 6. As $60 \times 7 = 420$, the smallest number is 420.

6 As $360 \div 4 = 90$, $360 \div 5 \times 3 = 216$ and $360 - (90 + 216 + 16) = 360 - 316 = 38$, there were 38 students who walked to school.

7 As $90 \times 4 = 360$, Ariarne could have scored 100%, 100%, 100% and 60%. The lowest possible score is 60%.

8 $8 + 6 + 4 + 2 = 20$. As $6 = 4 + 2$ and $2 = 8 \div 4$, the number could be 6842 or 6824.
As $42 - 24 = 18$, the difference is 18.

9 The rules are $b = a^2$, $c = 2 \times b - a$ and $d = c + 3a$. The * represents the number 60. The completed table is shown.

a	1	2	3	4	5
b	1	4	9	16	25
c	1	6	15	28	45
d	4	12	24	40	60

10 $(16 - 8) \div ($? + ? $) =$? means
$8 \div ($? + ? $) =$?. This means the missing number is 2.

11 In 2019 Jack receives \$60 000 + \$5000. In 2020 he receives \$60 000 + \$5000 × 2. In 2028 Jack receives \$60 000 + \$5000 × 10 = \$60 000 + \$50 000 = \$110 000.
As 110 000 ÷ 10 = 11 000, Jack gives away \$11 000.

12 As $168 \div 14 = 84 \div 7 = 12$, Haley will order 12 pizzas. As $12 \div 3 \times 8 = 32$, there will be 32 people at the party.

13 The sequence is 2, 4, 6, 8 … The 10th number is 20 and the 110th term is 220. As $220 \times 20 = 4400$, the result is 4400.

14 $360 \div 8 = 45$, and $3 \times 45 = 135$, the object has been rotated 135° clockwise.

15 As 45 minutes is $\frac{3}{4}$ of an hour, or 0.75 of an hour, Andrea took 4.75 hours to complete the job. Her profit is $360 - (120 + 24)$. Her hourly pay is $[360 - (120 + 24)] \div 4.75$.

16 The shape is a rectangle minus 2 small rectangles. As $10 \times 8 - 2 \times 4 \times 2 = 64$, the area is 64 cm^2.

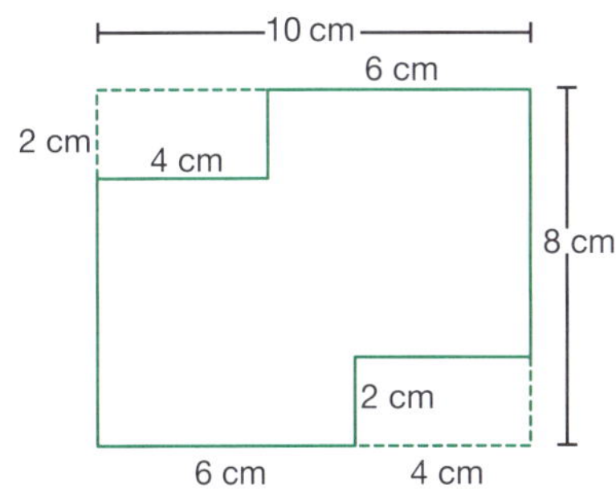

17 As $3600 \div 2 \times 3 = 1800 \times 3 = 5400$, the tank contains 5400 L when full. As $5400 \div 5 \times 2 = 1080 \times 2 = 2160$, the tank contains 2160 L when two-fifths full. As $3600 - 2160 = 1440$, the amount removed was 1440 L.

18 As $(30 - 4 - 4) \div 2 = 11$, the dimensions are 11 cm by 4 cm by 4 cm. As $16 \times 11 = 176$, the volume is 176 cm^3.

19 As $700 = 350 + 350$, $750 = 50 + 200 + 500$, $900 = 200 + 350 + 350$ and $950 = 50 + 200 + 350 + 350$, the only weight that cannot be weighed is 800 g.

20 6 m^2 in 12 minutes is 1 m^2 in 2 minutes.
As $16 \times 2.5 = 8 \times 5 = 40$, the wall has an area of 40 m^2. As $40 \times 2 = 80$, it will take 80 minutes, or 1 hour 20 minutes.

21 The speedometer shows a speed of 100 km/h. As 20 minutes is $\frac{1}{3}$ of an hour and $100 \div 3 = 33\frac{1}{3}$ Helga has travelled about 33 km.

22 5, 4, and 3 are factors of 60. $\frac{1}{5} = \frac{12}{60}$, $\frac{1}{4} = \frac{15}{60}$, $\frac{1}{3} = \frac{20}{60}$ and $12 + 15 + 20 = 47$. Cate spends $\frac{47}{60}$ of her wage. As $1 - \frac{47}{60} = \frac{13}{60}$, she saves $\frac{13}{60}$ of her wage. As $260 \div 13 \times 60 = 20 \times 60 = 1200$, Cate's wage is \$1200.

23 Let the distance $AB = X$.
As $X + 3 + 3 + X + 3 = 14$, then $X + X = 5$.
This means the distance is 2.5 km.

24 As $31 - 18 = 13$, the difference was 13°. But on Thursday the difference was 18°.
Statement 1 is not correct. As $31 - 4 = 27$, the difference was 27°. Statement 2 is correct. In order the maximums were 31, 30, 30, 28 …
This means 28 °C (Thursday) is the fourth warmest maximum. Statement 3 is not correct.
Statement 2 is the only correct statement.

25 2020 was a leap year. Summer (December to February): $31 + 31 + 29 = 91$. Winter (June to August): $30 + 31 + 31 = 92$. There was one more day.

26 Half of the spinner is purple and the other half is made up of the other 3 colours. As $\frac{1}{3}$ of $\frac{1}{2}$ is $\frac{1}{6}$, the probability of landing on red is $\frac{1}{6}$.

27 As 0.2 is $\frac{1}{5}$, and $60 \div 5 = 12$, it took 12 minutes to walk to the station. 7:56 am plus 12 minutes is 8:08 am, plus 3 minutes is 8:11 am. Adding 30 minutes is 8:41 am and another 9 minutes is 8:50 am.

28 12 more squares need to be shaded.

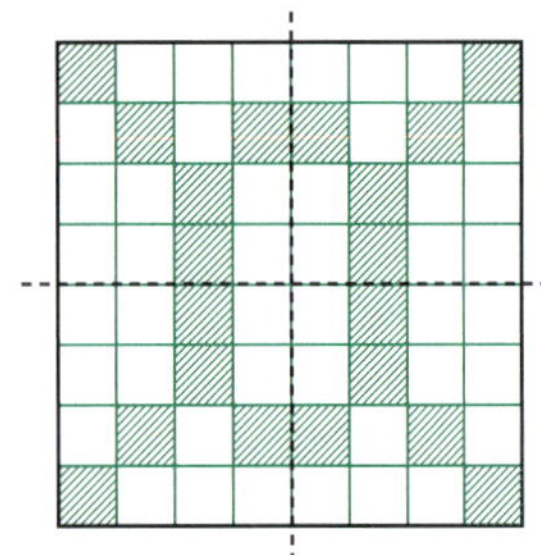

29 As 20 minutes = $\frac{1}{3}$ of an hour, and 60 ÷ 3 = 20, the distance is 20 km. As 20 ÷ 40 = $\frac{1}{2}$, the time taken to drive home was half an hour, or 30 minutes, which means a total of 40 km in 50 minutes. Now, dividing by 5 gives 8 km in 10 minutes. Multiplying by 6 gives 48 km in 60 minutes. This is an average speed of 48 km/h.

30 Luella divides the octagon into 6 triangles. As 180 × 6 = 1080, the angle sum is 1080°. As the 8 angles in a regular octagon are equal, and 1080 ÷ 8 = 135, each angle is 135°.

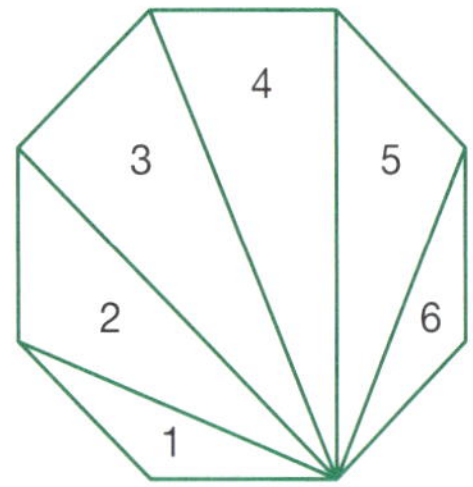

31 If a square has an area of 36 cm^2, the side length is 6 cm. As 6 × 6 = 36, the length of the rectangle is 36 cm. As there are 8 squares on the bottom row, and as 36 ÷ 8 = $4\frac{1}{2}$, each square in the bottom row has a side length of $4\frac{1}{2}$ cm. As 6 + $4\frac{1}{2}$ = $10\frac{1}{2}$, the dimensions of the rectangle are 36 cm by $10\frac{1}{2}$ cm.
As 2 × (36 + $10\frac{1}{2}$) = 93, the perimeter is 93 cm.

32 The probability of choosing a red card is 0.2 and choosing a yellow card is 0.4.
As 1 – (0.1 + 0.2 + 0.4) = 0.3, the probability of selecting a pink card is 0.3. Statement 1 is correct. As 0.4 × 40 is 16, there are 16 yellow cards in the box. Statement 2 is correct. As 0.1 + 0.3 = 0.4, the chance of selecting a blue or pink card is the same as selecting a yellow card. Statement 3 is correct. This means statements 1, 2 and 3 are correct.

33 As 240 ÷ 3 = 80, Jill's average speed is 80 km/h. As 80 ÷ 4 × 5 = 20 × 5 = 100, Jack's average speed is 100 km/h. As 240 ÷ 100 = 2.4, it takes Jack 2.4 hours. As 3 – 2.4 = 0.6, Jill takes 0.6 hour longer. As 0.6 = $\frac{6}{10}$ and 60 ÷ 10 × 6 = 36, it takes Jill 36 minutes more.

34 As 4 × 3 = 12, let the length be 12 units, width 3 units and height 4 units. As there are 4 'length' edges, 4 'width' edges and 4 'height' edges, then 4 × (12 + 3 + 4) = 4 × 19 = 76, which means the total length is 76 units. As 76 × 2 = 152, then each unit = 2 cm, so that the dimensions are 24 cm, 6 cm and 8 cm. As 24 × 6 × 8 = 144 × 8 = 1152, the volume is 1152 cm^3.

35 As 200 × 2 – 160 × 2 = 400 – 320 = 80, Ben drove 80 km more than Bill. Statement 1 is not correct. 11 am to 2 pm plus 3 pm to 4 pm is 4 hours. 1 pm to 2 pm plus 3:30 pm to 5 pm is 2 hours 30 minutes. As 4 hours is not twice 2 hours 30 minutes, statement 2 is not correct. Although Bill and Ben were stopped at the same time, they were not together. Statement 3 is not correct. No statement is correct.

SAMPLE TEST 15

Page 75

1 A **2** C **3** B **4** D **5** C **6** B **7** B **8** D **9** E
10 E **11** D **12** C **13** A **14** E **15** D **16** B
17 A **18** C **19** A **20** A **21** D **22** E **23** C
24 E **25** A **26** D **27** B **28** C **29** B **30** B
31 A **32** E **33** B **34** C **35** C

1 The sum of the two numbers is 52 and the difference is 6. The two numbers are 23 and 29. The 6th number is the middle number. As 23 – 2 = 21, the middle number is 21.

2 The numbers are 8432 and 2483.

$$\begin{array}{r} 8432 \\ -\ 2483 \\ \hline 5949 \\ \hline \end{array}$$

The difference is 5949.

3 As 108 ÷ 7 = 15, remainder 3 and 108 ÷ 8 = 13, remainder 4, the smallest number is 108.

4 As 60 is the smallest common multiple of 6, 4 and 5, the number of students is a multiple of 60. As 60 × 3 = 180, there could be 180 students surveyed.

5 As 100 – 40 = 60, the school population is 40% male and 60% female. For males, 50% of 40% is 20%. For females, 40% of 60% is 24%. As 20% + 24% = 44%, and 100 – 44 = 56, then 56% of the entire population do not play weekend sport.

6 As 99 is a multiple of 3 and 99 ÷ 3 = 33, there are 33 multiples of 3 between 1 and 100. Ignoring 3, 6, and 99 (as 1 more than these numbers are not 2-digit) there are 30 two-digit numbers with a remainder of 1 when divided by 3.

7 As $1 - \frac{3}{4} = \frac{1}{4}$, and 12 × 4 = 48, Madeline had 48 pumpkins available at the start of Sunday. As $1 - \frac{1}{3} = \frac{2}{3}$, then $\frac{2}{3}$ of the pumpkins she had available on Saturday equals 48.

As 48 ÷ 2 × 3 = 24 × 3 = 72, Madeline started with 72 pumpkins on Saturday morning.

8 $\sqrt{20 - 2^2} = \sqrt{16} = 4$, $\sqrt{10 - 3^2} = \sqrt{1} = 1$,

$\sqrt{74 - 7^2} = \sqrt{25} = 5$.

As $\sqrt{157 - 6^2} = \sqrt{157 - 36} = \sqrt{121} = 11$, the missing number is 11.

9 As 82 ÷ 2 = 41, the sum of the length and width is 41. As the length is 1 cm longer than the width, the dimensions are 21 cm and 20 cm. As 21 × 20 = 420, the area is 420 cm^2.

10 A hexagonal prism has 18 edges and 12 vertices. As 18 + 12 = 30, the total is 30.

11 As 36 ÷ 3 × 2 = 24, the ball rises to 24 m after bounce 1. As 24 ÷ 3 × 2 = 16, the ball rises to 16 m after bounce 2. The ball falls 36 m, rises and falls 24 m, then rises and falls 16 m. As 36 + 2 × 24 + 2 × 16 = 36 + 48 + 32 = 116, the ball has travelled 116 m.

12 45 + (? – 11) × 4 – 36 ÷ 4 = 60 can be rewritten as 45 + (? – 11) × 4 – 9 = 60. This means 36 + (? – 11) × 4 = 60, which is (? – 11) × 4 = 24. Now, ? – 11 = 6, so ? = 17.

13 As 12 × 12 ÷ 2 = 72, the area of each of the rectangles is 72 cm^2. The small triangle has a base of 6 cm and a height of 6 cm.

As $72 - \frac{1}{2} \times 6 \times 6 = 54$, the shaded area is 54 cm^2. Or, as the shaded area is $\frac{3}{8}$ of the square, and 144 ÷ 8 × 3 = 54, the area is 54 cm^2.

14 $1 - (\frac{1}{4} + \frac{1}{5} + \frac{1}{6}) = 1 - (\frac{15}{60} + \frac{12}{60} + \frac{10}{60})$
$= \frac{65}{60} - \frac{37}{60} = \frac{23}{60}$

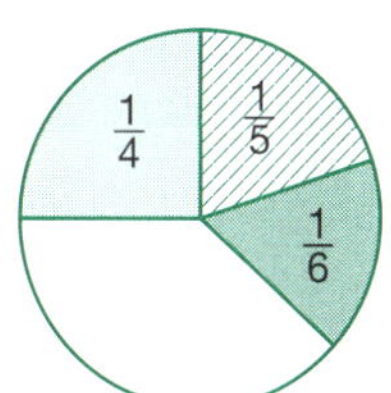

15 As 10 × 3 = 30, there are three times as many cars that passed the school as vans. Statement 1 is correct. As 10 + 12 + 5 = 27, which is less than 30, the total of vans, trucks and bikes was not more than the number of cars. Statement 2 is not correct. As 12 – 10 = 2, there were 2 more trucks than vans. As 6 × 2 = 12, after an hour there would be 12 more trucks than vans. Statement 3 is correct. Statements 1 and 3 are correct.

16

$$\begin{array}{r} 400\,000 \\ -\quad 400 \\ \hline 399\,600 \end{array} \qquad \begin{array}{r} 70\,000 \\ -\quad 70 \\ \hline 69\,930 \end{array} \qquad \begin{array}{r} 399\,600 \\ +\ 69\,930 \\ \hline 469\,530 \end{array}$$

The sum is 469 530.

17 As 80 ÷ 4 = 20, the length of each side of the smaller squares is 20 cm. When formed, the large square has side length 60 cm. As 60 × 60 = 3600, the area is 3600 cm^2.

18 Calculator + notebook = $27.10
Calculator – notebook = $15.80
Adding these two calculations gives
2 calculators = $27.10 + 15.80 = $42.90.
Cost of 1 calculator = $21.45. This means the cost of a notebook is $5.65 and so the cost of 2 notebooks is $11.30.

19 As 210 ÷ 15 = 420 ÷ 30 = 42 ÷ 3 = 14, Kieran needs to take 14 doses of medicine.
As 24 ÷ 8 = 3, he takes 3 doses a day. At 2 pm on Sunday Kieran will have his last dose.

20 As the diagonals meet in the middle of the rectangle, the diagonals always bisect each other. Statement 1 is correct. There are 4 triangles but they are only identical for a square (or rhombus). Statement 2 is not correct. The diagonals are perpendicular only if the shape is a square (or rhombus) but not always for a rectangle. Statement 3 is not correct. Only statement 1 is correct.

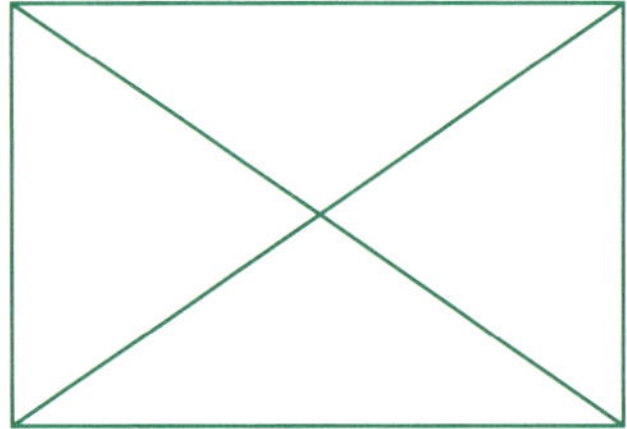

21 As 100 + 80 = 180, the time to drive 360 km at 180 km/h is 2 hours. This means they meet at 9 am. Statement 1 is correct.
As $360 \div 80 = 36 \div 8 = 4.5$, Holly takes 4 hours 30 minutes. She arrives in Lithgow at 11:30 am. Statement 2 is correct. As $360 \div 100 = 3.6$, Mia takes 3.6 hours, which is not half an hour less than Holly. Statement 3 is not correct. Statements 1 and 2 are correct.

22 As a pineapple has the same mass as 3 oranges, 2 pineapples have the same mass as 6 oranges. As 2 oranges have the same mass as 4 apples, then 6 oranges have the same mass as 12 apples. This means 2 pineapples have the same mass as 12 apples.

23 As 1.06 kg = 1060 g, and 1060 – 80 = 980, the total mass of the potatoes is 980 g. As $980 \div 4 = 245$, the average mass is 245 g.

24 The sum of the length and width is 20 cm, which means the width is 8 cm. For triangle *A*, the area is $\frac{1}{2} \times 12 \times \text{height} = 12$, which means $6 \times \text{height} = 12$, and so the height is 2 cm. This means the height of triangle *B* is 6 cm.

As $\frac{1}{2} \times 12 \times 6 = 36$, the area of triangle *B* is 36 cm^2. Or drawing two dotted lines shows that the sum of the areas of the shaded triangles is exactly half the area of the original rectangle. This means the sum of the area of triangles *A* and *B* is half of 96 cm^2 = 48 cm^2.

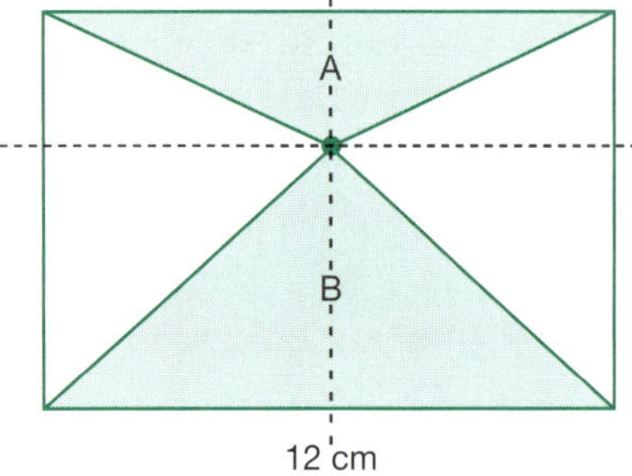

As 48 – 12 = 36, the area of triangle *B* is 36 cm^2.

25 There are 5 red cubes out of 20. This means the probability is $\frac{1}{4}$. Statement 1 is not correct. There are 6 green cubes out of 20. This means the probability is $\frac{6}{20} = \frac{3}{10} = 0.3$. Statement 2 is correct. If 2 are removed, there would be 9 blue cubes out of 18. This means the probability is $\frac{1}{2}$, or 50%. Statement 3 is correct. This means statements 2 and 3 are correct.

26 Three-quarters of 80 is $80 \div 4 \times 3 = 60$.
$120 \times 60 \times 70 = 7200 \times 70 = 504000$. The volume is 504 000 cm^3 which is 504 000 mL = 504 L. As $504 \div 6 = 84$, it will take 84 minutes, or 1 hour 24 minutes.

27 8:45 pm Wednesday plus 8 hours 25 minutes is 5:10 am Thursday. Adding 5 hours 50 minutes gives 11:00 am Thursday. Adding 13 hours 40 minutes gives 12:40 am Friday. Subtracting 9 hours gives 3:40 pm Thursday.

28 Ingrid needs 2 more triangles.

29 The angles inside a triangle add to 180° and there are 180° in a straight angle.
As 180 – (40 + 105) = 35, the missing angle is 35°.

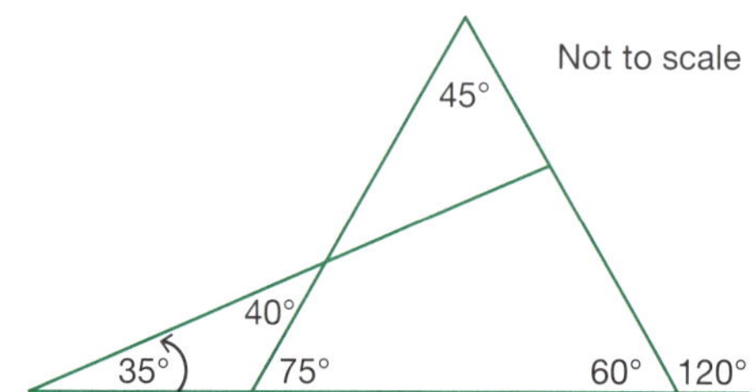

30

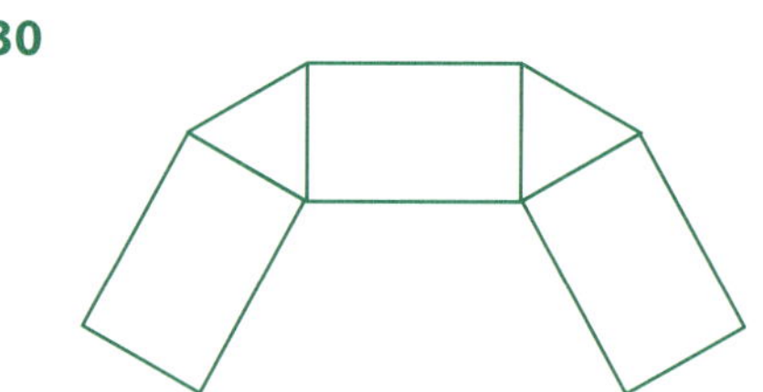

31 As 90° is one-quarter of 360°, and $360 \div 4 = 90$, there were 90 students who use Brand Y. Statement 1 is correct.

As 360 – (150 + 90 + 75) = 360 – 315 = 45, then the angle for Brand *W* is 45°.

As $45 \times 2 = 90$, twice as many students use Brand *Y* as use Brand *W*. Statement 2 is correct. $150 + 45 = 195$, which is more than 180. This means that more than half of the students use Brand X or Brand W. Statement 3 is correct. Statements 1, 2 and 3 are correct.

32 8 goals + 12 outers = 64, which means 4 goals + 6 outers = 32. As 4 goals + 10 outers = 40, then 4 outers = 8 points. This means 1 outer = 2 points. Also, 8 goals + $12 \times 2 = 64$ means 8 goals = 40, and so 1 goal = 5 points.
As $10 \times 5 + 5 \times 2 = 60$, the Cats scored 60 points in the second game.

33 As 1 m = 100 cm, the roof is a rectangle with dimensions 1200 cm by 1000 cm. As the depth of water is 10 mm = 1 cm, and $1200 \times 1000 \times 1 = 1\,200\,000$, the amount of water is 1 200 000 mL which is 1200 L.

34 As $4 + 4 \times 4 = 4 + 16 = 20$, then ☆ = 4.
Also ⃠ ÷ 4 = 3 means ⃠ = 12.
Finally ☺ − 2 × (12 + 4) = 8, then
☺ − 2 × 16 = 8. This means ☺ = 40.

35 There are 360° in a revolution.
As $360 - (90 + 120) = 360 - 210 = 150$, and $\frac{150}{360} = \frac{5}{12}$, the probability is $\frac{5}{12}$.

NOTES